NICHOLSON

THE ORDNANCE SURVEY GUIDE TO THE BROADS & FENS

River Ouse River Nene
Middle Level Navigations

Editor: David Perrott

Robert Nicholson Publications

Also available in this series:

Nicholson/Ordnance Survey Guide to the River Thames
Nicholson/Ordnance Survey Guide to the Waterways 1 South
Nicholson/Ordnance Survey Guide to the Waterways 2 Central
Nicholson/Ordnance Survey Guide to the Waterways 3 North

The indication of a towpath or footpath in this book does not necessarily imply a public right of way. If you are in any doubt, check before you proceed with the latest published Ordnance Survey map.

Pathfinder Series (2½in to 1 mile scale or 1:25 000). These OS walker and rambler maps show the countryside in great detail, including rights of way in England and Wales.
Landranger Series (1¼in to 1 mile scale or 1:50 000). This OS series covers the country in 204 sheets and is ideal for detailed exploring by car or on foot.

First published in 1986 by **Robert Nicholson Publications Limited**, 62–65 Chandos Place, London WC2N 4NW and
Ordnance Survey, Romsey Road, Maybush, Southampton SO9 4DH.

© Text, Robert Nicholson Publications Limited 1986

© The maps in this publication are reproduced from Ordnance Survey maps with the permission of the Controller of HMSO. Crown Copyright Reserved.

Cover photograph: Derek Pratt

Natural history information: Alwyne Wheeler
Sailing information: David Craig
Photographs: David Perrott
Line drawings: Towler Cox
Boat plans: Morag Perrott
Research assistants: Janet Davies, Morag Perrott

Many people and organisations have assisted in the preparation of this book. Special thanks are extended to: Alan and Janet Royall of Wroxham; Charlie Norman of West View Marina; Richard Allen of Buckden Marina; Dennis Barrett of Upwell; John Barford, Peter Cotton, Chris Klee and Dr Chris Spray of Anglian Water; Geoffrey Facer of the River Cam Conservancy; The Middle Level Commissioners; J A D Hart of the Great Yarmouth Port and Haven Commissioners; Maurice Gowan and Joe Neve of Hoseasons Holidays; Colin Prentice of Blakes Holidays. Others who gave considerable help include: The Broads Authority; the local Tourist Information Centres; The Norfolk Wherry Trust; The Norfolk Windmills Trust; The Well Creek Trust; The National Trust; The Nature Conservancy Council; The Norfolk Naturalist's Trust; The Royal Society for the Protection of Birds; The Wildfowl Trust; CAMRA; Stella Vayne; Margaret Hughes.

Great care has been taken throughout this book to be accurate, but the publishers cannot accept any responsibility for any errors which appear or their consequences.

Typeset by Rowland Phototypesetting Ltd, Bury St Edmunds, Suffolk
Printed in Great Britain by Chorley and Pickersgill Ltd, Leeds and London

Nicholson ISBN 0 905522 97 4
Ordnance Survey ISBN 0 319 00046 X

INTRODUCTION

Flowing gently through the lowlands, the rivers and broads of eastern England harbour many pleasant surprises for those who choose to come and explore.

Each year the Norfolk Broads – Britain's best-known holiday boating area – plays host to many thousands of water-borne visitors. Yet conservation interests are being maintained alongside those of commerce, in order to preserve the region's unique appeal. There is, of course, plenty to see and do, but if you prefer a quieter time, a secluded corner can always be found, or you can visit in the spring or autumn. You could consider having a *traditional* Broads holiday, mooring not only at some of the many fine pubs, but also anchoring sometimes at the edge of a reed-fringed broad to see the wildfowl and watch the sun setting. You might contemplate hiring a sailing craft (conditions are ideal for novices) and kindle thoughts of times passed, when sturdy wherries with billowing sails brought their cargoes to the village staithe.

Separate from the Broads and linked to the main waterways network are the rivers Ouse and Nene. With a rich history and varied wildlife, not to mention friendly pubs and unspoilt villages, their potential has yet to be fully realised. Between these two rivers are the fascinating Middle Level Navigations, where you can easily imagine yourself cruising in the heart of the Netherlands.

So take this book, with its superb Ordnance Survey maps, and see for yourself. You will surely not be disappointed.

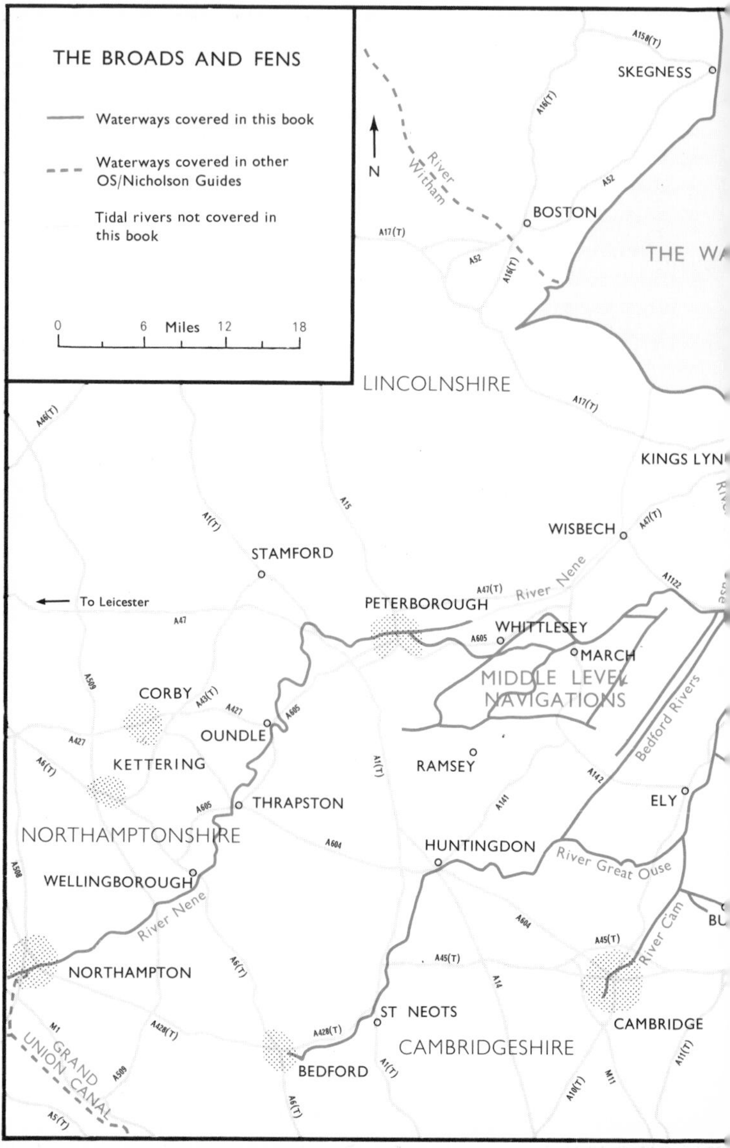

4

THE BROADS AND FENS

——— Waterways covered in this book

- - - Waterways covered in other
OS/Nicholson Guides

Tidal rivers not covered in
this book

N

0   6   Miles   12   18

A158(T)

SKEGNESS

A16(T)

River Witham

A52

BOSTON

A17(T)

A52

A16(T)

THE WA

LINCOLNSHIRE

A17(T)

A46(T)

KINGS LYN

A15

A1(T)

STAMFORD

WISBECH

A47(T)

A122

A47(T)   River Nene

← To Leicester

A47

PETERBOROUGH

A605

WHITTLESEY

°MARCH

MIDDLE LEVEL
NAVIGATIONS

A598

CORBY

A45(T)

A427

A605

OUNDLE

A1(T)

RAMSEY

A141

Bedford Rivers

A142

ELY

A427

A4(T)

KETTERING

A605

THRAPSTON

NORTHAMPTONSHIRE

A604

HUNTINGDON

River Great Ouse

A598

WELLINGBOROUGH

River Nene

A604

A45(T)

River Cam

BU

NORTHAMPTON

A45(T)

A45(T)

CAMBRIDGE

A14

M1

A428(T)

A43(T)

ST NEOTS

A45(T)

CAMBRIDGESHIRE

A11(T)

GRAND
UNION CANAL

A598

A1(T)

BEDFORD

A6(T)

A428(T)

A1(T)

A46(T)

M11

A5(T)

CONTENTS

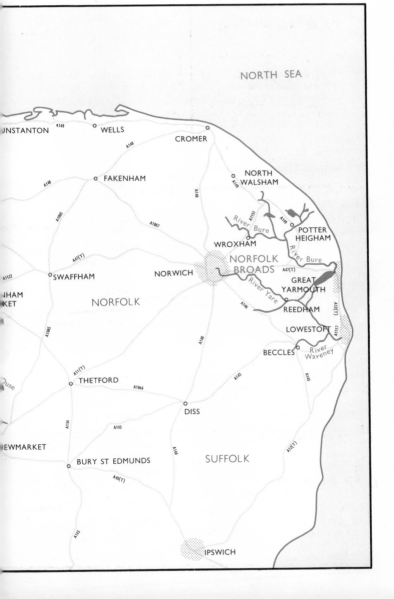

GENERAL CRUISING INFORMATION

Specific information relating to the Norfolk Broads, the River Great Ouse, River Nene and Middle Level Navigations is given in the introduction to each section.

Course to steer

Keep to the right (starboard), to pass oncoming craft port (left) to port.

Speed

Obey the speed limits and do not allow your wash to break. Go slowly past moored craft, rowing boats, punts and dinghies.

Locks

River locks are used to allow craft to pass by the weirs which control the flow of water and maintain levels suitable for navigation. They consist of a box with gates at each end, and a means of letting water in at the top (higher level) and out at the bottom (lower level). This is controlled 1) by slackers, which open and close either holes in the mitre gates or underground culverts, or 2) by gradually raising a guillotine gate and letting the water flow underneath. A windlass is usually needed to operate the slackers and wind up the guillotine.

To pass through a lock Tie your boat up a short distance away and check the state of the lock. If you need to fill it, make sure everything is closed at the bottom end, if you need to empty it, make sure all is secure at the top.
Drive or tow your boat in and steady it with the mooring lines, allowing for the change in level.
Empty or fill the lock as necessary, taking care and not allowing the boat to be bumped around.
Close the slackers, put your windlass back on the boat, pick up the crew and carry on with your journey.
Bear in mind the following: fenders should be raised in locks, or they may get caught; keep your boat away from the lock cill when going down; don't rush around at locks, especially in slippery conditions. Make the safety of the crew and boat your prime concern.
If the lock is operated by a keeper, follow any instructions given, and *always* be courteous and patient.

Bridges and bends

Pass through the bridge arch indicated as the navigation channel, or the right hand arch if there are two and neither is marked. Those travelling upstream must give way to those travelling downstream, who have less control over their craft. Do not cut corners – it is usually shallow on the inside of a bend.

Mooring

It is good practice to appproach a mooring with your boat facing upstream into the current, in order to maintain steerage at very low speeds. Do not approach the bank or quayside quickly, relying on reverse to stop the boat – if the propeller is fouled or the engine stalls, disaster will ensue. The golden rule is – go dead slow – then if things do not go quite as planned (a not uncommon occurrence) the result will be only a gentle bump. Avoid fending off with hands and feet, and take care to keep fingers and feet out of ropes. Do not moor against private ground, or where you will cause an obstruction. Do not allow your ropes to obstruct paths. Leave sufficient line, and depth of water under the boat, to allow for a possible rise or fall overnight.

Knots

A simple and easy way of securing a rope to a bollard or mooring stake is to use a couple of round turns and a half hitch made with a loop and pulled tight. This can be released quickly by pulling the loose end, which will have been left tidily coiled.

When leaving a mooring, coil all the ropes up again, ready for use when you need them.

Sound signals

It is important to know the basic signals in order to issue or recognise warnings. Remember that starboard is right and port is left when facing towards the bows (front).
One short blast: I am going to starboard
Two short blasts: I am going to port
Three short blasts: I am going astern
Four short blasts: I am unable to manoeuvre
Four short blasts followed by one short blast: I am turning round to starboard
Four short blasts followed by two short blasts: I am turning round to port
Continuous sounding of the horn indicates distress.

Sailing vessels

Power gives way to sail. If a power boat cannot manoeuvre, the correct sound signal is four short blasts. Those sailing must remember that many power craft drivers are inexperienced, and should plan their tacks accordingly.

Sub-aqua divers

Keep well clear of divers, who should fly code flag A to indicate their presence.

Code flag A

Weirs

There is a weir at every river lock – keep well away from the 'pull' of the weir above the lock, and allow for a possible cross current below.

Strong stream conditions

After prolonged heavy rainfall, the water level on a river will rise, the current will increase and the weirs will become very fierce indeed. When it is judged that this represents a hazard to navigation, warnings are usually displayed and all hire craft should then moor up out of the main current and telephone their base for instructions. To those with no experience of boat handling and navigation these strong stream conditions are DANGEROUS, so be cautious and obey the advice of those better qualified. Owners of private craft may proceed as they see fit. If you should experience engine failure or a fouled propeller in these conditions and carry no anchor, the consequences could be serious.

Care of the boat and engine

Those who own their own craft will have developed a suitable routine. Those with hire craft should follow the company's instructions each day before setting off. These are normally:
– Check the engine oil
– Check the cooling water level in the header tank, or the water inlet filter
– Pump the water from the bilges.
Start the engine *before* casting off, and check that the batteries are being charged, by reference to the warning light or ammeter.
After completion of each day's cruising, grease the stern gland.

Drinking water

Fill up every day. Drinking water is available from public water points or from boatyards, who may not unreasonably ask a small fee to offset their water rates.

Toilets

Many craft now have pump-out toilets, which have to be emptied with a special machine. This facility is indicated in the boatyard entries accompanying the maps. The symbol below is often displayed at boatyards offering this facility. Expect to have to pay.

Chemical 'bucket' type toilets and their more modern counterparts should only be emptied at boatyards offering 'chemical toilet disposal' or at a recognised sanitary station. Never throw the contents into the bushes or river. If the use of a sea toilet is permitted on a particular waterway, it is desirable that it be flushed where there is a current to take the waste away, since in the still water of, say, a small marina, there would be an accumulation.

Fuel

All boatyards offering fuel are indicated in the text. Boaters with diesel engines should take special care not to run out of fuel as the engine may need specialist attention before it will start again. Most hire craft carry fuel sufficient for at least two weeks normal cruising – your boatyard will advise.

HIRING A BOAT

It can be very disappointing to find the boat you have hired for a week or a fortnight does not live up to your expectations. Minor niggles may cause amusement, but major defects can mar your holiday. So how do you choose? Ideally, if you can see a particular boat before you book it, and talk to the hire company, you will know that all is OK. But for the majority of people this is impractical, as it would likely as not involve an additional long journey to the boatyard. No boatyard worth its salt, however, would turn down a request to view.

Second only to actually viewing the boat is the recommendation of a friend who has personal experience of a particular company, and can give you a first-hand account. All the best hire companies get a good percentage of their bookings either as repeats or by recommendation.

If you are starting from scratch, here is some general advice.

1 A well-produced brochure showing detailed plans, interior photographs and a full specification is a great help. Virtually all boat-hire companies on the Broads, and many elsewhere, have their bookings handled by two major agencies – Hoseasons Holidays and Blakes, who both produce comprehensive colour brochures. If you want to know more about a particular craft, do not be afraid to ask them, or to get in touch directly with the boatyard concerned. They are keen to do business with you and will prove extremely helpful.

2 The size of a company is no indication of quality – some of the largest companies have grown because they are good, some of the smaller ones maintain that by remaining small they can offer a better service.

3 Choose a boat suitable for your needs (and see below for special information regarding young children). For example, four large adults could feel very cramped in a small four-berth fibreglass cruiser, whereas two adults and two children might find it satisfactory. A four-berth steel narrow boat would usually offer more space.

4 Make sure you know what you will have to pay. With companies that quote an all-inclusive price you know exactly what your commitments are. However, if your itinerary is not very ambitious, you could be better off with a less expensive boat where the fuel cost is extra. Returnable security deposits are normal practice.

5 Fibreglass cruisers, while admirably suited to river navigations and the Broads, feel distinctly wrong on narrow canals, where the steel narrow boat, based upon traditional designs, is a much more suitable craft.

6 Modern pump-out toilets are preferable to the old chemical type, and virtually all hire craft are now equipped with them. A 'fresh water' flush is preferable to the recirculating type.

7 A water-cooled diesel engine is usually quieter than the air-cooled type.

8 If you are cruising early or late in the year, a boat with central heating (and an airing cupboard) will be more comfortable than one with just cabin heaters.

9 Generally, a newer boat will be better than an older one.

10 Sailing craft, available on the Norfolk Broads, are worth considering (see page 24).

Choosing a hirecraft, with children in mind

With a little forethought, babies who are not yet walking can be coped with easily on a boating holiday. Children between the ages of one and five are probably the most difficult to deal with, and the following points may be helpful:

1 Mum, Dad and two toddlers on a heavily locked length of canal or river will have problems. If you cannot gather a larger crew, then choose a navigation with very few or indeed no locks. The Norfolk Broads are ideal in this respect.

2 Ensure buoyancy aids are available for the children, and make sure they are worn when on deck.

3 Airing cupboards are useful for drying all the washing generated by small children.

4 Order cot sides to stop young children falling out of their bunks.

5 Pack the favourite toys and games.

6 Make plenty of stops so the children can run off their excess energy.

From the age of six or seven, children, properly supervised, become valuable and helpful crew members.

A typical wide beam holiday boat, common on rivers and the Norfolk Broads

A typical compact four berth cruiser

A typical narrow boat, most common on the canal system

PLANNING A CRUISE

The enjoyment you derive from a cruise on the inland waterways will depend on many things, but perhaps none more than the schedule you set yourself. The essence of a boating holiday is that it should be leisurely; taken at a pace that allows time to stop and explore villages and churches, lunch at friendly pubs, and go for a walk before breakfast. With time in hand, queuing at a lock or waiting to top up your water can be a pleasant break rather than a frustrating delay.

Speed limits on the waterways vary and are mentioned where appropriate: in practice your speed will usually be much less than the limit specified – remember the excessive 'wash' caused by speeding damages the banks and inconveniences other waterway users. When passing moored craft your boat should barely ripple the water, travelling at a speed of 2mph or less. You may assume your average speed to be 3mph on narrow or shallow stretches and perhaps 4mph where it is wider and deeper. Locks will slow down your progress, especially at peak times when you may have to queue before entering. But assuming no untoward delays, it will take about 20 minutes to pass through a lock, or about the same amount of time it takes to travel 1 mile at a speed of 3mph. Here we have the means to calculate an approximate journey time (miles plus locks), although other factors, such as whether you are travelling upstream (slower) or downstream (faster) will affect the result.

For example, if you have planned to moor for the night at a pub 18 miles away, and this involves passing through 6 locks, the calculation is as follows: 18 miles + 6 locks = 24 'lock miles'. Dividing this by an average speed of 3mph results in 8 hours cruising time – rather a lot for one day. Perhaps you could choose somewhere closer. However, if you feel you want to keep this 8-hour schedule, then an early start is preferable to a late finish – tempers invariably become a little frayed when, at dusk, you arrive at your destination only to find all the moorings taken.

So, remember, if your planned journey requires more than 6 hours cruising each day then your stops will have to be limited. More than 8 hours cruising each day is probably too ambitious.

Those who are taking to the inland waterways for the first time may think this all sounds painfully slow, but a few hours of gentle cruising on a fine day is usually enough to convert most people to the pace. For only by proceeding gently can you appreciate the peace and beauty of the countryside, watch the bird life and study the riverside architecture.

Should you consider venturing into waters subject to *strong* tidal influences, then your journey will have to be planned using tide tables. If you are not used to this more serious type of navigation, you should not make the passage without qualified assistance. You should also be certain that your boat and engine (and crew) are up to the standards required. Lock-keepers on the tidal sections will be pleased to advise you, but most hire companies impose strict limits to your cruising area, and rarely let you get anywhere near the sea. The confluence of the rivers Bure and Yare is, for instance, the limit for hire-craft on the Norfolk Broads.

NATURAL HISTORY

The wetlands of eastern England comprise one of the most fascinating regions of the British Isles, a world of open skies and wide vistas contrasting with dense reeds beds and woodland. Although lacking the drama of mountains and rolling hills, this area provides in its rivers and marshlands the ideal habitat for numerous animal, bird and plant species. Those on boats are sure to see lapwing, snipe and sandpiper using the water's edge; mallard, coot and moorhen on rivers and dikes; and great crested grebe and dabchick on the open water. While cruising gently through the 'unspoilt' countryside, it is easy to forget that these areas represent transitory, unstable habitats; much altered by man but also changing gradually as a result of natural processes.

The Norfolk Broads offer a classic example of the impermanence of open-water sites. Most broads are between 9 and 12 feet deep, and were at one time rich with aquatic plants. Fringed with Norfolk reed or reed sweet grass in the tidal reaches, the reed-swamps encroach on the open water by the gradual accumulation of dead vegetation and the trapping of mud in root systems; on the landward side the swamp becomes drier and the land surface is gradually built up, to be colonised by other plants such as marsh pea, marsh fern and marsh orchid. These plants form the cover in which seedlings of alder and various willow species thrive, replacing the fen by a shrubby mixture of alder in the shallows, with oak, birch and ash in the drier areas. The alder *carr*, which is typical on the boundaries of the least disturbed broads, is the nearest thing in Britain to impenetrable jungle – a dense shrubby growth, its roots hidden beneath the surface, all growing in a black glutinous mass which will bear your weight on one step but not the next. Perhaps it is because the reed-swamp, fen and carr are all so difficult for man to explore that they have become such a haven for wildlife.

Regrettably in the 1950s and 1960s there was a deterioration in the water quality of many of the broads (and also in the reed-swamp areas, though for different reasons), which led to a decline in the richness of plant and animal life. The major problem was one of water chemistry. An increase of plant nutrients – nitrates and phosphates derived from sewage treatment works, and drainage of chemical fertilisers from farmland – stimulated a massive growth of algae which had several detrimental effects. The water became turbid in summer – looking rather like thin pea soup – thus preventing the light penetrating more than an inch or so below the surface. The submerged water plants, once such a feature of the clear waters of the broads, were shaded out; without light they could not survive. An additional problem caused by the massive increase of algae is due to the fact that they precipitate calcium carbonate out of the water. This sinks, together with the great mass of dead algae generated each year, and the resultant build-up of soft mud means that virtually nothing except a small range of mud-dwelling insect larvae can live on the bottom. Sedimentation in the sheltered off-river broads has increased ten-fold in the last 30 years, at the rate of half an inch each year. In the relatively shallow waters of the broads this has meant that in some places it has become impossible even to row across them; for animal life it is disastrous, as virtually nothing

'a world of open skies and wide vistas'

can live in the oxygen-deficient water.

A secondary problem is the use (now well past its peak and declining on the Broads) of powered boats. Unwittingly even the most conservation-minded boat user causes disturbance to the ecosystem. Propellers stir up the mud, adding to the diminution of light in the already cloudy water. The wash from a boat driven too quickly causes erosion of the river banks, which in turn adds to the mud deposits in the river or broad. Such erosion has caused the loss of important reed beds which previously sheltered many bird species and some mammals. Shy species of birds will quit areas in which they were once common, due to general increased disturbance. Litter, while undesirable, is not as damaging to the environment as other less visible problems.

Within the present decade, however, considerable progress has been made in overcoming the problems of the area. Sewage treatment works are being modified to remove the nitrates and phosphates from their effluent; in other situations discharges are being directed away from the broads, and river flows diverted so as not to affect the still-water areas. Direct action is also being taken. At Cockshoot Broad, which had only a few inches of free water above feet of semi-liquid sludge, the mud was pumped out until a depth of three feet of clear water was achieved, and drainage into the broad was diverted. At Alderfen Broad the mud was left but the enriching inflow was likewise diverted. The object of these two schemes was to compare which method of treatment allowed quickest recovery for aquatic plants. As neither of these broads is navigable it has been possible to deal with the enrichment problems without the added complication of boat traffic.

Elsewhere, management plans have been agreed with farmers to limit the amount of fertiliser used, as well as the type and quantity of herbicides and insecticides, thus controlling the amount of pollutants leaching through the soil and into the water. In some broads, such as Barton, where recovery has begun, there are concerted efforts being made to restock with the native plants which were once so common.

Before Britain became an island in post-glacial times, its rivers were connected to those of mainland Europe and received elements of their rich and varied flora and fauna. When the sea flooded the North Sea basin this connection was broken and those animals which depend on fresh water were trapped, being unable to disperse westwards into other rivers. This is particularly noticeable in the distribution of freshwater fish. Both the Broads and the Fenland rivers have more fish species than the rivers of western Britain, and are distinguished by the presence of silver bream and ruffe (a relative of the perch). The burbot was also found in these rivers at one time – the only member of the cod family to live in fresh water, it occurs eastwards across Europe, central Asia and north America, but is now thought to be extinct in Britain; the last reported examples occurring in the River Ouse system near Cambridge nearly 20 years ago.

The Norfolk Broads are famous for their pike, with fish of up to 40lbs being caught. Perch, bream and roach are also common. The Middle Level Navigations are now inhabited by zander, along with the other more usual species. Introduced from central Europe, the zander is a predator which grows to 30 inches in length. A relative of the perch, it became exceedingly abundant after its introduction, making the smaller fish which it preys on, such as roach, very scarce. Fortunately its numbers are now stabilising. Another introduction, the coypu, became extremely common and caused a good deal of damage on the Norfolk Broads by eating reeds and rare plants such as the great water dock. Coypu look like giant guinea pigs and may weight up to 25lbs. Although mainly active at night they can occasionally be spotted during daylight hours, in quiet waters on warm summer days. While the coypu has multiplied in number, the more interesting native otter has become rare, but it is unlikely that there is any connection between these two events. Water voles, another native aquatic mammal, have also become less common as has the harvest mouse, which lives in the reeds; the coypu's depridations having had considerable effect on its preferred habitat.

The rivers Nene and Ouse run through what was once a great natural fen. While contributing to the immense present-day agricultural richness of the area they also provide a refuge for a fascinating array of wildlife, although the most specialised fenland animals and plants are now confined to the few jealously guarded nature reserves such as Woodwalton Fen and Wicken Fen, both in Cambridgeshire.

Woodwalton Fen is the home of the large copper butterfly, and is the only place in Britain where it can still be seen, although it once occurred throughout the Fens and the Broads. The population of this striking and brilliant insect is not native, the true British copper having become extinct about 1851. The Woodwalton butterflies are an introduced European relative, only subspecifically distinct, and identical except for the minutest differences. Attempts were made in the past to naturalise it on some of the broads but these were unsuccessful, due in some respect to the scarcity of the great water dock, the food-plant of the larva.

The most exciting of all British insects, the swallow-tail butterfly, is a native of Broadland and is unique to the area – these insects are recognised as a distinct sub-species found only in this country. The first swallow-tails to emerge can be seen on sunny May days with their wings spread as they bask on reeds and sedges. During a fine summer they become more common, beating along the reed beds and occasionally flying inland high over the alder carr as they mate. They lay their eggs on the milk parsley plant (another fenland native) and as they grow become bright green with black and orange spotted rings on their bodies. They are hard to find, even when one knows where the correct plants grow, but are easy to identify once located. If alarmed, these larvae erect a bright orange horn just behind the head, which gives off a smell of pineapple.

The birdlife of the wetlands is still very rich, for while some species have declined, many others have increased. Typical of the reed beds is the bittern, a beautifully marked brown bird rather like a small heron in appearance. Although hard to spot, it can be recognised by its characteristic booming call. The reed beds also offer shelter to reed and sedge warblers, and the grasshopper warbler's distinctive song can be heard by those who can distinguish it from the chirruping of a grasshopper or the ratchet on a fishing reel. Much rarer is Savi's warbler, which has a similar song and has recently become established in Britain. Other inhabitants of the reed beds are bearded tits and the marsh harrier, a large and rather uncommon bird of prey, which is gradually increasing its numbers on the Broads and Fenlands.

By proceeding quietly, all these and more can be seen, a source of endless fascination for the naturalist and layman alike.

Barbel

Bleak

Common Bream

Bullhead

Common Carp

Chub

Dace

Freshwater Eel

Gudgeon

River Lamprey

Perch

Minnow

Roach

Pike

Ruffe

Rudd

Stickleback

Tench

Brown Trout

FISHING

You will be pleased to discover that on a boating holiday there is always plenty to do. But if you think you might have some spare time, and are tempted to try your luck at fishing, there are a few things you should know.

Permission to fish

You *must* have a water authority rod and line licence, and in many cases you will also need a local permit – tackle shops and, quite often, boatyards can advise. On many waters the angling rights are private – respect these rights and do not fish without permission. A large number of riverside pubs and hotels own fishing rights and will sell you a day ticket. You must not fish during the close season, from *14 March to 16 June*.

Tackle

It need not be expensive, and a long rod is unnecessary if you are fishing from a boat. You will also need a simple reel; a line of 5 to 8lbs breaking-strain; a quill float; weights (more about these later); some hooks, size 14 is usually alright – preferably without a barb; and a tin for your bait. A disgorger is handy if the fish swallows the hook, and a landing net is useful if you think you might catch a big one! The tackle shop will explain how to assemble it all.

Bait

Maggots from a fishing shop, small worms from your garden (please do not dig up the river bank), or a pinch of white sliced bread squeezed onto the hook are the most common alternatives. A few morsels of whatever you are using thrown around your float will help to attract the fish.

Where

Fish are shy creatures, so choose a spot where you think they might find shelter – under lilies, close to reeds, or on the edge of clumps of weeds.

When

Early morning or evening is best.

What you might catch, and how

All the usual species of coarse fish are present in the waterways included in this book. Near the surface you may catch bleak, dace, small roach, perch; on the bottom you will generally find bream, gudgeon, eels, tench and larger roach – but there are no hard and fast rules. On the Middle Level Navigations you might hook a zander (see the Natural History section), on the Norfolk Broads a 40lb pike! If you do not seem to be getting any bites – that is the float is not dipping – try something different. Position the hook shallower or deeper, or change the bait. When you do get a bite, just a prompt *gentle* tug will secure the hook. Pull the fish out slowly, using a landing net if you have one, and handle the fish carefully with wet hands or a wet cloth. Remove the hook, admire the specimen, then put it back (do not throw it) straight away.

Cruising past Coldham Hall, Brundall

By following these instructions you will cause the minimum of injury to the fish.

The environment

It is regrettable, but true, that quite a few anglers leave litter (which is unsightly and sometimes harmful); nylon line, discarded or tangled in bushes (which traps birds); trampled riverside vegetation (habitat destruction); injured fish (from being kept in a small keep-net) and lost or dropped lead weights (which have poisoned thousands of swans and are now banned by Anglian Water). Make sure you set a better example by respecting the countryside, being gentle with the fish you catch, and by using lead-free weights, or at least making sure NO lead weights are dropped into the water or left on the bank.

HOW TO USE THIS GUIDE

MAPS

There are two map scales used within the descriptive sections of this book. The Norfolk Broads are shown at 2½ inches to 1 mile.
The River Nene, River Ouse and Middle Level Navigations are shown at 1¼ inches to 1 mile.

SYMBOLS used on the maps:

Ⓑ	Boatyard, marina or boatyard services
W	Water point
M	Public overnight mooring – Norfolk Broads only
	Lock
	Navigable water
	Unnavigable water
26	Mileage (main rivers only)
- - -	Footpath (public right of way)
— —	Bridlepath (public right of way)
- - - -	Path
☕	Public house

Various standard Ordnance Survey symbols also occur on the maps; these are explained on any OS map in the Pathfinder Series (Norfolk Broads area) or Landranger Series (remaining areas).

SYMBOLS AND ABBREVIATIONS
used in the text:

Ⓑ	Boatyard, marina or some boatyard services.
Ⓡ	Refuse disposal
Ⓢ	Chemical toilet (Elsan-type) disposal
Ⓦ	Water
Ⓟ	Petrol
Ⓓ	Diesel
Ⓔ	Electric boat recharging
☕	Public house
Ⓜ	Overnight mooring
✕	Restaurant
�	Licensed to sell alcohol
L	Open for lunch
D	Open for dinner
BA	Broads Authority
NT	National Trust
NCC	Nature Conservancy Council
NNT	Norfolk Naturalists Trust
RSPB	Royal Society for the Protection of Birds

MOORING

Public overnight moorings are marked on the Norfolk Broads maps only – these are also mentioned in the text along with other suggestions. Moorings on the rivers Ouse and Nene are not difficult to find.
Always check that you are not mooring against private property, and remember that many waterside pubs and boatyards also offer moorings, but seek permission first.

NAVIGATIONAL NOTES

These appear where necessary to point out potential hazards, navigational limits, lock-keepers' telephone numbers and any other relevant details.

BOATYARDS

Within the descriptions all the essential services you need are listed, but do not expect these to be available at a hire-craft base when their fleet is being 'turned around' (usually Saturday). They will have no room for your boat, and no staff free to help you. Any other day you will surely be made to feel very welcome.

BOAT TRIPS

These are listed where appropriate, and are an excellent way of sampling the waterways before you commit yourself to a longer period of hire, or simply a nice day out.

PUBS AND RESTAURANTS

Virtually all pubs close to waterways, and many in the surrounding villages, are included and described. If they offer food, have a garden or a children's room, this is also mentioned. Most of the pubs we mention offer real ale (as defined by CAMRA); we make no excuse for this bias, since they usually offer a keg beer or lager as well, thus ensuring the widest choice. Our selection of cafés and restaurants is more restricted – those included are generally above the usual standard, or have something special to offer in their area. Quite a few pubs offer excellent restaurant meals, and this information is also included. If you need to book, the telephone number is there. Finally, waterside pubs and restaurants often have their own good moorings – Ⓜ following the entry indicates this facility.

THE
NORFOLK BROADS

The present-day holiday industry of the Norfolk Broads is far removed from the traditional forms of marshland survival which preceded it. Wildfowlers, eel catchers and wherrymen could never have imagined a time when each year 250,000 visitors would take a boating holiday on the rivers and broads, supporting 6000 jobs which would otherwise disappear. With tourism on this scale it would seem likely that the natural environment must suffer, and a decade ago this was indeed the case. However, those with commercial interests in the region have recognised that unless the special characteristics of the Norfolk Broads are preserved, their industry will disappear. Conservation and restoration are now the main objectives of all concerned.

To fully appreciate and enjoy this unique area, it is necessary to understand a little of its history. In eastern Norfolk, sands, clays and gravels overlie a bed of chalk which slopes gently eastward. Three rivers, the Bure, the Yare and the Waveney drain the area and all find their outlet to the sea at Great Yarmouth, where they have formed a narrow peninsula and a sheltered tidal harbour. This network of rivers, and their tributaries, were natural water highways at a time when all else was rough tracks passable only by pack horse and mule; thus enabling the region to support a large population of relatively prosperous peasant farmers around the time of the Norman Conquest.

The origins of the Broads themselves long remained unclear, and it was fashionable for a time to believe they were evidence of a large estuarine complex which had drained as the sea level fell, leaving flooded depressions. However, investigations revealed them to have vertical edges cut some 12 feet deep through peat, often in almost geometric patterns; a glance at a map of the area will show each one to be in the immediate vicinity of a settlement. It therefore became clear that the Broads were manmade, having been created at a time when peat was dug for fuel.

About 7000 years ago, when the climate was much colder than it is now, wet and acid conditions caused the growth of sedge, moss and grass to outstrip the rate at which the dead plants decomposed, gradually forming the thick fibrous layer known as peat. Cut and dried, it has a calorific value about two-thirds that of coal, and was used in Norfolk during the 12th–14thC to heat the towns and monasteries (it is still used to this day in Ireland and the western islands of Scotland). It is also likely that peat was used in Yarmouth to heat the brine pans and thus extract salt – there was at that time a vast export industry in salted herrings. In places such as Heigham Sound the underlying clay was also dug out for brick and pot making – a practice recalled in the name Potter Heigham and dating from Roman times.

During the 15thC the land began to sink (and still does, at the rate of about 6 inches every 100 years); the peat workings flooded and, being separate from the scouring action of the rivers, soon silted up. Once this silt and organic matter had reduced the depth to about 18 inches, reed-mace and bulrush found a foothold and accelerated the process. Mud accumulates around the stems and this in turn is colonised by smaller wetland plant species. On this foundation, albeit still unstable, alder and willow take root, gradually increasing in size until they become too heavy for their fragile bases and topple over, further consolidating the floor of what then becomes typical Broads woodland or *carr*. Left untouched all the Broads would gradually become overgrown and disappear – indeed several already have.

Coal later supplanted peat as the local energy source; shipped down from the mines adjacent to the Aire and Calder Navigation and distributed via the natural water highways, which were becoming ever more complex as broad joined river and dykes were cut to connect the villages to the main arteries. Every parish, every settlement and many of the farms had their own staithe (landing stage). As well as local traffic, which would even include corpses for burial, there were imports of coal in exchange for large quantities of grain to support the burgeoning industrial populations of the north. Reeds were a particularly local product, cut by the ton for thatching and exported by water. The early trading vessels used were keels, with a central mast and square sail, later to be replaced by the wherry, with its mast stepped forward and gaff rigged. The distinctive Norfolk Wherry is the craft traditionally associated with the Broads, and was built to carry between 14 and 40 tons depending on which parts of the system they served. They are described in detail on page 23.

The Broadland soil – away from the marshland – is amongst the best in the country – a deep fertile sandy loam with the odd outcrop of sandy heathland. Naturally in an area so well endowed with water and marshland, there is a wide variety of birdlife and mammals to be observed, including the infamous coypu (see Natural History, page 12).

Today the Broads are a pleasure-boater's paradise – gently flowing lock-free rivers meandering through varied countryside under a vast expanse of sky, punctuated with pretty villages and the reed-fringed broads themselves.

Horsey Drainage Mill

Navigation authority

The Great Yarmouth Port and Haven Commissioners
21 South Quay
Great Yarmouth
Norfolk NR30 2RE

Great Yarmouth 855151

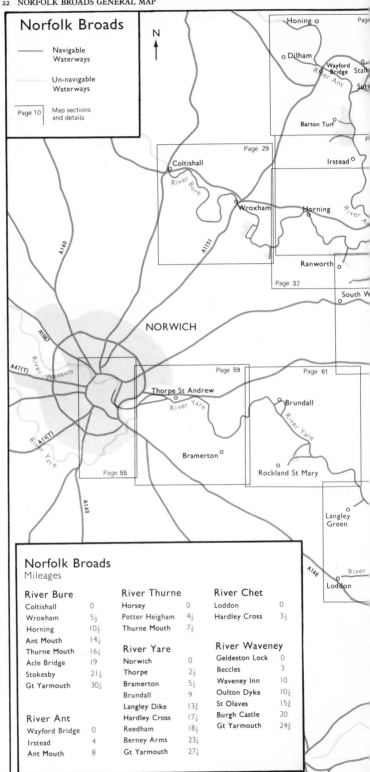

Norfolk Broads

N ↑

———— Navigable
Waterways

———— Un-navigable
Waterways

| Page 10 | Map sections and details |

Honing o

o Dilham

Wayford Bridge   Stal

River Ant

Sut

Barton Turf

Page 29

Coltishall

River Bure

Wroxham

Horning

Irstead o

River A

Ranworth o

Page 32

South W

NORWICH

A140

A1067

A47(T)

River Wensum

A11(T)

River Yare

A140

Page 59

Thorpe St Andrew

River Yare

Page 61

Brundall

River Yare

Bramerton o

Page 55

Rockland St Mary o

Langley Green

A146

River

Loddon o

Norfolk Broads
Mileages

River Bure		River Thurne		River Chet	
Coltishall	0	Horsey	0	Loddon	0
Wroxham	5½	Potter Heigham	4½	Hardley Cross	3½
Horning	10½	Thurne Mouth	7½		
Ant Mouth	14¼				
Thurne Mouth	16¼	River Yare		River Waveney	
Acle Bridge	19	Norwich	0	Geldeston Lock	0
Stokesby	21¼	Thorpe	2½	Beccles	3
Gt Yarmouth	30¼	Bramerton	5½	Waveney Inn	10
		Brundall	9	Oulton Dyke	10½
		Langley Dike	13¾	St Olaves	15¾
River Ant		Hardley Cross	17¼	Burgh Castle	20
Wayford Bridge	0	Reedham	18½	Gt Yarmouth	24¾
Irstead	4	Berney Arms	23¼		
Ant Mouth	8	Gt Yarmouth	27¼		

Sea Palling

Page 48

Brograve Bridge

Hickling Heath

Horsey Mere

West Somerton

North Sea

Potter Heigham

River Thurne

Winterton-on-Sea

Page 50

Thurne

Page 53

Ormesby Broad

Page 37

Rollesby Broad

Page 39

A1064

River Bure

Filby Broad

Caister-on-Sea

oton

Acle Bridge

Stokesby

Acle

River Bure

Page 41

GREAT YARMOUTH

Page 67

Breydon Water

Berney Arms

Burgh Castle

Page 65

River Yare

River Waveney

A12

Reedham

Hardley Cross

Haddscoe New Cut

Page 77

Fritton Decoy

St Olaves

A143

River Waveney

Somerleyton

Page 75

Page 71

LOWESTOFT

Waveney Inn

Oulton Dyke

A1117

eston

Beccles

River Waveney

Oulton Broad

Page 73

0   3   6
Miles

Registration and licensing

All craft must be registered with, and licensed by GYPHC. Craft visiting the Norfolk Broads for periods of less than 28 days may pay a toll at a concessionary rate, details of which may be obtained from the Collector of Tolls at the above address.

Water supply

Water supply, flood control, drainage, sewerage, pollution and fisheries are the responsibility of:

The Anglian Water Authority
Yare House
62–64 Thorpe Road
Norwich
Norfolk NR1 1SA

Norwich 615161

The Broads Authority

This body co-ordinates the activities of the local councils, the Countryside Commission, GYPHC, Anglian Water and other such organisations, in order to ensure the successful management and conservation of this unique area.

The Broads Authority
Thomas Harvey House
18 Colegate
Norwich
Norfolk NR3 1BQ

Norwich 610734

As we go to press, a bill is before Parliament, proposing that the Norfolk Broads be given equivalent status to a National Park, and be controlled by a newly constituted Broads authority.

Navigation rules and hints

Complete copies of the bye-laws can be obtained from the GYPHC (address above). The following notes are in addition to the general hints on page 6.

Speed limits

These are 3, 5 and 7mph and are clearly indicated. They are necessary to protect the river banks from erosion, to avoid undue disturbance to other river bank users and as an aid to navigation in difficult areas.

Trading vessels

Their ability to manoeuvre is limited by the confines of the river, so keep well clear at all times.

Channel markers

Keep to the marked channel at all times, however inviting the water outside may appear.

THE NORFOLK WHERRY

The Norfolk Wherry was a trading craft which evolved to suit the particular conditions encountered on the Broads. Its precursor was the keel, a square-rigged sailing barge dating from the time of William the Conqueror. This type of rig made the craft difficult to sail in anything but a following wind, and together with the absence of paths from which to bank-haul, made for slow progress and frequent delays.

It was the Dutch who first introduced the fore and aft rig – the sort of rig we see on yachts today – to Britain during the 16thC, allowing craft to sail much closer to the wind (ie with the wind almost against the direction of travel) than had hitherto been possible.

The hull of the Norfolk Wherry has as its distant ancestor the passenger rowing boat, clinker-built, which was married to the new sail configuration giving a highly manoeuvrable craft which could operate under most conditions. The first such craft to be recorded was the 'Spread Eagle', constructed in the early 17thC. Gradually they were built larger and larger, culminating in the 40 tonners of the early 20thC. The original low-peaked gaffsail was eventually replaced by a high-peaked sail upon a long gaff, with the mast well forward. Even this mast was built to a special design. Unstayed, it pivoted at the top of the tabernacle and was counter-balanced by an enormous metal weight of up to 2 tons, which meant it could be lowered quickly when passing under bridges, then raised again without the boat losing way. Crewed by a skipper and mate (who may also have been his wife or mistress) the Norfolk Wherry had achieved the elegant simplicity of all good functional design.

Cargoes of virtually every description were carried, and the wherrymen knew every inch of the Broads they sailed on, using every trick in the book to reach their destinations. But, alas, with the building of the railways and the roads, their days were numbered. By 1949 the last wherry had finally furled its sail and ceased trading. As usual, most were scrapped before their worth was realised, and it was only the timely intervention of the (then) newly formed Norfolk Wherry Trust which saved the 'Albion'. Although not wholly typical, being carvel-built, she is a wonderful reminder of bygone days. On most weekends during the summer, parties of enthusiasts are taken on sailing trips in this unique craft – if you would like to share this experience, or contribute to the survival of the 'Albion', contact the Norfolk Wherry Trust Secretary, Miss Pamela J. Oakes, at 63 Whitehall Road, Norwich (624642). More recently the 'Maud' has also been rescued and is currently being restored at Upton.

SAILING ON
THE NORFOLK BROADS

No-one will dispute that the best way to see the Norfolk Broads is from the water – although there may be argument about the best sort of boat to use. However, a sailing boat does seem so much more a part of the scenery than a boat with a diesel engine can ever be. Certainly the ducks and other wildlife think so.

Don't be deterred if you haven't done much sailing. If you have a little experience – even in the smallest sailing dinghy – you will quickly learn to handle one of the sailing cruisers available for hire. If you have no experience at all, some of the boatyards offering sailing craft can provide a short tuition session with an expert helmsman, well-worth the small extra charge. The waters of the Broads are an ideal area to learn to handle a large sailing boat. There is usually enough wind and seldom too much, and although the waters are tidal there is no great rise and fall, neither are there waves of any size, so you can concentrate on the art of sailing without worrying about the problems of navigation or even sheer survival which are sometimes present at sea.

The boat hire companies issue brochures from which you can select a boat with confidence – the boatyard entries in the guide list those with sailing craft for hire. The descriptions and specifications are usually accurate and it is worth noting that where they say 'suitable for yachtsmen with some experience' they mean someone who has sailed before – not necessarily Chay Blyth!

When you have committed yourself and confirmed the booking, you will be sent a little handbook with hints and tips. Read this carefully – all of it! The information is well presented, certainly worth having, and can make the difference between a successful holiday and a disappointment.

Before you go to collect your boat, decide which of the party is the skipper. It doesn't matter if he isn't a Nelson – the important thing is that you can't sail a boat by committee.

The boatyard will explain the boat to you. Make sure you pay attention and understand how everything works. Note how the boat is prepared for sailing so that you can reverse the process when you moor up for the night.

This is not intended to be an instruction manual, but a few dos and don'ts may not be out of place:

1 Keep the boat tidy – this helps to avoid accidents and breaking crockery.

2 Hoist and lower sails only with the boat pointing into the wind.

3 Make sure you know how to lower and raise the mast.

4 Make sure you know how to reef sails. If it is very windy and you are apprehensive, then stay where you are until the wind drops a bit. There are no prizes for foolhardiness.

5 Don't try to sail into a leeward mooring. Lower sails head to wind first, and then motor or drift in to moor.

6 Try to help the motor cruisers by signalling your intentions (if you're sure you know what they are).

THE RIVER BURE

Rises south of Melton Constable in Norfolk and flows generally south east to Great Yarmouth. The Rivers Ant and Thurne join below Horning. In 1773 a bill was passed by Parliament to extend the existing navigation of 31 miles which ended at Horstead Mill, up as far as Aylsham. Locks were built at Coltishall, Buxton Mill, Oxnead Mill, Burgh-near-Aylsham Mill and Aylsham, and the work was completed in October 1779. It was soon found that silting had occurred, reducing the depth to 3 feet in places – in view of this regular dredging or 'didling' had to be carried out. Thirteen-ton wherries carried timber, coal, bricks (from Oxnead), agricultural produce, flour (from the mills) and marl from the Horstead Hall Estate.

The navigation prospered until the coming of the Wroxham to Aylsham railway in 1880 and the North Walsham to Melton Constable line in 1883, and survived until 1912, when severe flooding damaged all the locks and funds for their repair could not be raised. Formal abandonment came in 1928. Today the river is once again navigable only as far as Horstead.

In 1825 work began on the North Walsham & Dilham Canal to extend navigation on the River Ant from Wayford Bridge to Antingham. John Millington was employed as the engineer, and he cut a true canal (not an improved river navigation) through difficult, marshy land. The official opening took place in August 1826 – when built, it was 8¾ miles long with six locks. The cargoes carried were those typical of an agricultural area. As early as 1830 it became clear the canal would not be financially viable and in 1886 the company was forced to sell the navigation for £600. The initial share capital raised had been £29,300! Inevitably things went from bad to worse – the section above Swafield Locks was abandoned in 1893 and damage was sustained in the 1912 floods. Ownership passed to the North Walsham Canal Company, but in spite of improvements made below Swafield Locks in the 1920s the end came in 1934, when the last wherry left the canal. Today only the short section to Tonnage Bridge remains navigable (smaller craft to Honing Common). The North Walsham Canal Company still exists.

Coltishall

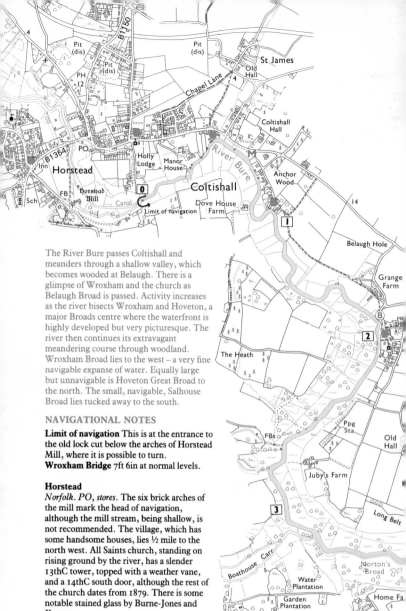

The River Bure passes Coltishall and
meanders through a shallow valley, which
becomes wooded at Belaugh. There is a
glimpse of Wroxham and the church as
Belaugh Broad is passed. Activity increases
as the river bisects Wroxham and Hoveton, a
major Broads centre where the waterfront is
highly developed but very picturesque. The
river then continues its extravagant
meandering course through woodland.
Wroxham Broad lies to the west – a very fine
navigable expanse of water. Equally large
but unnavigable is Hoveton Great Broad to
the north. The small, navigable, Salhouse
Broad lies tucked away to the south.

NAVIGATIONAL NOTES

Limit of navigation This is at the entrance to
the old lock cut below the arches of Horstead
Mill, where it is possible to turn.
Wroxham Bridge 7ft 6in at normal levels.

Horstead

Norfolk. PO, stores. The six brick arches of
the mill mark the head of navigation,
although the mill stream, being shallow, is
not recommended. The village, which has
some handsome houses, lies ½ mile to the
north west. All Saints church, standing on
rising ground by the river, has a slender
13thC tower, topped with a weather vane,
and a 14thC south door, although the rest of
the church dates from 1879. There is some
notable stained glass by Burne-Jones and
Kempe.

Coltishall

Norfolk. EC Wed, PO, stores. ½ mile from
the moorings by the common. The church of
St John Baptist has a 12thC chancel and a
curious circular Victorian window on the
north side. Facing the church along the main
street is a rich selection of pretty 18thC
red-brick houses, built at a time when
Coltishall was more important than
Wroxham. Note the flint-built school, and
The Limes, at the east end, which dates
from 1692 and is particularly handsome.
Browsers will find the antique and craft
shops delightful.

Blickling Hall (NT) 1½ miles north west of
Aylsham (bus from Coltishall). (Aylsham
733084). An important Jacobean mansion
built 1616–27 for Sir Henry Hobart (Lord
Chief Justice) by Robert Lyminge, who
designed Hatfield House 12 years earlier.
Red brick with stone dressings, the house
stands in gardens surrounded by massive
yew hedges. The interior is notable for the
plasterwork ceiling in the great gallery and
the State Bedroom. The park is open all
year, and fishing permits are available for the
large lake. Shop, tearoom, lunches and teas.
Textile Conservation Workshop. *The house is
open afternoons Apr–Oct, closed Mon & Thur.*
Admission charge.

Belaugh

Norfolk. Store. A tiny village around the
Norman church of St Peter, which stands on
a hill by the river. The cauldron-shaped font
is made of blue stone, and the tapestry-work
hassocks were made locally.

Wroxham (and Hoveton)

Norfolk. PO, stores, launderette, BR station.
Two villages divided by the river, but
colloquially lumped together as Wroxham –
the major Broads holiday centre, bustling
with boats and boaters during the summer
months. Before the coming of the railway
(c1880) Wroxham was a tiny settlement
around the church and the manor house,
facing the river and open country to the west
and even today still surprisingly intact. The
mostly Perpendicular church of St Mary has
a gloriously decorated Norman south
doorway and many monuments, of which
the one to Daniel Collyer, 1774, is
outstanding – both pretty and graceful. The
gabled manor house is to the south east of
the church. St John's church, Hoveton,

cleaning ladies who care for the boats. *On
some summer Sunday afternoons* there are rides
to be had on the miniature steam railways at
Barton House – check at the Information
Centre before you go.

Information Centre Station Road,
Wroxham (2281). Situated in a renovated
cottage, there is a small display and public
toilets close by. *Open Apr–Sep.*

Wroxham Barns Tunstead Road, Hoveton
(Wroxham 3762). 1½ miles north of
Wroxham. Group of Norfolk barns and
courtyards. Craft workshops, gift shop and
tea room. Set in parkland with adventure
playground and picnic area.

Hoveton Great Broad Nature Trail (NCC)
Access by boat only to this ½ mile walk
around the island in the Broad. Likened to a
tropical swamp, the trail passes a 9 foot
depth of liquid mud at one point, so be sure
to stay on the railway sleeper path. There is a
bird observation point and a platform upon
which terns nest. *Open weekdays May–mid
Sep.* Admission charge. Ⓜ

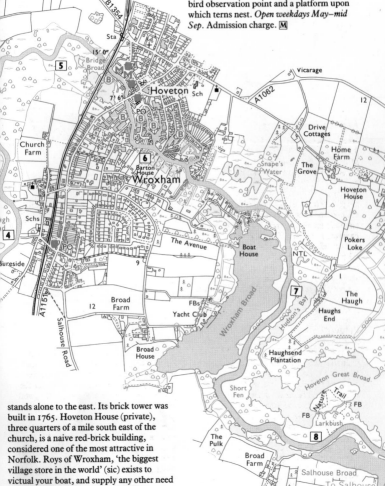

stands alone to the east. Its brick tower was
built in 1765. Hoveton House (private),
three quarters of a mile south east of the
church, is a naive red-brick building,
considered one of the most attractive in
Norfolk. Roys of Wroxham, 'the biggest
village store in the world' (sic) exists to
victual your boat, and supply any other need
you may have. There are no less than 15
boatyards offering craft for hire, and
summer Saturdays – turn around day – are a
hectic time for the army of mechanics and

Salhouse

Norfolk. PO, stores. A short walk south from the excellent moorings at Salhouse Staithe brings you to this typical Broadland village, which has two fine pubs. The church of All Saints dates partly from the 12thC; unfinished later work has left it with a curiously lopsided appearance. The Old Bakehouse opposite the post office is now a craft shop and tearoom.

BOATYARDS

Ⓑ **Belaugh Boats** (Hoseasons Holidays) Belaugh (Wroxham 2802). Ⓡ Ⓢ Ⓦ Ⓓ Ⓔ Pump-out, Butagas, cruiser hire, winter storage, books and maps, boatbuilding, engine sales and repairs, public toilets. Ⓜ *Closed Sun afternoons.*

Ⓑ **Sabena Marine** (Hoseasons Holidays) Marsh Road, Wroxham (2552). Ⓡ Ⓢ Ⓦ Ⓓ Pump-out, Butane gas, cruiser hire, long-term mooring, winter storage, slipway, books and maps, boatbuilding and sales, boat and engine repairs, public toilet. Ⓜ *Closes 15.00 Suns.*

Ⓑ **Royall & Son** (Hoseasons Holidays) Riverside Road, Hoveton (Wroxham 2743). Ⓡ Ⓦ Ⓓ Pump-out, Butagas, Hudson gas, cruiser hire, day hire boats, slipway, boatbuilding and sales, engine repairs, towage Ⓜ. An old established, helpful and knowledgeable company.

Ⓑ **Fineway Cruisers** (Blakes) Riverside Road, Hoveton (Wroxham 2309). Ⓡ Ⓦ Ⓓ Pump-out, Unigas, cruiser hire, sailing dinghy hire, day hire boats, slipway, provisions, books and maps, boatbuilding, boat and engine repairs, public toilet. Self-drive excursion boat for 11 persons. Ⓜ

Ⓑ **Barnes-Brinkcraft** (Blakes) Riverside Road, Hoveton (Wroxham 2625/2333). Ⓡ Ⓦ Ⓓ Pump-out, Unigas, cruiser hire, sailing craft hire, long-term mooring, winter storage, slipway, books and maps, boatbuilding, boat and engine sales and repairs, public toilet. Ⓜ *Closed Sun afternoons.*

Ⓑ **Jack Powles** Staitheway Road, Hoveton (Wroxham 2101). Ⓡ Ⓦ Ⓓ Pump-out, Unigas, AIG gas, cruiser hire, long-term mooring, winter storage, slipway, books and maps, boatbuilding and sales, boat and engine repairs, public toilet, showers, 70-seater excursion boat, scheduled service to Potter Heigham. Ⓜ *Closed Sun.*

Ⓑ **L L Cruisers** (Blakes) Burecroft, Brimbelow Road, Hoveton (Wroxham 2069). Ⓡ Ⓦ Ⓓ Pump-out, Unigas, cruiser hire, sailing dinghy hire, slipway, books and maps, boatbuilding, light engine repairs, toilets, houseboat. Ⓜ *Closed winter Suns.*

Ⓑ **Bernard Press** (Blakes) Riverside Road, Hoveton (Wroxham 2642). Ⓡ Ⓢ Ⓦ Ⓓ Pump-out, Unigas, cruiser hire, sailing dinghy hire, slipway, boat and engine repairs, toilets. Specialist sailing dinghy builder. Ⓜ

Ⓑ **Porter & Haylett** (Hoseasons Holidays) Viaduct Boatyard, Wroxham (2472). Ⓡ Ⓢ Ⓦ Ⓟ Ⓓ Pump-out, Unigas, Butagas, cruiser hire, sailing dinghy hire, long-term

mooring, winter storage, books and maps, boatbuilding and sales, boat and engine repairs, toilets, showers. Ⓜ *Closed winter weekends.*

Ⓑ **Geo Smith & Sons** (Blakes) The Rhond, Riverside Road, Hoveton (Wroxham 2527). Ⓡ Ⓦ Ⓓ Pump-out, AIG gas, cruiser hire, day hire boats, boatbuilding, boat and engine sales and repairs, toilets, showers. Ⓜ

Ⓑ **Brister Craft** (Hoseasons Holidays) The Rhond, Hoveton (Wroxham 3783). Ⓡ Ⓦ Ⓓ Pump-out, Butagas, cruiser hire, sailing dinghy hire, slipway, maps, boatbuilding, boat and engine repairs, toilets. Ⓜ

Ⓑ **Moore & Co** (Blakes) Grange Walk, Wroxham (3311). Ⓡ Ⓦ Ⓓ Unigas, cruiser hire, day hire boats, long-term mooring, slipway, books and maps, boat and engine repairs, houseboats. Ⓜ

Ⓑ **Faircraft Loynes** (Blakes) The Bridge, Hoveton (Wroxham 2280). Ⓡ Ⓦ Ⓓ Pump-out, Unigas, cruiser hire, day hire boats, books and maps, boatbuilding and sales, boat and engine repairs, public toilets. Ⓜ

Ⓑ **Summercraft** (Hoseasons Holidays) Brimbelow Road, Hoveton (Wroxham 2809). Ⓡ Ⓢ Ⓦ Ⓓ Pump-out, gas, cruiser hire, slipway, chandlery, boatbuilding and sales, boat and engine repairs, public toilet, houseboats. Ⓜ *Closed Sat afternoons.*

Ⓑ **Zodiac Cruisers** (Blakes) Brimbelow Road, Hoveton (Wroxham 3012). Ⓡ Ⓢ Ⓦ Ⓓ Pump-out, Unigas, cruiser hire, slipway, boatbuilding and sales, boat and engine repairs. Ⓜ

BOAT TRIPS

Broads Tours (Wroxham (2207). Regular trips leave from their base close to the station. Restaurant and shop. Two of their boats have hoists for wheelchairs.

MOORING

There are public overnight moorings at Coltishall Common; Belaugh Staithe; Hoveton, near Wroxham Station and also the Kings Head; Salhouse Broad. Also possible are: north bank above Belaugh; at Wroxham for Blakes and Hoseasons craft; between Hoveton Great Broad and Salhouse Broad on both sides of the river. You may find it possible to moor in Wroxham Broad, but it is not recommended.

PUBS AND RESTAURANTS

🍷 **Recruiting Sergeant** Norwich Road, Horstead. Handsome 16thC pub ¼ mile north west of Horstead Mill. Meals (*L&D*), snacks, garden and Norwich Brewery real ale.

🍷 **Railway** Station Road, Coltishall (Norwich 738316). 19thC inn serving Norwich Brewery real ale and meals (*L&D*). Garden. The railway now carries only freight, so there is no longer a station.

🍷 **Red Lion** Church Street, Coltishall (Norwich 737402). Friendly old beamy pub which is deservedly busy in summer. Meals (*L Mon–Fri, D Tue–Sat*) and snacks, Whitbread Wethered real ale and a garden.

Rising Sun Wroxham Road, Coltishall (Norwich 737440). Comfy and welcoming riverside pub, noted for the quality of its food, which may include fresh Cromer crab, pizzas and grills. There is also a children's menu. Norwich Brewery and Websters real ales are served, and there is a terrace and garden by the Staithe. The Granary Bar may be used by families. M

Anchor Anchor Street, Coltishall (Norwich 737214). A fine riverside pub with ¼ mile of moorings, and fishing rights. Bar meals (*L&D*) snacks. Websters real ale. M

Hotel Wroxham Wroxham (2061). Varied selection of real ales in a quiet modern hotel which has a solarium. Meals (*L&D*), afternoon teas and riverside terrace.

King's Head Station Road, Wroxham (2429). Meals (*L&D*), snacks, garden and Norwich Brewery real ale. Children's room.

Horseshoes Station Road, Wroxham (2352). Modern pub with a garden, close to the river. Norwich Brewery and Websters real ales, meals (*L&D*).

Broads Hotel Station Road, Wroxham (2869). Smart hotel bar. Food (*L&D*).

Bell Lower Street, Salhouse (Norwich 721141). 17thC inn with low-beamed ceilings, dispensing Norwich Brewery real ale, food (*L&D Mon–Thur*) and snacks. Garden and children's room.

Lodge Vicarage Road, Salhouse (Wroxham 2828). Until 1975 this was a Georgian vicarage, now it's a popular pub serving a good selection of real ales and single malt whiskies. Buffet (*L*), carvery (*D Mon–Sat*) and large garden.

Buckinghamshire Arms Blickling (Aylsham 732133). A visit to Blickling Hall would not be complete without a stop (or a stay) at this traditional English 17thC pub. Balanced choice of real ales, excellent restaurant food (*D and carvery Sun L*) and bar meals (*L&D*). Garden with play area. Three bedrooms with four-poster beds. Children welcome in the restaurant.

Midweek at Wroxham

Typical carr woodland persists on each bank, with the occasional, small, unnavigable broad just visible through the thick growth.

Horning lies to the north after Hoveton Little Broad (*navigable summer only*), outlying villas and chalets gradually giving way to the more substantial but equally charming dwellings in the village. It's a busy place with plenty of boatyards, and many private craft. Then once again the woodland takes over, thinning on the north bank to allow a sight of Horning church. At Horning Hall the view at last widens, and the River Ant joins from the north. (See page 47).

NAVIGATIONAL NOTES

Hoveton Little Broad *Open Easter Sat–2nd Sat Sep.* No landing, except by dinghy where specified.

Dinghy sailing Weekends at Horning. Needs careful and steady navigating.

condition – 100 years ago all the broads were like this. The half-mile walkway follows Cockshoot Dike to a hide overlooking the broad. *Open all year.* Ⓜ at the mouth of the dike.

Horning

Norfolk. EC Wed, PO, stores. A Broadland holiday centre, but perhaps less commercially so than Wroxham. Thatched Edwardian lodges fronted by lawns and thatched boathouses lend a touch of elegance to the riverside with new, bijou, executive residences in between. The church of St Benedict stands separate from the village, a mile to the east. Dating from the 13thC, its north aisle and porch were dismantled and sold off in the mid 18thC to pay for a new roof. Horning Hall (private) lies a further mile to the east – the barn (visible from the river) was once the Chapel of St James's Hospital, connected to St Benet's Abbey Gatehouse by a causeway. The remains of

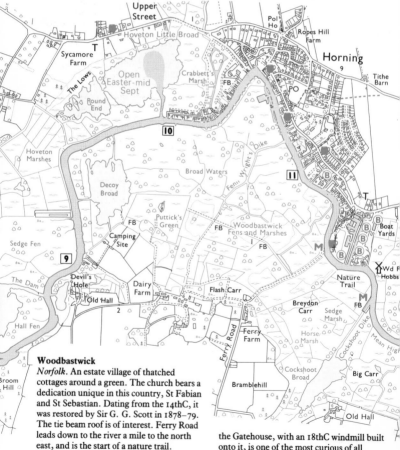

Woodbastwick

Norfolk. An estate village of thatched cottages around a green. The church bears a dedication unique in this country, St Fabian and St Sebastian. Dating from the 14thC, it was restored by Sir G. G. Scott in 1878–79. The tie beam roof is of interest. Ferry Road leads down to the river a mile to the north east, and is the start of a nature trail.

Cockshoot Broad Nature Trail (NNT and NCC). Starts from the end of Ferry Road, north east of Woodbastwick. In 1982 the Broads Authority dammed off the broad and pumped out three feet of mud and ooze, restoring the water to its former clear

the Gatehouse, with an 18thC windmill built onto it, is one of the most curious of all Broads landmarks. *A regatta is held in Horning each August, and the Three Rivers Race starts from here in early June.* The ferry to Woodbastwick no longer operates.

Hobbs Mill Horning. An open-framed trestle windpump standing by the river.

Ranworth

Norfolk. EC Sat, PO, stores. The tall square tower of St Helen's church is visible for miles, and those who climb to the top will be rewarded with magnificent views. The 15thC rood screen, with its 12 delicately painted saints; dogs, ducks, swans and lions, is considered the finest in Norfolk; the reredos of the two side altars also have painted figures. It was all discovered during the last century when whitewash was removed. The *Sarum Antiphoner* – a leather book brilliantly illuminated with burnished gold – is kept in the church during the summer months. Created by the monks of Langley Abbey, it was sold to the church for 50 guineas after being lost for many years.

Information Centre Ranworth Staithe (South Walsham 453). *Open Apr–Sep.*

Broadlands Conservation Centre (NNT) Ranworth (South Walsham 479). A ½ mile nature trail which starts to the north of the church, leads through Ranworth Marshes to a thatched building floating on pontoons between Ranworth and Malthouse Broads. An exhibition shows the natural life of the Broads, emphasising the need for conservation. The upstairs gallery, where you may hire binoculars, offers excellent views. *Open daily Apr–Oct. Closed Mon and Sat mornings. Wed afternoons are reserved for visiting parties.* No dogs.

BOATYARDS

Ⓑ **Southgates** Lower Street, Horning (630306). Ⓡ Ⓦ Pump-out, Unigas, cruiser hire, sailing dinghy hire, day hire boats, slipway, books and maps, toilets, showers. Ⓜ *Closed Sun.*

Ⓑ **Ferry Boatyard** (Blakes) Ferry Road, Horning (630392). Ⓡ Ⓦ Ⓟ Ⓓ Pump-out, Unigas, cruiser hire, day hire boats, long-term mooring, winter storage, slipway, books and maps, boatbuilding and sales, boat and engine repairs, public toilet, showers, houseboats. Ⓜ Also Helska Leisure Centre, with swimming pool, jacuzzi and gym (not inexpensive).

Ⓑ **Blue Line Cruisers** (Hoseasons Holidays) Ferry View Estate, Horning (630366/630128). Ⓡ Ⓦ Ⓓ Ⓔ Pump-out, AIG gas, cruiser hire, sailing dinghy hire, boat hoist, boat and engine repairs, public toilet. Ⓜ *Closed Sun afternoons and winter weekends.*

Ⓑ **King Line Cruisers** (Hoseasons Holidays) Ferry View Estate, Horning (630297). Ⓦ Ⓓ Ⓔ Pump-out, Unigas, cruiser hire, day hire boats, dry dock, books and maps, boat and engine sales and repairs. Ⓜ *Open May–Oct. Closed Sun.*

Ⓑ **Ellis Frost Marine** Ferry Road, Horning (630498). Ⓢ Ⓦ Ⓟ Ⓓ Pump-out, Unigas, cruiser hire, day hire boats, slipway, books and maps, boat and engine sales and repairs. *Open Jun–mid Sep.*

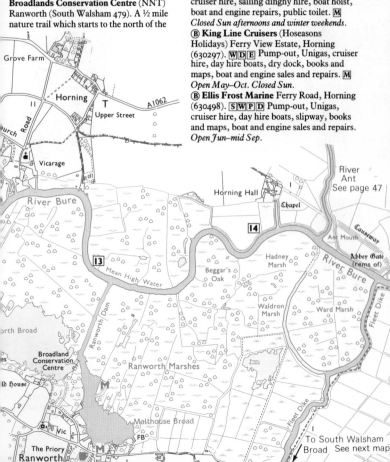

Ⓑ **Chumley & Hawke** (Hoseasons Holidays) Burehaven Marina, Lower Street, Horning (630214). ⓇⓌⓅⒹⒺ Pump-out, Butagas, cruiser hire, sailing craft hire, day boat hire, long-term mooring, slipway, dry dock, boatbuilding, boat and engine repairs, public toilet. Ⓜ *Closed Sun in winter.*

Ⓑ **Compass Craft** (Blakes) Ferry View Estate, Horning (630401) ⓇⓌⒹ Pump-out, Unigas, cruiser hire, winter storage, slipway, gantry, boatbuilding, engine sales and repairs. Ⓜ *Closed Sun.*

Ⓑ **Nerina Cruiseways** Horning (630443). ⓌⒹ Pump-out, AIG gas, long-term mooring, dry dock, boatbuilding, boat and engine repairs, public toilet.

Ⓑ **Colin Facey Boats** (Blakes) Ferry Road, Horning (630302). ⓌⒹ Pump-out, Butagas, cruiser hire, sailing dinghy hire, day hire boats, crane, boatbuilding, boat and engine repairs, toilets, showers, houseboats. Ⓜ *Closed Sun afternoons and winter weekends.*

BOAT TRIPS

Nerina Cruiseways Horning (630443). 32-seater boat with cold buffet and bar, *leaves daily in summer at 11.00, 15.00 & 19.30 for 2-hour trips.* Available for private charter.

Southern Comfort Mississippi River Boat, Hill House, Ropes Hill, Horning (630262). Trips from the Swan at Horning.

Olive To book trips on this lovely little steam launch based at the Swan, ring Horning 630123.

MOORING

There are public overnight moorings at Woodbastwick, opposite the Ferry pub, Horning; Cockshoot Dike; Upper Street Staithe; Ranworth Staithe and east bank of approach from Ranworth Dam. There are many other opportunities for mooring on this section: by Hoveton Marshes and Decoy Broad; around Horning (although many moorings are private); opposite Ranworth Broad. Do not try to moor by St Benet's Abbey.

PUBS AND RESTAURANTS

🍺 **Black Horse** Horning Road, Upper Street (Horning 630271). Modern pub serving Whitbread Wethered real ale, food (*L&D*) and snacks. Children's room.

🍺 **Swan** Lower Street, Horning (630316). Large pub next door to the Sailing Club. One timbered bar, serving Norwich Brewery and Wethered real ales. Bar meals (*L&D*), restaurant (*L summer only*). Children's room and garden. Ⓜ

🍺 **New Inn** Lower Street, Horning (630309). Riverside pub with a playground in the garden. Bar snacks. Ⓜ

🍺 **Petersfield House Hotel** Lower Street, Horning (630741). Comfortable bar in a residential hotel. Adnams real ale, meals (*L&D*), snacks and large garden. Ⓜ

🍺 **Ferry Inn** Ferry Road, Horning (630259). An imposing Chef & Brewer pub offering bar meals (*L&D*), snacks, and Norwich Brewery beers. Games room, garden. Ⓜ

🍺 **Maltsters** Ranworth (South Walsham 241). Popular pub with a nautical theme. Food (*L&D*) in the lounge. Norwich Brewery real ale, garden, children's play area. Ⓜ

The steam launch 'Olive' at Horning

Marshland now begins to predominate as the river passes what little remains of St Benet's Abbey; parts of the old walls showing clearly in the river bank.

At Thurne Mouth the Bure makes a sharp turn south towards Acle, and the distant windmills define the course ahead. There are posts marking a measured ¼ mile here, and you can check your speed: multiply your time between the posts by 4 and divide the result by 60. If the answer is more than 7, slow down!

Upton Dyke provides access to the village, and the opportunity to examine a unique drainage mill.

After passing the handsome Clippesby Mill, Acle Bridge is reached, attended by cruiser bases and a pub – the town is a mile away at this point.

Leaving the bridge a useful farm shop M is passed; a flurry of boats marks the entrance to Acle Dike before the reed-fringed river enters open country once again.

NAVIGATIONAL NOTES

Tides If you are making the passage through Great Yarmouth and Breydon Water to the southern broads, you should arrive at the Yacht Station within one hour after low water slack. If you are unfamiliar with tide tables consult your own boatyard or ring the Yacht Station on Great Yarmouth 842794. *DO NOT attempt to make the passage at full ebb or flow – it is potentially dangerous.*

River Bure Fleet Dike to Thurne Mouth. This is a special angling area. Avoid cruising here prior to 09.00 Sun.

St Benet's Abbey

There are but scant remains of this foundation, which may have existed even before it was endowed with three manors by King Canute (Cnut) in 1020. Overwhelmed by floodwater in 1287, most of the site was rebuilt, including the gatehouse and wall, and these defences were tested in 1381 when the monastery was attacked by peasants.

By Acle Bridge

Palmers Hollow Post Mill Upton Dyke. A
tiny hollow-post drainage windpump,
unique in that it has a plunger action. It was
moved here from Acle, and can be viewed
from the footpath.

Clippesby Mill Just below the entrance to
Upton Dyke. A four-storey tower
windpump. Although not open to the
public, the machinery is intact.

Acle

*Norfolk. EC Wed, MD Thur/Sun. PO, stores,
BR station.* Half way between Norwich and
Great Yarmouth, Acle is a pleasant market
town (general goods and livestock), with
some nice houses around the crossroads. St
Edmund's church has a round tower dating
from the 13thC – the battlements were added
in 1472 at a cost of £16. The tall screen is
very fine and the font is dated 1410 – four
lions and four wild men adorn the stem.
Acle Bridge, a mile north east, was the site of
many executions, the luckless criminals
being hanged from the parapets. Concrete
has replaced medieval stone, but the ghosts
apparently remain . . . Ⓡ

BOATYARDS

Ⓑ **R & C Bondon** (Blakes) Fleet Lane,
South Walsham (262) ⓇⓌⒹ Pump-out,
AIG gas, cruiser hire, long-term mooring,
winter storage, gantry, boatbuilding, boat
and engine repairs, toilets. Ⓜ *Closed Sun
afternoons and winter.*

Ⓑ **Eastwood Whelpton** (Blakes) Upton
Yacht Station (Great Yarmouth 750430)
ⓇⓈⓌ Butagas, sailing craft hire, winter
storage. Ⓜ *Closed Sun afternoons.*

Ⓑ **Bridgecraft** (Hoseasons Holidays) Acle
Bridge (Great Yarmouth 750378). ⓌⒹ
Pump-out, Butagas, Unigas, cruiser hire,
day hire boats.

Ⓑ **Horizon Craft** (Hoseasons Holidays) Acle
Bridge (Great Yarmouth 750283). ⓇⓌⒹ
Pump-out, Unigas, cruiser hire, maps, boat
and engine repairs, toilets. Ⓜ *Closed Sun and
winter weekends.*

Ⓑ **Alan Johnson** (Hoseasons Holidays) Acle
Bridge (Great Yarmouth 750481). ⓇⓈⓌⒹ
Pump-out, Unigas, Butagas, cruiser hire,
slipway (*not Fri or Sat*), maps. *Closes 15.00
Sun, closed winter.*

Ⓑ **Anchor Craft** (Blakes) Acle Bridge (Great
Yarmouth 750500). ⓇⓌ Pump-out, AIG
gas, cruiser hire, day hire boats, slipway,
maps, boatbuilding, boat and engine repairs.
Ⓜ *Closed in winter.*

Ⓑ **Easticks Yacht Station** (Blakes) Boat
Dyke Lane, Acle (Great Yarmouth 750264).
ⓇⓌⒹ Pump-out, Hudson gas, cruiser hire,
sailing craft hire, long-term mooring, winter
storage, slipway, dry dock, chandlery (old
style yacht fittings), books and maps,
boatbuilding, boat and engine sales and
repairs, houseboats. Ⓜ *Closed Sat, & Sun
afternoons.*

After the Dissolution the site was quarried
for building materials, leaving only the
gatehouse, joined to Horning Hall by a
causeway, onto which an 18thC windmill has
been built. There are also fragments of the
church to be seen. The last Abbot became
Bishop of Norwich – a service held here on
the *first Sunday in August* when the Bishop
arrives by boat, commemorates this fact.
Mooring by this site is inadvisable.

South Walsham

Norfolk. PO, stores. A pleasant village south
of the broad, which has two churches
sharing one churchyard, the result of an
amalgamation of parishes a century ago. St
Lawrence lies partly in ruins, having been
burnt out in 1827, St Mary survives and is an
extremely handsome, mainly Perpendicular,
building. The screen is notable and many of
the pew ends are carved with poppy heads,
some 600 years old.

The walk by South Walsham Broad along
Fleet Dike to the river is excellent.

Fairhaven Garden Trust (South Walsham
449). By South Walsham Inner Broad.
Gardens of rare plants and shrubs, especially
primulas and rhododendrons, best seen in
early summer. *Open Wed–Sun, Apr–Sep.*
Teas. Admission charge.

Upton

Norfolk. PO, store. Scattered houses around
a green, with the church of St Margaret, a
large Perpendicular building, standing apart
to the south. Some of the pew ends are
carved with poppy heads. A stone in the
graveyard is carved with a wherry, the
traditional Broadland sailing vessel.

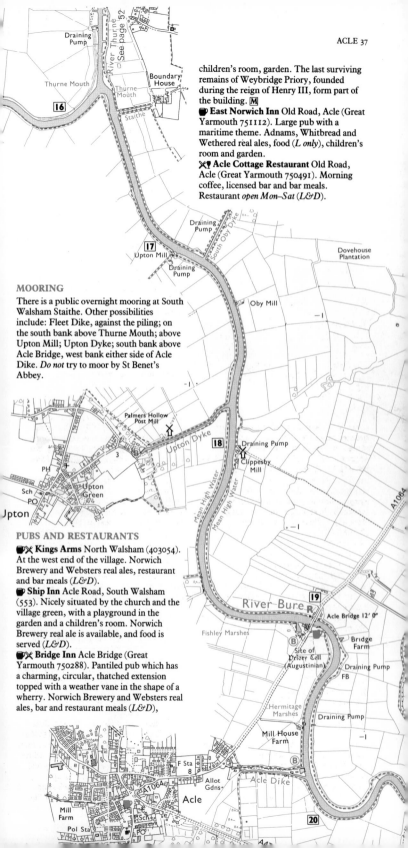

children's room, garden. The last surviving remains of Weybridge Priory, founded during the reign of Henry III, form part of the building. M

East Norwich Inn Old Road, Acle (Great Yarmouth 751112). Large pub with a maritime theme. Adnams, Whitbread and Wethered real ales, food (*L only*), children's room and garden.

Acle Cottage Restaurant Old Road, Acle (Great Yarmouth 750491). Morning coffee, licensed bar and bar meals. Restaurant *open Mon–Sat* (*L&D*).

MOORING

There is a public overnight mooring at South Walsham Staithe. Other possibilities include: Fleet Dike, against the piling; on the south bank above Thurne Mouth; above Upton Mill; Upton Dyke; south bank above Acle Bridge, west bank either side of Acle Dike. *Do not* try to moor by St Benet's Abbey.

PUBS AND RESTAURANTS

Kings Arms North Walsham (403054). At the west end of the village. Norwich Brewery and Websters real ales, restaurant and bar meals (*L&D*).

Ship Inn Acle Road, South Walsham (553). Nicely situated by the church and the village green, with a playground in the garden and a children's room. Norwich Brewery real ale is available, and food is served (*L&D*).

Bridge Inn Acle Bridge (Great Yarmouth 750288). Pantiled pub which has a charming, circular, thatched extension topped with a weather vane in the shape of a wherry. Norwich Brewery and Websters real ales, bar and restaurant meals (*L&D*),

STRACEY ARMS

RIVER BURE 38

The river passes the isolated village of
Stokesby and soon resumes its lonely course
until the main Norwich–Yarmouth road
closes in at Stracey Arms. This is, however,
but a brief encounter and once again the
marshes dominate; the flat skyline broken by
the towers of ruined windpumps and the
distant chimneys of Great Yarmouth.
Imperceptibly the character of the river
changes – the exposed riverbed becomes
muddier and the piling heavier. The harbour
at Great Yarmouth cannot be far away.

Stokesby
Norfolk. PO, store. A charming and unspoilt
red-brick riverside village. The thatched
church of St Andrew is a short walk to the
east. It is mainly Decorated and contains
benches with openwork tracery backs, ends
carved with poppy heads, and arm rests with
animals and a kneeling woman. There are
some excellent brasses. Glebe Farmhouse,
across the road, has a medieval stone
doorway. Candles are made in a workshop in
the village.

Stracey Arms Windpump
Built on piles
sunk some 40 feet between the road and the
river, this pump is fully restored and the
brakewheel and gears can be examined.
Open daily Apr–Oct.

Runham
Norfolk. A small farming community. Set
apart to the east is the church of St Peter and
St Paul, its north tower topped with
battlements and pinnacles. Parts of the
building date from the 14thC.

Ormesby, Rollesby and Filby Broads
Lying about 3½ miles south east of Heigham
Bridge or 3 miles north east of Acle Bridge.
Known as the 'Trinity Broads' these isolated
but very beautiful broads abound with
wildlife, and their surrounding villages make
a fascinating area well-worth exploring. If
you do not feel energetic enough to walk
there you can catch buses from Heigham
Bridge to Rollesby, or to Ormesby St
Margaret via Martham, Winterton on Sea,
Hemsby Beach and Rollesby (a good
sightseeing tour); from Acle Bridge buses
run to Fleggburgh, Filby and Caister. For
times, ring Eastern Counties Bus Company,
Norwich 660421.

Rollesby
Norfolk. A quiet village west of Ormesby
Broad (rowing boat hire in summer). The
church of St George has a Norman round
tower, the rest of the building being of 14thC
origin.

Ormesby St Margaret (and St Michael)
Norfolk. A larger village to the east of the
Broad, with some handsome houses. The
church has a Perpendicular battlemented
tower and a Norman south doorway. Down
by Rollesby Broad is Ormesby St Michael,
where you will find the Eels Foot pub, a very
pleasant place in which to relax. Its wooded
garden stretches down to the water's edge –
there are some toys for the children, and
ducks to feed.

Filby
Norfolk. A pretty village with some
charming old cottages and a pub. The
church is worth a second look – you will find
inside this mainly Decorated building a fine
rood screen, with eight painted saints, and
no less than seven locks on the belfry door,
which was probably once used as a
strongroom. The north door is embellished
with foliated 14thC ironwork.

Thrigby Hall Wildlife Gardens
Just south
of Filby on the Stokesby road (Fleggburgh
477). Mature landscaped gardens containing
Asian mammals, birds and reptiles. Tropical
house, bird house, deer paddock, snow
leopards, gibbons and a lake. Children's
playground, café and gift shop. *Open daily.*
Admission charge.

To the west of Filby Broad is Fleggburgh
(Burgh St Margaret) where you will find the
King's Arms, a good village pub with a log
fire on cold days (real ale).

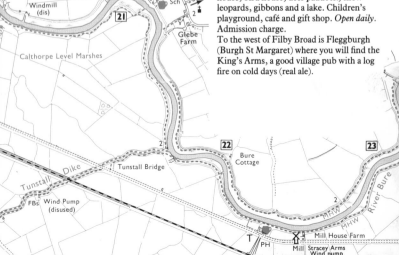

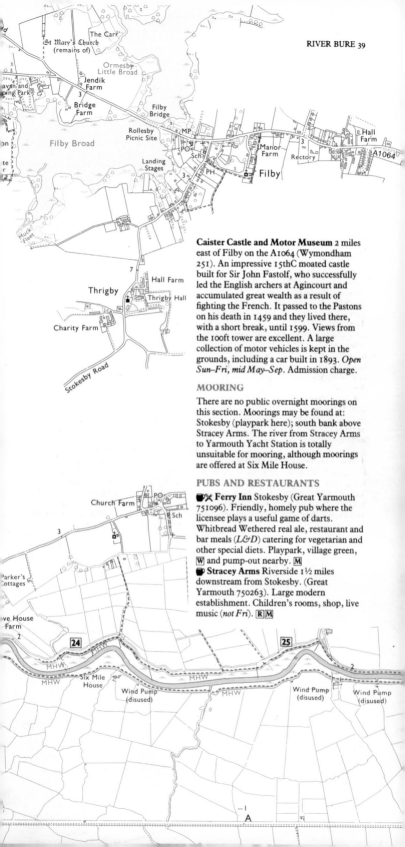

Caister Castle and Motor Museum 2 miles
east of Filby on the A1064 (Wymondham
251). An impressive 15thC moated castle
built for Sir John Fastolf, who successfully
led the English archers at Agincourt and
accumulated great wealth as a result of
fighting the French. It passed to the Pastons
on his death in 1459 and they lived there,
with a short break, until 1599. Views from
the 100ft tower are excellent. A large
collection of motor vehicles is kept in the
grounds, including a car built in 1893. *Open
Sun–Fri, mid May–Sep*. Admission charge.

MOORING

There are no public overnight moorings on
this section. Moorings may be found at:
Stokesby (playpark here); south bank above
Stracey Arms. The river from Stracey Arms
to Yarmouth Yacht Station is totally
unsuitable for mooring, although moorings
are offered at Six Mile House.

PUBS AND RESTAURANTS

Ferry Inn Stokesby (Great Yarmouth
751096). Friendly, homely pub where the
licensee plays a useful game of darts.
Whitbread Wethered real ale, restaurant and
bar meals (*L&D*) catering for vegetarian and
other special diets. Playpark, village green,
W and pump-out nearby. M

Stracey Arms Riverside 1½ miles
downstream from Stokesby. (Great
Yarmouth 750263). Large modern
establishment. Children's rooms, shop, live
music (*not Fri*). R M

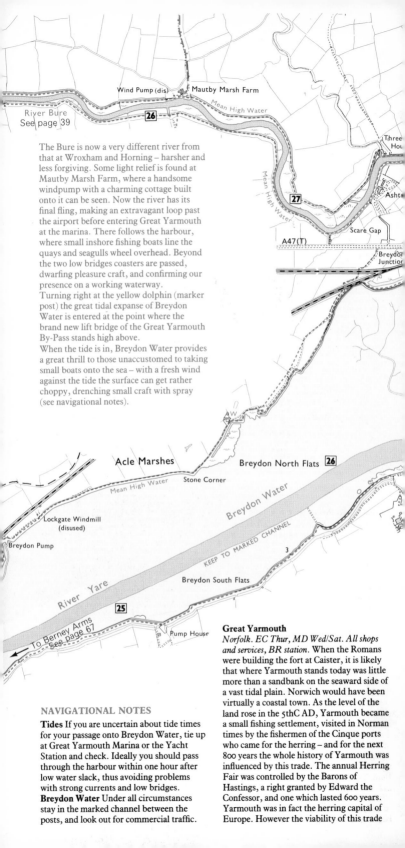

Wind Pump (dis)   **Mautby Marsh Farm**

River Bure
See page 39

Mean High Water

`26`

The Bure is now a very different river from
that at Wroxham and Horning – harsher and
less forgiving. Some light relief is found at
Mautby Marsh Farm, where a handsome
windpump with a charming cottage built
onto it can be seen. Now the river has its
final fling, making an extravagant loop past
the airport before entering Great Yarmouth
at the marina. There follows the harbour,
where small inshore fishing boats line the
quays and seagulls wheel overhead. Beyond
the two low bridges coasters are passed,
dwarfing pleasure craft, and confirming our
presence on a working waterway.
Turning right at the yellow dolphin (marker
post) the great tidal expanse of Breydon
Water is entered at the point where the
brand new lift bridge of the Great Yarmouth
By-Pass stands high above.
When the tide is in, Breydon Water provides
a great thrill to those unaccustomed to taking
small boats onto the sea – with a fresh wind
against the tide the surface can get rather
choppy, drenching small craft with spray
(see navigational notes).

Three
Hou

Mean High Water

`27`

Asht

Scare Gap

A47(T)

Breydon
Junction

Acle Marshes   **Breydon North Flats** `26`

Mean High Water   Stone Corner

Breydon Water

Lockgate Windmill
(disused)

Breydon Pump

KEEP TO MARKED CHANNEL   3

Breydon South Flats

River Yare

`25`

To Berney Arms
See page 67   Pump House

See page 39

See page 67

NAVIGATIONAL NOTES

Tides If you are uncertain about tide times
for your passage onto Breydon Water, tie up
at Great Yarmouth Marina or the Yacht
Station and check. Ideally you should pass
through the harbour within one hour after
low water slack, thus avoiding problems
with strong currents and low bridges.
Breydon Water Under all circumstances
stay in the marked channel between the
posts, and look out for commercial traffic.

Great Yarmouth
*Norfolk. EC Thur, MD Wed/Sat. All shops
and services, BR station.* When the Romans
were building the fort at Caister, it is likely
that where Yarmouth stands today was little
more than a sandbank on the seaward side of
a vast tidal plain. Norwich would have been
virtually a coastal town. As the level of the
land rose in the 5thC AD, Yarmouth became
a small fishing settlement, visited in Norman
times by the fishermen of the Cinque ports
who came for the herring – and for the next
800 years the whole history of Yarmouth was
influenced by this trade. The annual Herring
Fair was controlled by the Barons of
Hastings, a right granted by Edward the
Confessor, and one which lasted 600 years.
Yarmouth was in fact the herring capital of
Europe. However the viability of this trade

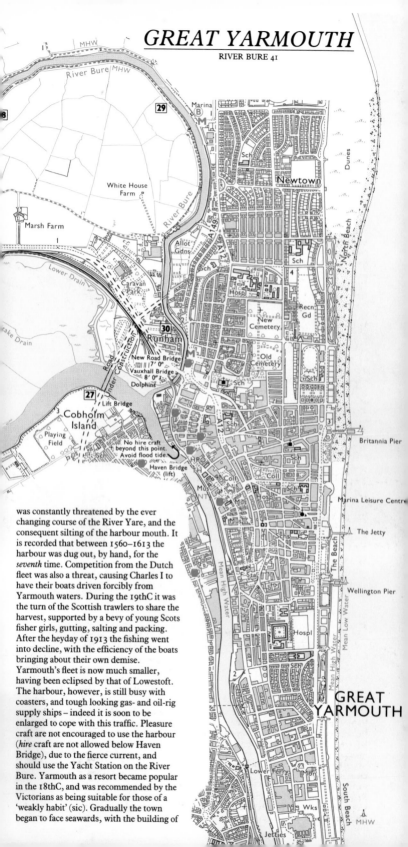

GREAT YARMOUTH

RIVER BURE 41

was constantly threatened by the ever changing course of the River Yare, and the consequent silting of the harbour mouth. It is recorded that between 1560–1613 the harbour was dug out, by hand, for the *seventh* time. Competition from the Dutch fleet was also a threat, causing Charles I to have their boats driven forcibly from Yarmouth waters. During the 19thC it was the turn of the Scottish trawlers to share the harvest, supported by a bevy of young Scots fisher girls, gutting, salting and packing. After the heyday of 1913 the fishing went into decline, with the efficiency of the boats bringing about their own demise. Yarmouth's fleet is now much smaller, having been eclipsed by that of Lowestoft. The harbour, however, is still busy with coasters, and tough looking gas- and oil-rig supply ships – indeed it is soon to be enlarged to cope with this traffic. Pleasure craft are not encouraged to use the harbour (*hire* craft are not allowed below Haven Bridge), due to the fierce current, and should use the Yacht Station on the River Bure. Yarmouth as a resort became popular in the 18thC, and was recommended by the Victorians as being suitable for those of a 'weakly habit' (sic). Gradually the town began to face seawards, with the building of

The Yacht Station, Great Yarmouth

hotels and piers. Parts of the old town wall
survive – this once enclosed over 140 'rows',
narrow alleys between 2ft 6in and 6ft wide.
Only a few of these survived the terrible
pounding the town suffered during both
world wars.

Those who moor at the Marina or Yacht
Station and visit the town will easily find
plenty of seaside amusements and
diversions. But by far the most interesting
part of the town is to be found by walking
from St Nicholas Church (up Fullers Hill
from North Quay), through the market and
the 'rows' and on down the South Quay,
where there are many attractive period
houses and a choice of museums.

St Nicholas Church Church Plain. The
largest parish church in England, dating
from the 12thC and once attached to a
Benedictine Priory. Having been restored
from a ruined condition in 1847 and 1862, it
was gutted by fire in 1942. During the period
1957–60 it was rebuilt within the 13thC
walls in a disappointing imitation Gothic –
the result is impressive but lacking in
authenticity and coherent style.

The Rows To the east of the Market Place,
Market Row and Broad Row are notable
survivors of the bombing.

Fisherman's Hospital Church Plain. A
handsome single-storey building, founded in
1702.

Anna Sewell House Church Plain. Anna
Sewell (1820–78), the author of *Black
Beauty*, was born here. The house has been
restored to its 17thC condition with the
original inglenooks. Collection of
memorabilia. *Open daily*. Admission charge.

South Quay Some fine period houses,
including the Customs House, built by John
Andrews, 'the greatest herring merchant in
Europe', in 1720.

Elizabethan House Museum South Quay,
Great Yarmouth (855746). 16thC merchant's
house. Room settings and displays of
Victorian life. *Open Sun–Fri, Jun–Sep;
Mon–Fri, Oct–May*. Admission charge.

**Old Merchant's House, The Row 111
Houses and Greyfriars** Off South Quay,
Great Yarmouth (857900). A worthwhile
tour starting at the Row 111 Houses. The
Old Merchant's House is a 17thC brick
building with wooden mullioned windows –
inside is a collection of 17th–18thC domestic
ironwork. Greyfriars was founded by the
Franciscans in 1226. Little now remains.
Open 09.45–15.45 Mon–Fri, Apr–Sep.

Admission charge. Parties by appointment
only.

Tolhouse Museum Tolhouse Street, Great
Yarmouth (842267). Maritime history in the
old shipwrecked sailors home, built in 1858.
*Open Sun–Fri, Jun–Sep; Mon–Fri,
Oct–May*. Admission charge.

The Piers Wellington Pier was built in 1853,
Brittania Pier in 1857 (rebuilt in 1901). Both
have theatres and the usual attractions. The
Jetty dates from 1560, having since been
rebuilt and extended several times.

Tourist Information 1 South Quay, Great
Yarmouth (856100), Hall Plain (844313) and
Marine Parade (842195).

Breydon Water Nature Reserve
An expanse of tidal water on the River Bure.
Once a favourite haunt of wildfowlers and
'punt-gunners', it became a Local Nature
Reserve in 1968. In spring and autumn
migrating ducks, waders and geese can be
seen. Public footpaths skirt the whole of
Breydon Water, and there are hides on the
north bank (keys from Great Yarmouth and
Gorleston Central Libraries and Great
Yarmouth Town Hall). *Open all year*, access
to the reserve is best from under the railway
bridge at Great Yarmouth or turn right past
the church at Burgh Castle.

BOATYARDS

ⓑ **Great Yarmouth Marina** Great
Yarmouth (842253). Ⓡ Ⓢ Ⓦ (75p) Ⓟ Ⓓ
Pump-out, long-term mooring, provisions,
books and maps, toilets, showers, licensed
clubhouse, snack bar, amusements,
playpark. Ⓜ up to 2 hours: £2; Ⓜ 24 hours:
£3.50 (1985 prices).

ⓑ **Great Yarmouth Yacht Station** Lawn
Avenue, Great Yarmouth (842794). Advice
regarding tides. Ⓜ 24 hours: £4.80 (1985).
Open summer season only.

BOAT TRIPS

Pleasure Steamers Two boats offering
a regular programme of Broads trips
throughout the summer, starting
from Haven Bridge. (Great Yarmouth
850378).

MOORING

The only recommended moorings are those
on the River Bure; at Great Yarmouth
Marina; at South Quay (Yacht Station)
above the White Swan (moor facing
upstream into the strong current). In an
emergency it may be possible to moor on the

south bank at Scare Gap or opposite Mautby Marsh Farm.

PUBS AND RESTAURANTS

It is not difficult to find a pub or a café in Great Yarmouth. Unfortunately a great many are geared to the seasonal holiday trade and lack quality or imagination. The pubs which follow have been chosen for their proximity to the river, the eating places because their menu extends further than hamburgers or fish and chips with peas.

🍺 **White Swan** North Quay, Great Yarmouth (859679). Pleasantly geared towards those in boats, this riverside pub serves Websters real ale, snacks and meals (*L&D*). Garden.

🍺 **St John's Head** North Quay, Great Yarmouth (843443). Whitbread Wethered real ale, good food (*L only*) and snacks in a modernised pub.

🍺 **Talbot** 4 Howard Street North, Great Yarmouth (843175). No less than 16 real ales in a small comfortable one bar pub next to the Police Station and close to the 'Rows'. Bar snacks.

🍺 **Star and Garter** Hall Quay, Great Yarmouth (842740). Whitbread real ale in a single bar pub by Haven Bridge. Bar snacks.

🍺 **Gallon Can** South Quay, Great Yarmouth (852687). Adnams and Bass real ales in an old pub facing the River Yare. Meals (*L&D*) and snacks. M

✕🍷 **Friends Bistro** 55 Deneside, Great Yarmouth (852538). A good range of excellent savoury dishes – chicken and asparagus quiche, barbecued spare ribs – and tempting sweets. *Open Mon–Sat 10.00–16.00 (L), Tue–Sat 19.00–22.00 (D).*

✕🍷 **Zak's Yankee Traveller** 36 King Street, Great Yarmouth (57065). The theme is travel in the US, and the food, not surprisingly, is solid American fare – Manhattan clam chowder and a choice of burgers. *Open midday to after 23.00, Sun 16.00–22.30.*

🍺 **Cobholm Tavern** Mill Road, Cobholm, Great Yarmouth (650554). Whitbread Wethered real ale in convivial surroundings. Bar snacks (*L*).

🍺 **Anson Arms** Southtown Road, Great Yarmouth (603874). Olde worlde interior in which to enjoy Norwich Brewery and Websters real ales, and perhaps a snack (*L, Mon–Fri*).

✕🍷 **Rambouillet Restaurant** North Drive, Great Yarmouth (842000). Fine cuisine created around local specialities such as lobster, oysters and game (in season), also French dishes. *Open daily (L&D).*

A fresh breeze at Stracey Arms

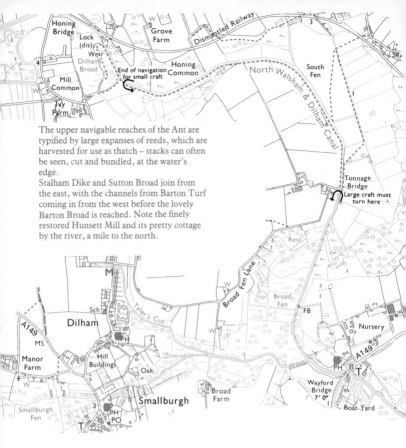

The upper navigable reaches of the Ant are typified by large expanses of reeds, which are harvested for use as thatch – stacks can often be seen, cut and bundled, at the water's edge.

Stalham Dike and Sutton Broad join from the east, with the channels from Barton Turf coming in from the west before the lovely Barton Broad is reached. Note the finely restored Hunsett Mill and its pretty cottage by the river, a mile to the north.

NAVIGATIONAL NOTES

Wayford Bridge 7ft 0in at normal levels.
Barton Broad Keep in channel between posts.

Dilham

Norfolk. Store. A brief respite from obscurity came to Dilham with the opening of the North Walsham and Dilham Canal on 29 August 1826. Regrettably the venture was never a financial success and the last wherry took a cargo from Bacton Wood Staithe in 1934, since which time the canal and the village have remained very much a backwater.

Stalham

Norfolk. EC Wed, MD Tue. PO, stores. Stalham Staithe is a popular holiday venue, separated from this busy Georgian market town by the main A149 road. The squat, mainly Decorated church of St Mary contains a remarkable 15thC font, standing on three steps, one decorated with a catherine wheel motif. The Trinity, Christ's Baptism and 12 Apostles are depicted on the bowl.

Sutton

Norfolk. PO, stores. The village lies to the east of Sutton Staithe, across the main A149, at the head of Sutton Broad, now so overgrown the navigation channel has to be maintained with regular clearing. A crop of reeds is taken regularly for thatch. The small church of St Michael, to the east of the main street, is 14thC.

Sutton Windmill ½ mile east of the village, on the back road to Hickling (Stalham 81195). Nine storeys, machinery and sails rescued from dereliction by the present owners. Splendid views from the top. Local museum, tea rooms. *Open afternoons Apr–mid May, daily mid May–Sep.* Admission charge.

Barton Turf

Norfolk. A tiny village whose origins probably lie in the seasonal migration to dig peat (or turf), but whose pride must rest in its church, St Michael. The large west tower has a superb entrance door, but of particular interest is the rood screen, considered by some to be amongst the finest in England. Dating from the 15thC, the paintings depict three saints and a set of Heavenly Hierarchies (order of angels). There is also a fine brass to Thomas Amys, 1445. Barton Broad is a nature reserve, administered by the NNT. Once by-passed by the Ant, the river was diverted to flow through it.

BOATYARDS

Ⓑ **Bowerscraft** (Blakes) Wayford Bridge, Stalham (80260). Ⓡ Ⓢ Ⓦ Ⓟ Ⓓ Pump-out, Calor, Unigas, Butagas, Shell gas, cruiser hire, sailing craft hire, long-term mooring, crane, winter storage, boat and engine repairs, boat sales, houseboats. Ⓜ *Closed Sun afternoons and winter.*

Ⓑ **Neatishead Boatyard** (Blakes) Wayford Bridge, Stalham (80465). Ⓦ Ⓓ Butagas, cruiser hire, long-term mooring, winter

storage, crane, maps, toilets. Ⓜ *Closed winter weekends.*

Ⓑ **Stalham Yacht Services** (Blakes) The Staithe, Stalham (80288). ⓇⓌⓅⒹ Pump-out, Calor, Unigas, cruiser hire, day hire boats, long-term mooring, winter storage, slipway, boatbuilding, boat and engine repairs, toilet, houseboats. Ⓜ *Closed Sun afternoons and winter weekends.*

Ⓑ **John Williams Boats** (Blakes) The Staithe, Stalham (80953). ⓇⓌⒹⒺ Pump-out, Unigas, cruiser hire, sailing craft hire, day boat hire, winter storage, boatbuilding, boat and engine repairs, toilet. Ⓜ *Closed Sun afternoons.*

Ⓑ **Mixer Marine** (Hoseasons Holidays) Mill Road, Stalham (80355). ⓌⓅⒹ Pump-out, Unigas, cruiser hire, day hire boats, provisions, books and maps, toilets, showers, houseboats. Ⓜ *Closed Sun afternoons in summer, all day Sun in winter.*

Ⓑ **Richardsons New Horizon** The Staithe, Stalham (81522). ⓇⓌⒹ Pump-out, gas, cruiser hire, day hire boats, long-term mooring, winter storage, slipway, provisions, books and maps, boatbuilding, boat and engine repairs, toilets, showers, children's playground, café. Ⓜ *Closed Sun afternoons and winter weekends.*

Ⓑ **Tuncraft** (Blakes) Sutton Staithe (Stalham 81653). ⓇⓈⓌ Pump-out, Butagas, cruiser hire, slipway (nearby), books and maps, boatbuilding, boat and

engine repairs, toilets. *Closed Sun afternoons and winter weekends.*

MOORING

There are public overnight moorings at Dilham. Other suitable moorings may be found below Wayford Bridge; at the head of Stalham Dike; Sutton Staithe; west bank of river opposite Longmoor Farm; Barton Turf.

PUBS AND RESTAURANTS

🍺 **Cross Keys** Dilham (Smallburgh 398). Large friendly village local serving Norwich Brewery real ale, meals (*L&D*) and snacks. Children's room, garden and bowling green.

🍺 **Crown** Smallburgh (314). Small village pub with stuffed pike on display. Norwich Brewery and Websters real ales, including Bullard's Mild, meals (*L&D*) and snacks. Children's room, garden.

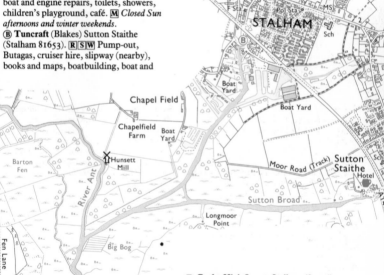

🍺 **Grebe** High Street, Stalham (80376). Welcoming newish pub on the site of the Railway Hotel, once the 'Gallon Pot'. Norwich Brewery real ale, bar meals (*L&D*), snacks, garden and games room.

🍺 **Swan** High Street, Stalham (81492). Comfortable pub offering Whitbread Wethered real ale, meals (*L&D*) and snacks.

🍺 **Sutton Staithe** Sutton (Stalham 80244). Once the haunt of smugglers and poachers to the extent that it was closed during the 1850s. Fortunately for us it re-opened during the 1930s, and now Adnams real ale, good food (*L&D*) and snacks can be enjoyed in traditional surroundings. Antique settles, cosy alcoves and Windsor chairs. Children welcome in eating area, terrace with roses, accommodation, country and western music *Sun.* Ⓜ

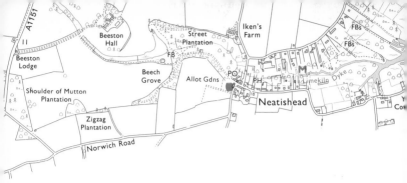

The western arm of Barton Broad extends to Neatishead: the narrow southern exit is marked by a large sign – it would otherwise be easily missed.

Continuing south, the amiable mixture of carr woodland and open fields makes for a lively journey. At How Hill two fine windpumps are passed before Ludham Bridge is approached. Once through, the views across miles of open farmland are splendid – the mill of St Benet's Abbey Gatehouse being clearly visible, indicating the proximity of the parent river.

NAVIGATIONAL NOTES

Ludham Bridge 7ft 6in at normal levels.
Limekiln Dyke From the entrance to Neatishead Staithe it is very narrow. Large craft will have difficulty turning.

Neatishead
Norfolk. EC Wed, PO, stores. A charming Georgian village to the west of Barton Broad. From here it is just a short walk to Beeston Hall.
Beeston Hall (Horning 630771). A pleasant ½ mile walk west of Neatishead. An unusual Gothic house built in 1786 and faced with squared knapped flint. Georgian interiors, furniture and portraits associated with the Preston family, Norfolk squires who built the house. *Open Fri afternoons, Sun and B. Hol Mons from Easter to mid-Sep.* Teas. Admission charge. The nearby church at Beeston St Laurence has a round tower and a 14thC nave. Inside are many monuments to the Preston family.
Irstead
Norfolk. A tiny settlement with a fine river frontage around the thatched church of St Michael. Mainly Decorated, it has a fine 14thC octagonal font depicting the Head of Christ, the Hand of God and leaf motifs on a stem with eight statuettes. The bench ends are carved with poppy heads and the rood screen has three saints painted on a light background. Note the medieval ironwork on the south door.
How Hill Nature Reserve (How Hill Trust

and BA) Ludham (St Benet's 555). A microcosm of Broadland habitat – reed and sedge beds, marshland fields, clear dikes, carr woodland. The estate also includes Reedham Water and Cromes Broad. A tiny thatched cottage, Toad Hole, was once the home of the local marshman and is now an environmental centre for the Broads. The nature trails are *open all year.* Enquire at the fine Edwardian house if you are interested in fishing the river.
Boardman's Mill On the How Hill estate, this open-framed trestle windpump with turbine is in working order. *Open daily.*
Turf Fen Windpump Also on the How Hill estate, the double scoop wheel here is of special interest. Currently being restored to working order.
Ludham Bridge There is a useful store here.

BOATYARDS

Ⓑ **Ludham Bridge Services** (Horning 630486). Ⓡ (close by) ⓌⓅⒹ Pump-out, Calor, Butagas, Unigas, AIG gas, day hire boats, winter storage, crane, chandlery, provisions, books and maps, boatbuilding, boat and engine repairs and sales, wire rigging, towage, toilets. Ⓜ (close by). *Closed winter Suns.*

MOORING

There are public overnight moorings at Neatishead. Other suitable moorings may be found at: Irstead Staithe; below Irstead on east bank; at the entrance to Cromes Broad Dike; above Ludham Bridge on west bank; Ludham Bridge to old causeway on west bank.

PUBS AND RESTAURANTS

🍺 **White Horse** Neatishead (Horning 630828). Comfortable pub dispensing Norwich Brewery and Websters real ales, snacks (*L*) and meals (*D*).
🍺 **Dog** ¼ mile north east of Ludham Bridge (Wroxham 3117). Welcoming pub serving Norwich Brewery real ale and good food (*L&D*). Children's room, garden, barbecues *Fri eves Jul & Aug.*

Hunsett Mill

IRSTEAD
RIVER ANT 47

Dead Man's Hole
KEEP TO MARKED CHANNEL

Pleasure Hill

Great Fen

NTL

Herons' Carr

Turkey Broad

Irstead Road

Camer Shetland Pony Stud

The Shoals

River Ant

Mud Point

Cobb's Farm

Snipe Marsh

Irstead

MHW

Old Hall

Hall Fen

Hall Fen

Crome's Broad

Crome's Farm

Irstead Street

Reedham Hill

How Hill Road

Reedham Marsh

The Skeleton Mill (disused)

Boardmans Mill

How Hill

The Mill House

Turf Fen Wind Pump

Nature Trail

Page's Farm

Reedham Water

Turf Fen

How Hill Farm

FB

T

Pol Ho

shead

Browns Hill Cottage

8

A1062
To Ludham

ter's Carr

Browns Hill

Pipe Line

Blind Lane (Track)

The Limes

River Ant

Whitehouse Farm

ewage Works

Draining Pump

Chapel

Ludham

Johnson Street

Horning Marshes

Hall Road

W

MS

Bridge Farm

Horning

T

A1062

Upper Street

Horning Falgate

2

Ludham Bridge
8' 6"

B T

Wd Pp (dis)

Hundred Dike

Hall Farm Cottages

Horning Hall

Mean High Water

Chapel

See page 33

River Bure

Ant Mouth

Causeway

The passage across the great expanse of Hickling Broad is extremely pleasurable – above the reed-fringed edges often as many as five windpumps can be seen beneath towering skies. On leaving the broad the thatched Royal Shooting Lodge is passed at White Slea. The channel narrows through Deep-Go Dyke, then spreads out into Heigham Sound. To the north east is Meadow Dyke, an intimate channel through extensive reed beds – if you are lucky you may see them being cut and stacked by hand, and taken out by punt. Suddenly you are on the remote and lovely Horsey Mere. Waxham New Cut, a narrow cul-de-sac, heads off due north; in time east is Horsey Mill – it is an easy 30-minute walk to the sea from here.

NAVIGATIONAL NOTES
Hickling Broad and Heigham Sound
Keep to the marked channel between the posts.

Hickling
Norfolk. EC Wed, PO, stores. A popular if undistinguished Broads village, best approached via the Pleasure Boat Inn.

Standing alone in a field is the tall sail-less tower of Hickling Mill, while to the north east are the scant remains of an Augustinian priory, founded 1185.

Hickling Broad (NNR) A 1361-acre site of astonishing beauty acquired by the NNT in 1945, which became a NNR in 1958. Reed and sedge beds, oak woodland and wader scrapes (artificial ponds) attract a wide variety of birdlife, including such unlikely migrants as ospreys, spoonbills and avocets. In May and June you may possibly see colourful swallowtail butterflies. Famous for its large pike and shoals of bream, the Broad has in the past suffered from outbreaks of the alga *prymnesium* and many fish have died. It has, however, subsequently been restocked. There are three nature trails and a fee is charged for each. They are: **Dearys Trail** (1¼ miles) and **Skoyles Marsh Trail** (2½ miles) which both start from the Warden's House, Stubb Road. Booking is essential at weekends (Hickling 276). The **Water Trail** starts from Pleasure Boat Staithe. Visitors, who should be well wrapped up, travel in a replica lighter, the traditional boat used to carry out cut reeds, sedge and marsh hay. It lasts 2½ hours and booking is essential (Hickling 503). *Reserve open 09.00–18.00 Apr–Oct.*

Horsey
Norfolk. A remote settlement described in 1842 as 'a most desolate place' when it was inhabited by marshmen and wildfowlers. All Saints church has a round tower (of 180 such round towers in England, almost 120 are in Norfolk) and bench ends carved with poppy heads. A mile to the east, past the pub, is the seashore. It was here in 1287 that a disastrous storm broke through the sea defences causing severe flooding and damaging, amongst other buildings, St Benet's Abbey, Horning. More recent floods occurred in 1938 when half a mile of dunes were lost and 7000 acres flooded, and in 1953, when the sea broke through at Sea Palling. Swimming in the sea along here is not recommended.

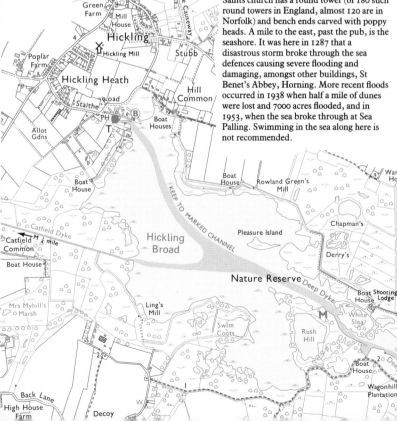

Horsey Mere (NT) A slightly brackish but very attractive expanse of water, rich in ducks, waders and geese. The entrance to the narrow Waxham New Cut is to be found in the north west corner.

Horsey Mill A four-storey red-brick windpump owned by the NT. There are splendid views from the top. *Open Apr–Sep.* Admission free. W R and toilets. M

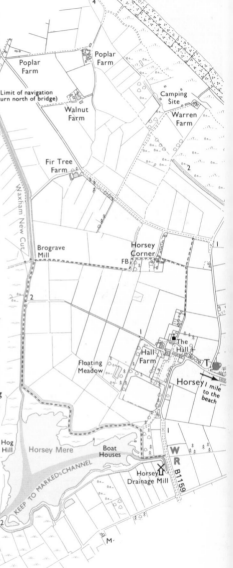

BOATYARDS

Ⓑ **Whispering Reeds Boats** (Hoseasons Holidays) The Staithe, Hickling (314). R S W P D Pump-out, Calor, Hudson gas, cruiser hire, sailing craft hire, day boat hire, long-term mooring, winter storage, slipway, chandlery, maps, boatbuilding, boat and engine repairs, toilet, showers, houseboats. M *Closed winter weekends.*

MOORING

There are public overnight moorings at Catfield Staithe; Deep Dyke and Deep-Go Dyke. Mooring may also be possible at: Pleasure Boat Inn Staithe, Hickling; Horsey Staithe, by Horsey Mill.

PUBS AND RESTAURANTS

🍺 **Greyhound Inn** The Green, Hickling (306). Bustling local serving Norwich Brewery real ale and snacks. Garden.

🍺 **Pleasure Boat** Hickling Staithe (Hickling 211). A large, old pantiled pub popular with both locals and tourists. Norwich Brewery real ale, meals (*L&D*), snacks, garden, children's room. Restaurant *in summer.* M

🍺 **Nelson's Head** Horsey. Remote, unspoilt country pub off the main road. Children's play area. Whitbread beers. A pleasant place to stop if you walk to the dunes and the sea. Note the thatched farm buildings next door. Delicious oak-smoked herrings can be bought nearby from a local fisherman.

As the River Thurne leaves West Somerton its slightly elevated position offers splendid views over rich farmland. Horsey Mill to the north and the Damgate Water Tower to the south are easily identifiable landmarks. After Martham Broad, the Hundred Stream joins amidst vast reed beds, and the main river heads south west to Martham Ferry, where there are some summer chalets and moored craft around the rusty floating bridge.

NAVIGATIONAL NOTES

Martham Ferry This is a floating swing bridge, which is opened by pulling a chain whilst standing on the bridge. There is no need to close it after you.
River Thurne A section above the entrance

to Candle Dyke is a special fishing area. Do not navigate here before *09.00 on Suns.*

West Somerton
Norfolk. PO, store. The thatched church of St Mary stands to the east of this small

rambling village. Its Norman round tower has a later octagonal belfry; inside there are 14thC wall paintings depicting Christ on a rainbow, and St Christopher, now rather faded. Look for the funny faces on the pulpit, and the 15thC backless bench in the airy chapel. In the graveyard lies Robert Hales, the Somerton Giant, who was 7ft 8in tall and weighed 33 stone. He died, aged 50, in 1863. Somerton Hall stands by the church; in the grounds there was once a leper hospital, owned by Bentley Priory in Suffolk.

Winterton-on-Sea
Norfolk. 1½ miles to the east of West Somerton, and a very pleasant walk. A charming little town with narrow streets, very much like the Yarmouth 'Rows', which has now succumbed to the holiday trade. To the north is Winterton Dunes (NNR), 259 acres of heath, bog and dune.

Martham
Norfolk. PO, stores. There are some fine Georgian houses around two large greens in this village which lies a mile to the south of Martham Broad (nature reserve). St Mary's church has a massive west tower, culminating in a spike. Beneath this edifice is a stone to Alice Burraway, put in place by her husband, which recalls that 'in this life, (she was) my sister, my mistress, my mother and my wife'. He was born as the result of an incestuous union between his father and sister. Unknowingly, following an affair, he later married Alice.

The old bridge at Potter Heigham

BOATYARDS

Ⓑ **Martham Ferry Boatyard** (Hoseasons Holidays) Ferrygate Lane, Martham (Great Yarmouth 740303). Ⓡ Ⓢ Ⓦ Ⓟ Pump-out, Butane and Propane gas, cruiser hire, sailing craft hire, day hire boats, winter storage, boatbuilding, boat and engine repairs, toilet, showers, houseboats. Ⓜ *Closed winter weekends.*

MOORING

No public overnight moorings on this section. Suitable moorings may be found at: West Somerton Staithe; River Thurne at Martham Ferry to below entrance to Sock Drain, both banks.

PUBS AND RESTAURANTS

🍺 **Lion** West Somerton (Winterton 289). A friendly village pub dispensing Greene King real ales, a wide range of excellent meals (*L&D*) and snacks. Children's room, garden.

🍺 **Victoria** Repps Road, Martham (Great Yarmouth 740774). Welcoming local where you can enjoy Norwich Brewery and Websters real ales, and bar meals (*L&D*). Garden, family room.

🍺 **Fishermans Return** The Lane, Winterton-on-Sea (305). An excellent place to rest if you have just walked 1½ miles from West Somerton. A pretty brick building with cosy bars, offering a choice of real ales and excellent meals (*L&D*). Children's room, garden, accommodation.

The approach to Potter Heigham is marked by ever increasing numbers of summer houses and chalets of indiscriminate vintage. Many are really quite attractive and virtually all have their own off-line mooring. After the low new bridge comes the tiny arch of the old, where bridge pilots squeeze large hirecraft through at high speed, while lesser mortals and land-lubbers look on. Now there are even more summer houses, over a mile of them on both sides, before the river is once again in open country.

A diversion to Ludham along Womack Water is most rewarding. Along its short length is a microcosm of Broadland scenery, with the chance of seeing the wherry 'Albion', moored by the sailing school. Continuing south the River Thurne passes the village that is its namesake, the entrance to the dyke is marked by a very handsome white windpump.

NAVIGATIONAL NOTES

Potter Heigham Old Bridge 7ft 0in high and very narrow. Larger hire craft are not allowed through unless in the charge of an official bridge pilot. *The new bridge is also low.*

Potter Heigham
Norfolk. PO, stores. The discovery of wood ash from the kilns of a Roman pottery reveal the origins of this unusually named village, the true centre of which is a mile north west of the holiday centre which has burgeoned around the medieval bridge. This bridge, with its notoriously low and narrow arch, is such an obstacle that Hoseasons and Blakes run a pilot service to help their unwary holiday boaters through. The church of St Nicholas dates from the 13thC and has a round tower topped with a 15thC belfry. Its hammer-beam roof is particularly handsome.

High's Mill Riverside, above Potter Heigham. Red-brick tower mill with a boat-shaped cap, converted into a dwelling.

Weavers Way A 29-mile cross-country walk from Cromer to Stalham, through what was the heart of the Norfolk weaving trade. Between Heigham Bridge and Thurne village it follows the south bank of the river.

Ludham
Norfolk. EC Wed, PO, stores. An attractive village with some good houses and a large 14thC church. Dedicated to St Catherine, who was put to death on a spiked wheel, her emblem has been incorporated into the roof. The font is decorated with wild men and lions; the screen painted with eleven saints and a king. There is also a fine 15thC painting of the crucifixion, and a large poor box of a similar age.

Wherry 'Albion' Womack, Ludham. For many years the only surviving trading wherry on the Broads, but soon to be joined by the 'Maud', being rebuilt at Upton. Interestingly, the 'Albion' was one of the few such craft to be carvel-built (ie having the planking joined flush at the seams), the great

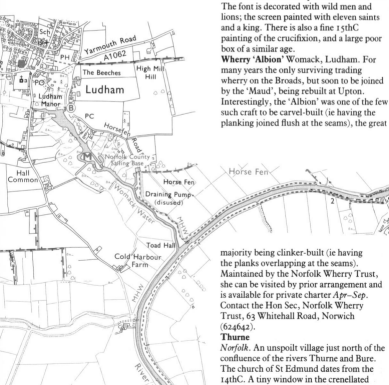

majority being clinker-built (ie having the planks overlapping at the seams). Maintained by the Norfolk Wherry Trust, she can be visited by prior arrangement and is available for private charter *Apr–Sep.* Contact the Hon Sec, Norfolk Wherry Trust, 63 Whitehall Road, Norwich (624642).

Thurne
Norfolk. An unspoilt village just north of the confluence of the rivers Thurne and Bure. The church of St Edmund dates from the 14thC. A tiny window in the crenellated tower looks out towards St Benet's Abbey – it is said that a lantern placed here could signal a warning to the monks at the Abbey.

See page 37

POTTER HEIGHAM

Thurne Dyke Windpump A very pretty and distinctive white-painted tower, housing a small exhibition. *Open daily Apr–Oct.* Another handsome windpump, privately owned, stands on the opposite bank.

Norfolk County Sailing Base Horsefen Road, Ludham (St Benets 263). A very fine collection of gleaming mahogany gaff-rigged sloops, used in the BBC's serialisation of Arthur Ransome's *Coot Club*. Available for hire to experienced yachtspersons.

MOORING

There are public overnight moorings at Womack Island. Other suitable moorings may be found at: entrance to Candle Dyke; either side of Heigham Bridge, south bank; Repps Staithe; Ludham Staithe; River Thurne, east bank, opposite Womack Water; both banks below Thurne Dyke; Thurne Dyke.

PUBS AND RESTAURANTS

Bridge 1 Station Road, Potter Heigham (670204). Popular pub with a fine riverside garden. Norwich Brewery real ale, meals (*L&D*) and snacks. Evening disco during the holiday season. Children's room.

Broadshaven Bridge Road, Potter Heigham (670329). Modern pub with a restaurant and night club. Norwich Brewery real ale, meals (*L&D*) and snacks. Children's room and garden. Friday evening disco during the holiday season.

Falgate Inn Potter Heigham (670003). Norwich Brewery real ale, bar meals (*L&D*) and snacks. Garden, accommodation.

King's Arms Ludham (St Benets 386). Village pub dispensing Norwich Brewery real ale and snacks. Garden.

Lion At the head of Thurne Dyke (Potter Heigham 670796). Brilliantly illuminated at night. Whitbread Wethered real ale and bar meals (*L&D*) are available in the down to earth bar, which has the suggestion of a nautical theme. Family room, garden.

BOATYARDS

ⓑ **Martham Boat Building and Development** Riverside, Cess Road, Martham (Great Yarmouth 740249). Ⓦ Pump-out, sailing craft hire, sailing tuition.

ⓑ **Maycraft** (Hoseasons Holidays) Potter Heigham (670241). Ⓦ Ⓟ Ⓓ Pump-out, Butagas, cruiser hire, sailing craft hire, day hire boats, boatbuilding and sales, boat and engine repairs. Ⓜ

ⓑ **Herbert Woods** (Blakes) Broads Haven, Potter Heigham (670711). Ⓡ Ⓦ Ⓟ Ⓓ Pump-out, Unigas, cruiser hire, sailing craft hire, day boat hire, long-term mooring, provisions, books and maps, boat and engine repairs. Ⓜ *Closed winter weekends.*

ⓑ **Ludham Marine** (Hoseasons Holidays) Womack Staithe, Ludham (Horning 62322). Ⓡ Ⓦ Ⓓ Pump-out, Calor, Hudson, Unigas, cruiser hire, sailing craft hire, day boat hire, canoe hire, long-term mooring, winter storage, slipway, provisions, books and maps, yachting clothing, boatbuilding, boat and engine sales and repairs, toilet. Ⓜ *Closed in winter.*

THE RIVER YARE

Rising south of Shipdham in Norfolk, the Yare has long been navigable from Norwich to Great Yarmouth where it joins the River Bure below the shallow tidal expanse of Breydon Water, to pass through Yarmouth Harbour to the sea. Indeed it was this lack of depth in Breydon Water which necessitated the trans-shipment of goods from sea-going vessels to smaller craft able to make the passage to Norwich, thus giving Yarmouth a stranglehold on all trade going inland. The Norwich merchants were anxious to free themselves from this obstacle and various schemes were mooted to improve the river, all to be blocked in one way or another by the men of Yarmouth, who obviously recognised a good thing when they saw it.

Finally, in 1827, after giving much evidence of malpractice at Yarmouth, Norwich finally got a Bill through Parliament enabling them to improve the navigation and by-pass Yarmouth by building the Haddiscoe New Cut and opening Oulton Broad and Lake Lothing to the sea at Lowestoft. The improved 32-mile navigation, which enabled sea-going vessels to reach Norwich, was officially opened in September 1833.

Unfortunately, receipts were not sufficient to recover the investment, and to add to the difficulties, Lake Lothing silted up. Railway building did not improve matters. By 1850 the traffic was once again passing through Yarmouth, with the New Cut little used. Today small coasters make the journey up river to Norwich (via Yarmouth), mooring in the town centre on the River Wensum.

Pulls Ferry, Norwich

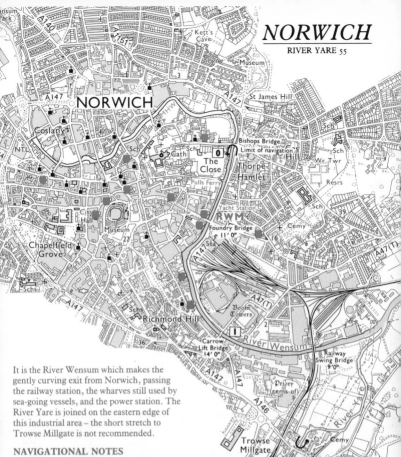

It is the River Wensum which makes the
gently curving exit from Norwich, passing
the railway station, the wharves still used by
sea-going vessels, and the power station. The
River Yare is joined on the eastern edge of
this industrial area – the short stretch to
Trowse Millgate is not recommended.

NAVIGATIONAL NOTES

Limit of navigation For cruisers: Bishopgate
Bridge on the River Wensum (if you have a
rowing dinghy it is worth exploring above
the bridge). Navigation on the River Yare
from its confluence with the Wensum to
Trowse Millgate is not recommended.
Keep a sharp watch for commercial craft.

Norwich

*Norfolk. EC. Thur, MD Mon–Sat. All shops
and services, BR station.* The county town,
social capital and market centre of Norfolk.
Its irregular street plan indicates Saxon
origins, while a wealth of surviving buildings
testify to its continued importance from the
early Middle Ages onwards. In addition to
its magnificent cathedral, Norwich could
once boast a church for every Sunday in the
year, and a pub for every other day of the
year. The Industrial Revolution, which dealt
the final blow to its hand-weaving industry,
saw the birth of the city as one of the chief
shoe manufacturing towns in the country.
The city centre is enclosed on three sides by
the old city wall, the curve of the River
Wensum defining the fourth. Modern
development has been judiciously restrained
(with a few exceptions) and many of the
city's old buildings have been saved and
restored. With its twisting streets and alleys,
glimpses of the great castle keep or the
cathedral spire around virtually every
corner, and a bustling market at its heart,
Norwich is the ideal town to explore on foot.

Norwich Castle (Norwich 611277, extn
279). From its high mound the castle
dominates the city centre. The magnificent
keep was built in the 12thC, but owes its
pristine condition to a refacing in the 19thC.
It had a turbulent early history and was
made into the city gaol in 1220, a function it
maintained until 1887 when it was converted
into the county museum. Although the
museum has recently been modernised, the
Great Hall on the first floor remains much as
it must have been 600 years ago. Of major
interest are a fine natural history section and
a comprehensive collection of paintings of
the Norwich school, as well as archaeological
exhibits, Lowestoft porcelain and Norwich
silver. There are regular conducted tours of
the castle battlements and dungeons. *Open
Mon–Sat & Sun afternoons.* Admission
charge.

Norwich Cathedral Tombland. This
beautiful example of Norman architecture
was begun in 1096 by Herbert de Losinga on
the Pope's orders, as a punishment for the
sin of simony. Herbert certainly paid his
penance well.
The splendid vaulted roof of the nave has
over 300 carved bosses, and there are more
in the cloisters, totalling 1200 in all. It is
thought that the Bishop's Throne, behind
the altar, may be 1000 years old, which

would make it the oldest in any English cathedral. The graceful, slender spire is second in height only to that at Salisbury, and is equally lovely. It's a 15thC replacement of an earlier spire which collapsed in 1362. The cathedral close stretches down to the River Wensum, and the 15thC river gate, Pull's Ferry. There are a number of excellent Georgian buildings in the close.

The two cathedral gates face the cobbled square of Tombland. The Erpingham Gate is regarded as one of the finest in the Perpendicular style. St Ethelbert's is slightly earlier, built jointly by the townspeople and monks as a penance after one of their periodic riots in the Middle Ages.

St Peter Mancroft Market Place. This 15thC church stands in splendour above the Market Place, with a lavishly panelled and substantial tower arched over the street. It is crowned by turrets and a charming Victorian Gothic spirelet, a little lost in the midst of such a spectacle. The clerestory forms a magnificent wall of light in the lofty interior, meeting the boss-studded roof in which the hammer beams are covered by coving. A fine panoply of 15thC stained glass fills the east window. Also of note are the impressive canopy over the font, the brasses and monuments, and the Mancroft Heritage Exhibition, displaying objects of great interest associated with the church. *Open weekdays*.

Stranger's Hall Charing Cross, Norwich (611277 extn 275). A 15thC merchant's house built upon an early 13thC undercroft. Its name derives from immigrant cloth-workers who lived here in the 17thC. Furnished rooms show a variety of fashions between the 16th and 19thC and it now houses a museum of costumes and period furniture. *Open weekdays*. Admission charge.

Bridewell Museum Bridewell Alley, Norwich (611277 extn 299). Built upon a 14thC vaulted undercroft, the museum has exhibits relating to local crafts and industries from the Middle Ages to the present day. *Open weekdays*. Admission charge.

Coleman's Mustard Museum 3 Bridewell Alley, Norwich (627889). Mustard cultivation, manufacturing techniques and associated printed ephemera. Shop. *Open daily, closed Thur & Sun*. Admission free.

Elm Hill 200 yards west of the cathedral, this is one of the most picturesque streets in the city. Pastel-painted, red-brick and irregular timbered buildings shoulder to shoulder along a narrow cobbled street. Lantern-lit by night.

Entertainment There are four theatres: Maddermarket; Theatre Royal; The Puppet Theatre and Premises at the Norwich Arts Centre – also four cinemas and several night clubs and discos. Details from:

Tourist Information Office Tombland, Norwich (66071/66072).

The Yacht Station, Norwich

BOATYARDS

Ⓑ **Norwich Yacht Station** Riverside Road, Norwich (622024). Ⓡ Ⓦ Showers, toilets, washrooms, public telephone. Advice and help on any boating matters, including tidal information. Ⓜ

MOORING

Visitors to Norwich should moor at the Yacht Station.

BOAT TRIPS

Southern River Steamers 43 Ebbisham Drive, Norwich (501220). Cruises from Roaches Court (off Elm Hill) and Thorpe Station (by Foundry Bridge), in 'Princess Victoria' and 'Empress'. *Mid May–mid Sep. Also private charter all year.*

PUBS AND RESTAURANTS

There are many very good places to eat and drink in Norwich – it would not be possible to list them all here. The pubs described here have been chosen because they are near the river, near the sights, or worth a longer walk. The eating places are a selection of those which offer something special and are close to the town centre.

🍺 **Ferry Boat Inn** King Street (near Carrow Road Lift Bridge), Norwich (613553). A comfortable rambling pub with an assortment of drinking areas – some with beams and antiques, others more open and airy. Greene King real ales, meals (*L&D*) and snacks; barbecues some summer weekends in the riverside gardens. Live music most evenings and some lunchtimes.

🍺 **Coach and Horses** 82 Thorpe Road, Norwich (620704). On A1074 east of the river. Friendly family-run pub with a children's room. Norwich Brewery real ale.

🍺✗ **Hotel Nelson** Prince of Wales Road, Norwich (628612). Adnams real ale in a friendly modern hotel by the river. Good food (*L&D*), snacks, garden.

🍺 **Compleat Angler** Prince of Wales Road, Norwich (622425). Close to the Yacht Station, this friendly pub offers Norwich Brewery real ale, and good bar meals (*L&D*). Garden.

🍺 **Adam & Eve** Bishopgate, Norwich (667423). The lower part of this pub was built some 700 years ago, making it the oldest in Norwich. It is an attractive Dutch-gabled building with a flower-decked terrace. The interior is wood panelled with high backed settles. A choice of real ales is available, and good food and snacks are served (*L only*). Children's room.

🍺 **Gardeners Arms** (also known as the 'Murderers') Timber Hill, Norwich (21447). Bustling pub popular with the young. A good range of real ales meals (*L only*) and snacks. Garden. *Closed Sun lunchtime.*

🍺 **Fruiterers Arms** 2 White Lion Street, Norwich (624860). Close to the market. A pleasingly modernised pub in which to enjoy Adnams and Bass Springfield real ales. Snacks. *Closed Sun lunchtime.*

🍺 **Norfolk Wherry** 8–10 Castle Meadow, Norwich (627431). Modern pub opposite

The River Yare in Norwich

the castle, offering Ind Coope real ale, food (*L only*) and snacks. Garden.

🍺 **Whites** 1 Queen Street, Norwich (625539). Large pub which was once a smart restaurant. Tolly Cobbold, Bass Springfield and Adnams real ales, meals (*L only*) and snacks. *Closed Sun evening.*

🍺 **Louis Marchesi** 17 Tombland, Norwich (613817). An old pub, once called the Waggon & Horses. Norwich Brewery and Websters real ales, bar food (*L only*) and snacks. *Evening opening 19.00.*

🍺 **Ten Bells** St Benedicts, Norwich (624571). A small pub often offering as many as 10 well kept real ales. Snacks.

🍺✗ **John W Stokes** Barrack Street, Norwich (621869). Modern riverside pub serving Norwich Brewery real ale and meals (*L&D*). Garden down to the water's edge.

✗🍷 **Bombay Restaurant** 9 Magdalen Street, Norwich (666618); 43 Timber Hill (20305); and Prince of Wales Road (621208). A good range of curries and tandooris. Vegetarians well catered for. *Open daily (L&D).*

✗🍷 **Assembly House** Theatre Street, Norwich (627526). South of Central Library. Morning coffee, lunches and teas, all home made in a fine Georgian building housing an art gallery and lounge bars. Also an art gallery and cinema. *Open 10.00–19.30 Mon–Sat.* Disabled access.

✗ **Briton's Arms Coffee House** 9 Elm Hill, Norwich (623367). Cosy, cottage-style coffee shop near the cathedral. Light lunches, nice teas. *Open 10.00–17.00 Mon–Sat.*

✗🍷 **Greens Seafood Restaurant** 82 Upper St Giles Street, Norwich (623733). West of City Hall. Very good fish and shellfish, all from Lowestoft. Vegetarians catered for. Smart dress preferred. Essential to reserve. *Open Mon–Fri (L&D), Sat D only.*

✗🍷 **Marco's** 17 Pottergate, Norwich (624044). Excellent Italian food, delicious sweets. Vegetarians well catered for. Essential to reserve. *Open Mon–Fri (L&D). Closed Aug.*

✗🍷 **Pizza One and Pancakes Too** 24 Tombland, Norwich (621583). A bright, lively restaurant with a courtyard where you can eat outside in fine weather. Interesting and delicious concoctions – savoury or sweet. *Open daily (L&D) 12.00–23.00.*

🍷✗ **Wine Press** Woburn Court, Guildhall Hill, Norwich (612874). Basement wine bar in a former silk merchant's house. Cold food, salads and hot meals too. Delicious fruit flans. Pastries with morning coffee. *Open 09.00–15.00 Mon–Sat.*

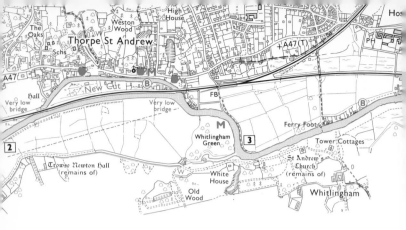

The New Cut offers the most direct route for those not wishing to visit Thorpe St Andrew. The course of the river is wide and deep, as you would expect on a navigation where a coaster might loom up around the next bend. Attractive woodlands flank the south bank at Whitlingham, followed by Whitlingham Marsh and gently undulating farmland to the north.

The pretty Bramerton Woods contrast starkly with Postwick Marsh before the Ferry House pub at Surlingham is reached. Both banks are thickly wooded below this point.

NAVIGATIONAL NOTES

New Cut Those who wish to follow the old course of the river should note that the two fixed railway bridges are *very* low, and of differing heights.

Thorpe St Andrew
Norfolk. EC Thur. PO, stores. A smart residential suburb of Norwich with some pleasant 18thC houses in close proximity to the river, but separated from it by the busy A47 trunk road. The direct course by boat from Norwich is along the New Cut, which keeps south of the railway and avoids Thorpe altogether. However, if headroom allows, you can take the original river route, now a quiet backwater of boathouses and pubs. St Andrew's church, built in 1866, is approached through the porch of an earlier building. Its spire, damaged during the second world war, was rebuilt in 1956. Thorpe Hall, now being rebuilt, is an early 17thC house incorporating parts of a 14thC building, and once belonged to the Bishops of Norwich. The Town House Hotel has a superb circular-domed conservatory, dating from the 1820s. This building has associations with the old Norwich School of painters, whose most celebrated artist was John Sell Cotman, born in Thorpe in 1782. Many of his paintings can be seen in the Castle Museum (see Norwich section, p 55). 'Garden House', a Tudor building, is now the Rush Cutters pub.

Kirby Bedon
Norfolk. The church of St Andrew, mainly 19thC but with a genuine Norman south doorway, faces the ruined round tower of St Mary's. Together with the Georgian rectory they form a compact group of buildings just off the main road.

Bramerton
Norfolk. PO. A 1-mile walk up from the delightful riverside area of Bramerton Woods End. The church of St Peter dates from the late 13thC, and has a nave built in the Decorated style.

Postwick
Norfolk. A village surrounded on three sides by the river and Postwick Marsh with the railway on the fourth. Parts of All Saints church date from the late 13thC. It has a Decorated tower and the piscina (used for washing communion vessels) is notable.

BOATYARDS

Ⓑ **Hearts Cruisers** (Blakes) The Island, Thorpe St Andrew, Norwich (33666). Ⓡ Ⓢ Ⓦ Ⓓ Pump-out, Unigas, cruiser hire, long-term mooring, winter storage, slipway, provisions (close by), books and maps, boatbuilding, boat and engine repairs, boat sales, toilets. Ⓜ *Closed winter weekends.*

Ⓑ **Classic Leisure Cruisers** (Hoseasons Holidays) Griffin Lane, Thorpe St Andrew, Norwich (32129). Ⓡ Ⓦ Ⓓ Ⓔ Pump-out, AIG gas, cruiser hire, long-term mooring, winter storage, slipway, boatbuilding, boat and engine sales and repairs, toilet. Ⓜ

Ⓑ **Highcraft** (Blakes) Griffin Lane, Thorpe St Andrew, Norwich (39372). Ⓡ Ⓢ Ⓦ Ⓓ Pump-out, Unigas, cruiser hire, day hire boats, long-term mooring, winter storage, slipway, chandlery, provisions, books and maps, boatbuilding, engine sales, boat and engine repairs. Ⓜ *Closed Sun afternoons.*

Ⓑ **Maiden Craft** (Hoseasons Holidays) Bungalow Lane, Thorpe St Andrew, Norwich (35173). Ⓡ Ⓢ Ⓦ Ⓓ Pump-out, Butagas, Unigas, cruiser hire, winter storage, slipway, books and maps, boatbuilding and sales, boat and engine repairs, outboard sales, toilet. Ⓜ *Closed Sun afternoons.*

MOORING

There are public overnight moorings at: Thorpe Green; Whitlingham Green; Bramerton Common. No other moorings are recommended.

PUBS AND RESTAURANTS

Kings Head 36 Yarmouth Road, Thorpe St Andrew, Norwich (33540). Pub and restaurant with large garden by the river. Whitbread Wethered real ale, meals (*L&D*) and snacks. Ⓜ

The Rush Cutters Yarmouth Road, Thorpe St Andrew, Norwich (35403). Fine Tudor building where Norwich Brewery and Websters real ales may be enjoyed. Restaurant meals (*L&D*) and snacks. Ⓜ

The Buck Adjacent to the church, Thorpe St Andrew. Picturesque pantiled pub serving real ale and food (*L&D*). Garden.

Woods End Riverside at Bramerton (Surlingham 296). Friendly and welcoming pub on a very pretty part of the river. Norwich Brewery real ale, food (*L&D*), snacks and garden. Ⓜ

Ferry House Inn Riverside near Surlingham (227). Built in 1725 and still thriving, although the chain ferry it once served has long since disappeared. A very attractive place in which to enjoy Norwich Brewery and Websters real ales, good food (*L&D*). Children's room and garden. Ⓜ

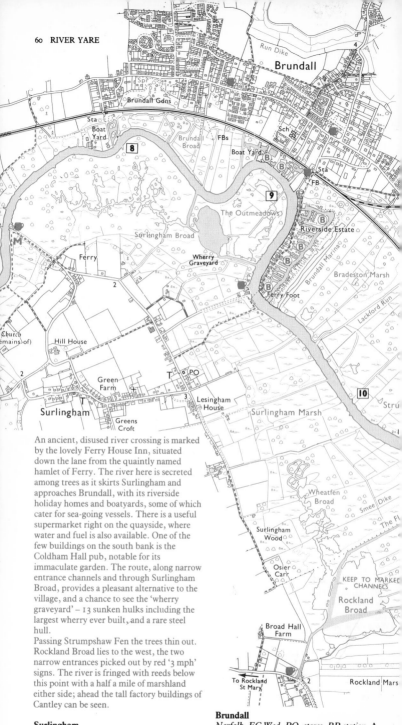

An ancient, disused river crossing is marked by the lovely Ferry House Inn, situated down the lane from the quaintly named hamlet of Ferry. The river here is secreted among trees as it skirts Surlingham and approaches Brundall, with its riverside holiday homes and boatyards, some of which cater for sea-going vessels. There is a useful supermarket right on the quayside, where water and fuel is also available. One of the few buildings on the south bank is the Coldham Hall pub, notable for its immaculate garden. The route, along narrow entrance channels and through Surlingham Broad, provides a pleasant alternative to the village, and a chance to see the 'wherry graveyard' – 13 sunken hulks including the largest wherry ever built, and a rare steel hull.

Passing Strumpshaw Fen the trees thin out. Rockland Broad lies to the west, the two narrow entrances picked out by red '3 mph' signs. The river is fringed with reeds below this point with a half a mile of marshland either side; ahead the tall factory buildings of Cantley can be seen.

Surlingham

Norfolk. PO, stores. A sprawling village to the south of Surlingham Broad (NNT nature reserve). The church is situated to the east of the village. Dedicated to St Mary, it has a round Norman tower topped with a 14thC octagonal belfry. A short distance to the north east are the ruins of St Saviour's, thought to have been built in the 12thC.

Brundall

Norfolk. EC Wed, PO, stores, BR station. A village of commuters and Broadland holidaymakers, distinguished for its abundance of charming cottages and riverside villas. A vast marina south of the station makes a base for many boat hire companies; on summer weekends the water is thick with craft. The tiny 13thC church of St Lawrence stands in the midst of fields to the east, aloof from such worldly doings. It has the only lead font in Norfolk and some nice 16thC stained glass.

Rockland St Mary
Norfolk. PO, stores. A linear village to the west of Rockland Broad. The church of St Mary dates from the 14thC, with much rebuilding. To the north is Wheatfen Broad, maintained as a private nature reserve.

Strumpshaw
Norfolk. A tiny village on the slopes of Strumpshaw hill. It is worth visiting the church of St Peter to have a look at the colourful 15thC screen.

Strumpshaw Fen (RSPB). A complete range of Broadland habitats with five miles of mown footpaths. Cetti's warbler, marsh harriers and bearded tits breed on the fen. Also to be seen are all the common species of wildfowl, woodland, marsh and reed-dwelling birds. The visitor centre/hide is by the entrance over the railway crossing at the head of Strumpshaw Broad. To the south of the river a public footpath over Rockland marshes starts opposite the New Inn. There is a public hide overlooking Buckenham Marshes for viewing bean geese (*open Oct–Mar*). Warden: Staithe Cottage, Low Road, Strumpshaw, Norwich (715191). Admission charge to non-RSPB members.

Strumpshaw Hall Steam Museum (Norwich 714535). All manner of steam engines, including a beam engine, a steam wagon, a showman's road engine and a fairground organ. *Also a steam railway on Sun. Open afternoons Sun–Fri, Jun–Sep.* Admission charge.

BOATYARDS

Ⓑ **Broom Boats** (Blakes) Riverside, Brundall (Norwich 712334). R S W P D Pump-out, Calor, Butagas, cruiser hire, long-term mooring, winter storage, slipway, provisions, boatbuilding and sales, boat and engine repairs. M

Ⓑ **Harvey Eastwood** (Hoseasons Holidays) Riverside, Brundall (Norwich 713345/715145). R W P D Pump-out, BOC gas, cruiser hire, sailing craft hire, day hire boats, long-term mooring, winter storage, slipway, books and maps, boatbuilding and sales, boat and engine repairs, toilets, houseboats. M

Ⓑ **Stellarcraft of Brundall** (Blakes) Riverside, Brundall (Norwich 712195, Potter Heigham 670544). W D Pump-out, Unigas, cruiser hire, day hire boats, long-term mooring, winter storage, slipway, books and maps, boat and engine sales, toilet. M

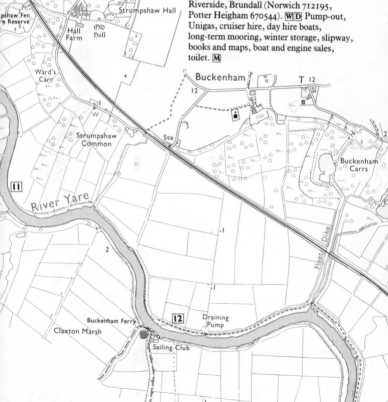

ⓑ **Bell Boats** (Blakes) Waterside, Brundall (Norwich 713109). Ⓡ Ⓦ Cruiser hire, day hire boats, winter storage, cranage, DIY facilities, chandlery, boat and engine repairs, engine sales, houseboats. Ⓜ *Closed Sun afternoons and B. Hols.*

ⓑ **Silverline Marine** (Hoseasons Holidays) Riverside Estate, Brundall (Norwich 712247). Ⓦ Ⓓ Pump-out, Butagas, cruiser hire, slipway, books and maps, boatbuilding, boat and engine repairs. Ⓜ *Closes 15.00 Suns.*

ⓑ **Bees Boats** (Hoseasons Holidays) Riverside Estate, Brundall (Norwich 713446). Ⓡ Ⓢ Ⓦ Ⓓ Pump-out, Butagas, Shell gas, cruiser hire, winter storage, slipway, towage, books and maps, boatbuilding, boat and engine repairs, toilets. Ⓜ *Closed winter weekends.*

ⓑ **Buccaneer Boats** (Hoseasons Holidays) Riverside Estate, Brundall (Norwich 712984). Ⓡ Ⓢ Ⓦ Ⓓ Pump-out, Butagas, cruiser hire, sailing dinghy hire, sailboard hire, day hire boats, long-term mooring, slipway, books and maps, boatbuilding, boat and engine sales and repairs, toilets, showers. Ⓜ

ⓑ **Bounty Boats** (Blakes) Riverside Estate, Brundall (Norwich 712070/715255). Ⓡ Ⓦ Ⓓ Pump-out, Butagas, cruiser hire, gantry, chandlery, boatbuilding and sales, boat and engine repairs. Ⓜ

ⓑ **Alpha Craft** (Hoseasons Holidays) Riverside Estate, Brundall (Norwich 713265). Ⓡ Ⓦ Ⓓ Pump-out, cruiser hire, boatbuilding, toilet. Ⓜ

ⓑ **BB Cruiser Co** (Blakes) Riverside Estate, Brundall (Norwich 713507). Ⓡ Ⓦ Ⓓ Pump-out, Butagas, cruiser hire, day hire boats, books and maps. Ⓜ *Closed in winter.*

ⓑ **Willow Cruisers** (Hoseasons Holidays) Riverside Estate, Brundall (Norwich 713952). Ⓡ Ⓦ Ⓓ Pump-out, Shell gas, cruiser hire, long-term mooring, slipway, boatbuilding, boat and engine repairs. Ⓜ

ⓑ **Fencraft** (Hoseasons Holidays) Riverside Estate, Brundall (Norwich 715011). Ⓡ Ⓦ Ⓓ Pump-out, Butagas, Unigas, cruiser hire, day hire boats, slipway, books and maps, toilets. Ⓜ

ⓑ **Swancraft Cruisers** (Blakes) Riverside Estate, Brundall (Norwich 712362). Ⓡ Ⓦ Ⓓ Pump-out, Unigas, cruiser hire, long-term mooring, winter storage, slipway, boat and engine repairs, toilets. Ⓜ *Closed Sun and B. Hol afternoons.*

MOORING

There are public overnight moorings at Surlingham Ferry Quay. Suitable moorings may also be found at: Coldham Hall; Brundall Marina; Rockland St Mary Staithe; Beauchamp Arms.

PUBS AND RESTAURANTS

🍺 **Ferry House Inn** Riverside near Surlingham (227). Built in 1725 and still thriving, although the chain ferry it once served has long since disappeared. A very attractive place in which to enjoy Norwich Brewery and Websters real ales, good food (*L&D*). Children's room and garden. Ⓜ

🍺 **Coldham Hall** Riverside near Surlingham (591). A smart red-brick and thatch pub with an immaculate garden, opposite Brundall Marina. Norwich Brewery real ale, food (*L&D*), and snacks. Ⓜ

🍺 **Ram** The Street, Brundall (Norwich 715280). 300-year-old village pub dispensing Norwich Brewery real ale to locals and visitors alike.

🍺 **White Horse** The Street, Brundall (Norwich 716003). Holiday pub serving Norwich Brewery real ale, food (*L&D*) and snacks. Children's room and garden. Ⓜ

🍺 **The Yare** Station Road, Brundall (Norwich 713786). Large popular pub with nautical theme. Encouraging range of real ales, food (*L&D*), snacks, children's room and patio.

🍺 **New Inn** New Inn Hill, Rockland (Surlingham 395). Close to Rockland St Mary Staithe, at the southern end of Rockland Broad. 17thC pub with brewery relics and an old punt gun on display. Norwich Brewery real ale, meals (*L&D*), snacks, family room and garden. Ⓜ *Evening opening at 19.00.*

🍺 **Beauchamp Arms** Buckenham Ferry. Stones ales, bar meals (*L&D*), wine bar, family room, pool tables and amusements. It doesn't look at all like a pub. Ⓜ

Commercial traffic on the River Yare

A generous meandering course is taken across the marshes by the wide reed-fringed river. Towers of disused windpumps are passed at frequent intervals, and more are seen in the distance. Langley Dike provides an interesting diversion before passing Cantley, where the sugar-beet factory brings a flavour of the industrial waterways to the Broads, reminding us that the whole of this network was once used as a commercial transport system, long before the coming of the railways and the roads.

Joining the main river by the Hardley Cross is the lovely River Chet; time should be found to visit Loddon and Chedgrave. Heading up this tributary the navigator cannot fail to notice the limited width and elevated position – rather like a canal on a low embankment. Twisting and turning it passes Hardley Flood, separated from it in one place only by a wooden footbridge carrying the path. Keep a look out for stacks of cut reeds, for use as thatch, lying at the water's edge. A guest-house and restaurant followed by a succession of boatyards signal the virtual limit of navigation, and the staithe is soon reached (WR, toilets). A clapboard mill finally closes the river. On the main river, the chain ferry, the last on the Broads, indicates the approach to Reedham.

NAVIGATIONAL NOTES

Hardley Dike Very narrow and difficult to turn. No facilities.
Reedham Chain Ferry Keep well clear while it is crossing – the chains stretch right across the river.

Cantley
Norfolk. PO, stores, BR station. A market town during the 13thC, Cantley is now a village dominated by the vast sugar-beet factory. Smoke from the chimneys during the autumn and winter months indicate that the crop is being processed and the sugar extracted. Sugar-beet is a major part of the local farming economy, and one of the few root crops grown amongst the cereal and rape which predominates here. The church of St Margaret dates mainly from the 14thC, incorporating some earlier Norman work.

Langley Green
Norfolk. PO, stores. Scattered village approached via Langley Dike. Just to the west are the few flint remains, some incorporated into farm buildings, of Langley Abbey, founded by Premonstratensian Canons in 1195. It is built on a gravel outcrop surrounded by peat. The church and Langley Park are over a mile to the south west.

Hardley Street
Norfolk. Just a little more than a quarter of a mile from Hardley Staithe is the church of St Margaret's. It has a round Norman tower and a 15thC wall painting of St Christopher. There are ample opportunities for walking in this area, with good public footpaths and quiet lanes – an excellent 3-mile ramble, starting at the church, would pass Hardley Hall, a 16thC house, progress east to the River Chet and then south along the river bank by Hardley Flood, a NNT reserve of 90 acres rich in birdlife, to finish at the White Horse pub in Chedgrave. Less energetic crew members could bring the boat round. Hardley Cross, at the confluence of the Chet and Yare, marks the limit of jurisdiction of the City of Norwich over the latter river. It was erected in 1676.

Loddon (and Chedgrave)
Norfolk. EC Wed, MD Mon. All shops and services. Loddon, to the south of the Chet, has a main street lined with attractive, mainly Georgian houses, with the market square and church to the east. Holy Trinity, late 15thC and much-restored Perpendicular, stands in a vast graveyard. Light floods in through the many windows, illuminating the unusual screen, decorated with scenes from the Life of Christ and Martyrdom of St William of Norwich, who is shown with blood gushing from his side. It is thought by some that the original church on this site was founded by St Felix in 630. The oak alms box is a relic thought to have come from this building. Anglo Saxon, it is carved from a solid block of wood. There are some excellent brasses (rubbings by arrangement, see notice in the porch) and monuments – that to Lady Williamson, patron of several London churches, is of particular note. A painting in the south aisle depicts Sir James Hobart and his wife against a background of Loddon Church and, interestingly, a fortified bridge at St Olaves. The Hobart family lived at Hales Hall (see below), and were responsible for the building of the church.

Chedgrave is the northerly continuation of

Loddon

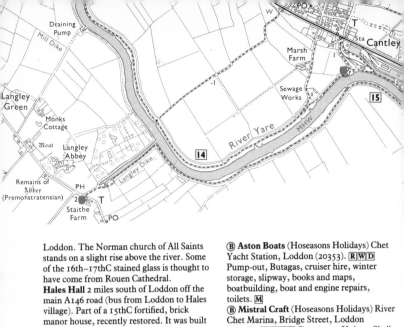

Loddon. The Norman church of All Saints stands on a slight rise above the river. Some of the 16th–17thC stained glass is thought to have come from Rouen Cathedral.

Hales Hall 2 miles south of Loddon off the main A146 road (bus from Loddon to Hales village). Part of a 15thC fortified, brick manor house, recently restored. It was built by Sir James Hobart, Attorney-General to Henry VII. Part of the Hall was demolished in the 17thC – this is now the site of an archaeological dig, with many of the finds on display. The barn, a magnificent structure, dates from 1478. Its roof timbers are of particular note. The moated garden is currently being restored, and many unexpected plants (orange and lemon trees, figs and vines) are for sale. *Open only four or five weekends during the year*. Admission charge. Teas in the old kitchen.

Opposite is St Margaret's, described as a 'perfect Norman village church'. It has a round tower and some 13th–15thC wall paintings. If you visit the hall, it's worth crossing the main road to have a look at this charming little building.

BOATYARDS

Ⓑ Worsley Craft (Hoseasons Holidays) Riverside, Loddon (20397). Ⓡ Ⓦ Ⓓ Pump-out, Unigas, cruiser hire, day hire boats, winter storage, boat lift (8 tons), books and maps, boatbuilding and sales, boat and engine repairs. Ⓜ *Closed Sun*.

Ⓑ Aston Boats (Hoseasons Holidays) Chet Yacht Station, Loddon (20353). Ⓡ Ⓦ Ⓓ Pump-out, Butagas, cruiser hire, winter storage, slipway, books and maps, boatbuilding, boat and engine repairs, toilets. Ⓜ

Ⓑ Mistral Craft (Hoseasons Holidays) River Chet Marina, Bridge Street, Loddon (20438). Ⓡ Ⓢ Ⓦ Ⓓ Pump-out, Unigas, Shell gas, cruiser hire, long-term mooring, winter storage, slipway, chandlery, boatbuilding and sales, boat and engine repairs, Interspray, blast cleaning. Ⓜ

Ⓑ Maffett Cruisers (Blakes) Riverside, Loddon (20344). Ⓡ Ⓦ Ⓓ Pump-out, AIG gas, cruiser hire, slipway, toilets, showers. Ⓜ

Ⓑ Broadland Cruisers (Blakes) Riverside, Loddon (20758). Ⓡ Ⓢ Ⓦ Ⓓ Pump-out, Butane gas, cruiser hire, day hire boats, slipway, books and maps. Caravan Club site. Ⓜ *Closed Sun afternoons*.

Ⓑ **Gale Cruisers** (Hoseasons Holidays) Riverside, Loddon (20300). Ⓡ Ⓦ Pump-out, Unigas, cruiser hire, overnight mooring, long-term mooring, winter storage, slipway, boatbuilding, boat and engine repairs, toilets, showers. Ⓜ

Ⓑ **Walklin Cruisers** (Blakes) Riverside, Loddon (20649). Ⓡ Ⓦ Ⓓ Pump-out, Butagas, cruiser hire, slipway, maps, boat and engine repairs, toilets (close by). Ⓜ *Closed Sun afternoons and winter weekends.*

MOORING

There are public overnight moorings at Loddon Staithe. Suitable moorings may also be found at: Langley Staithe; Red House Inn, Cantley; Hardley Staithe; Hardley Cross; Loddon Staithe; Ferry Inn, Reedham.

PUBS AND RESTAURANTS

🍺**Wherry Inn** Langley Green (Loddon 28427). At the head of Langley Dike. Norwich Brewery and Websters real ales, bar meals (*L&D*), snacks, garden.

🍺 **Red House** Riverside, Cantley (Great Yarmouth 700801). Next door to the sugar-beet factory, a good local for worker and visitor alike. Whitbread Wethered real ale, meals (*L&D*), snacks and garden. Ⓜ

🍺 **Ferry** Reedham Ferry (Great Yarmouth 700429). Popular family-run pub, white-painted with a pantiled roof, offering Adnams and Tolly Cobbold real ales, grills (*L&D*) and snacks. Children's room and garden. Ⓜ

🍺 **Top House** The Halfacre, Reedham (Great Yarmouth 700340). A connoisseur's choice of real ales. Bar meals (*L&D*), children's room, garden.

🍺 **White Horse** Norwich Road, Chedgrave (Loddon 20250). Fine unspoilt pub with tap room and bar. Norwich Brewery real ale, snacks, garden.

🍺 **Angel** High Street, Loddon (20763). Norwich Brewery real ale in convivial surroundings. Outstanding food (*L&D*), snacks and garden.

🍺 **Swan** High Street, Loddon (20239). 16thC inn where the Whitbread Wethered real ale is not cheap. Meals (*L&D*), snacks, children's room.

✕♟ **Loddon Water Mill** Bridge Street, Loddon (20693). A la carte restaurant with an art gallery, working waterwheel, machinery, bric à brac and antiques. (*L Sun only, D Tue–Sun*). Cream teas *Tue–Fri in summer.*

Below Reedham railway swing-bridge, Haddiscoe New Cut provides a (dull) shortcut to Oulton Broad and the Waveney, while the Yare meanders across a vast expanse of marsh to Berney Arms. To the north is Breydon Water, to the south is the Waveney, which makes its lonely course across the marshes to St Olaves.

NAVIGATIONAL NOTES

Do not cut the corner at Berney Arms – keep to the marked channel.
Mooring at Reedham Always moor against the tide, which is especially strong here.

Reedham

Norfolk. EC Wed. PO, stores, BR station. It was here that a 'King's Falconer' murdered Lothbroc the Dane; the bad feeling this generated caused 20,000 Danes to take Norfolk by force, thus ending the Saxon dynasty. Today, as the result of a minor blossoming of industry up to 1900, the village is mainly Victorian – and the riverside, as you would expect, is very busy during the summer. To the west is the chain ferry, the last on the Broads and the only road crossing of the Yare between Yarmouth and Norwich, while to the east is an unusual railway swing bridge, drawn aside for the trading vessels which ply inland to Norwich. The church of St John Baptist stands on higher ground to the north east.

Berney Arms Mill One of the finest mills in the country, built originally to grind cement clinker and later converted for marsh drainage. Constructed in 1870, with seven floors it is over 70 feet high. In perfect working order, it houses an exhibition. *Open Apr–Sep.* Admission charge. Access by boat, train (Berney Arms Station) or 3-mile walk from Wickhampton.

Burgh Castle

Suffolk. PO, stores. The village lies back from the river, behind the marina and holiday village. A short walk to the north, overlooking the Waveney, are the substantial remains of the Roman fort of Garianonum, encompassing an area of six acres and

Berney Arms Mill

affording good views towards Berney Arms, the marshes to the west and Breydon Water to the north. A short way beyond the fort is the church of St Peter and St Paul, which has a Norman round tower and bench ends decorated with poppy heads.

BOATYARDS

Ⓑ **Sanderson Marine Craft** (Blakes) Riverside, Reedham (Great Yarmouth 700242). Ⓟ Ⓓ Ⓔ Pump-out, Calor, Unigas, AIG gas, cruiser hire, sailing craft hire, long-term mooring, winter storage, maps, boatbuilding, boat and engine repairs. Ⓜ *Closed Sun afternoons and all day Sun in winter.*

Ⓑ **W Pearson (Marine Craft)** (Hoseasons Holidays) Holly Farm Road, Reedham (Great Yarmouth 700288). Ⓡ Ⓢ Ⓦ Ⓟ Ⓓ Pump-out, Calor, cruiser hire, long-term mooring, slipway, books and maps, boatbuilding, boat and engine repairs, towing, salvage, toilets. Ⓜ

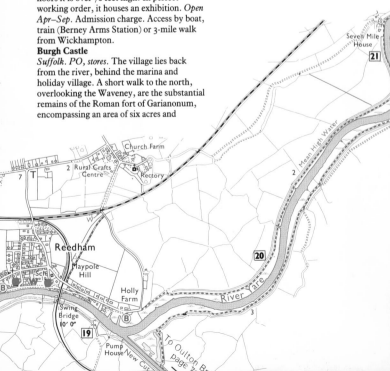

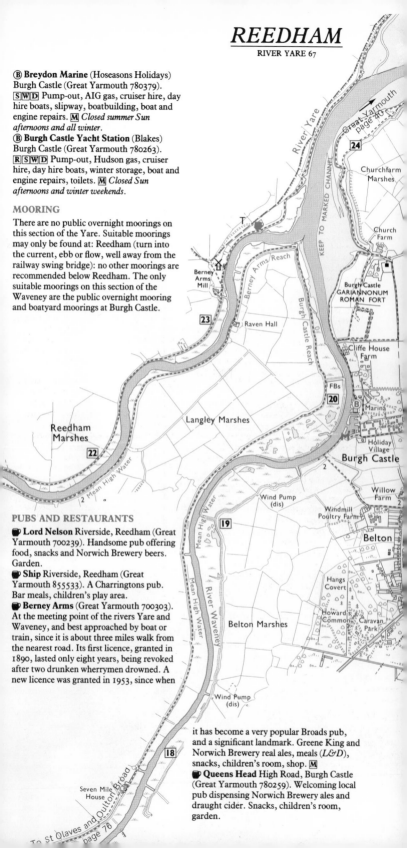

(B) **Breydon Marine** (Hoseasons Holidays) Burgh Castle (Great Yarmouth 780379). [S][W][D] Pump-out, AIG gas, cruiser hire, day hire boats, slipway, boatbuilding, boat and engine repairs. [M] *Closed summer Sun afternoons and all winter.*

(B) **Burgh Castle Yacht Station** (Blakes) Burgh Castle (Great Yarmouth 780263). [R][S][W][D] Pump-out, Hudson gas, cruiser hire, day hire boats, winter storage, boat and engine repairs, toilets. [M] *Closed Sun afternoons and winter weekends.*

MOORING

There are no public overnight moorings on this section of the Yare. Suitable moorings may only be found at: Reedham (turn into the current, ebb or flow, well away from the railway swing bridge): no other moorings are recommended below Reedham. The only suitable moorings on this section of the Waveney are the public overnight mooring and boatyard moorings at Burgh Castle.

PUBS AND RESTAURANTS

Lord Nelson Riverside, Reedham (Great Yarmouth 700239). Handsome pub offering food, snacks and Norwich Brewery beers. Garden.

Ship Riverside, Reedham (Great Yarmouth 855533). A Charringtons pub. Bar meals, children's play area.

Berney Arms (Great Yarmouth 700303). At the meeting point of the rivers Yare and Waveney, and best approached by boat or train, since it is about three miles walk from the nearest road. Its first licence, granted in 1890, lasted only eight years, being revoked after two drunken wherrymen drowned. A new licence was granted in 1953, since when

it has become a very popular Broads pub, and a significant landmark. Greene King and Norwich Brewery real ales, meals (*L&D*), snacks, children's room, shop. [M]

Queens Head High Road, Burgh Castle (Great Yarmouth 780259). Welcoming local pub dispensing Norwich Brewery ales and draught cider. Snacks, children's room, garden.

Cantley

THE RIVER WAVENEY

The source of the Waveney is to be found five miles west of Diss, less than half a mile from the point where the River Little Ouse rises to flow west from the watershed into the Fenlands. In 1670 an Act of Parliament was passed giving authority to improve the navigation from Beccles to Bungay by building locks at Geldeston, Ellingham and Wainford on what was a private navigation outside the jurisdiction of the Yarmouth Commissioners. After changing ownership several times, this section was finally abandoned in 1934.

During the early part of the 19thC the merchants of Beccles felt aggrieved, as did their counterparts in Norwich, that all goods had to be trans-shipped at Yarmouth, and were equally delighted when, in 1831, the new route through Oulton Dyke, Oulton Broad and Lake Lothing to the sea at Lowestoft was opened. However, by about 1850, due to silting, boats were once again trading via Yarmouth. Today only pleasure craft use the river, and have to turn below the site of Geldeston Lock. From its source to the junction into the Haddiscoe New Cut, the river constitutes the boundary between Norfolk and Suffolk.

Oulton Broad

The character of the River Waveney is soon established as it meanders across the flood plain, villages keeping their distance on the higher ground. Geldeston, however, can be reached via Geldeston Dyke. Beccles lies to the east behind an attractive but brief river frontage – once through the low bridge the river again enters marshland, with woodland below the Stanley Hills bringing a welcome change.

NAVIGATIONAL NOTES

Limit of navigation Geldeston Lock.
Beccles Bridge Only 6ft 6in headroom at mean high water springs.

Geldeston
Norfolk. PO, stores. A small village at the limit of navigation on the Waveney, notable for having two fine pubs, one of which is situated by the disused lock. This once marked the start of an extended navigation to Bungay. The church of St Michael has a round tower, but little other original work. There are some fine headstones in the churchyard. The footpath, which starts at Geldeston Dyke, makes a pleasant walk to Beccles.

Barsham
Suffolk. Walking south from Geldeston Lock to Barsham Hall, then south again for just a little over one mile you will find Holy Trinity church, Barsham. Its round tower is topped with a spike, but the real delight is the whole exterior of the east wall, an amazing stonework trellis (undated but pre-17thC) incorporating a stained glass east window by Kempe. Inside there are fine examples of more recent work: the stuccoed chancel roof (1906) and the gaily decorated rood canopy (1919).

Gillingham
Norfolk. A modern estate village. Separate, and to the north, is the Norman church of St Mary. The nave was rebuilt in 1859 in the Norman style. Only the tower remains of All Saints, its close neighbour. The rest of the building collapsed in 1748.

Beccles
Suffolk. EC Wed, MD Fri. PO, stores, BR station, launderette. A solidly Georgian town, rebuilt in red brick after four great fires in the 16th and 17thC. With lock-free access to the sea it was once a great port, with Norfolk wherries and bluff-bowed 'billyboy' ketches from the north east filling the quays. Today the waterfront has a more genteel air, with long gardens down to private moorings, each with its smart cruiser. Industry, including a large printing works, remains inconspicuous. From the river, the tower of St Michael's is dominant. Separate from the body of the church, it is 97 feet tall, square and solid. Sold for £1 in 1972 to the local council, who had to assume ownership before starting restoration, the view from the top is well worth the climb. The church has a very grand south porch, two storeys tall and with much detailed decoration – however, the interior, destroyed by fire in 1586, is of little architectural interest. It was here, on 11 May 1749, Rev Edmund Nelson and Catherine Suckling were married; their son was Horatio Nelson the British naval hero.
Beccles Museum Newgate, Beccles (712628). Rear of Post Office. Local industry and farming. Domestic implements, costumes, paintings and the original Beccles Town sign. *Open afternoons Wed, Sat, Sun & B.Hols, Apr–Oct (Sun only Nov–Mar).* Admission free.
Broads Information Centre The Quay, Beccles (713196). *Open daily Apr–Sep.*
Swimming A major attraction to boaters will be the heated outdoor pool right by the river at Puddingmoor, *open during the summer.*
The Otter Trust Bungay (3470). Off the A143 at Earsham. Bus from Beccles Old Market to Bungay Earsham Street, then 1½ miles walk west to Earsham, off A143. A collection of otters in natural surroundings. Three species of these fascinating creatures are bred here, some for release into suitable

wild habitats. Nature trail, wildfowl on three lakes, muntjac and Chinese water deer. Teas and gift shop. *Open daily Apr–Oct.* Admission charge.

If visiting the Otter Trust, you may well wish to explore Bungay (*EC Wed, MD Thur*), a handsome market town with over 1000 years of history – indeed the Mayor of Bungay is still known as Town Reeve, a Saxon term. Of interest are: the castle ruins; Holy Trinity church, which has an 11thC round tower, one of the oldest in the country; and the Butter Cross. Built in 1689, this octagonal domed shelter from which butter and other produce was sold, once contained a cage and dungeon for prisoners.

BOATYARDS

Ⓑ **Beccles Yacht Station** Beccles (712225). ⓇⓌ Pump-out, toilets, showers, launderette. Friendly and helpful advice regarding tides and boathandling. Ⓜ

Ⓑ **H E Hipperson** (Hoseasons Holidays) West bank, below Beccles Bridge. Beccles (712166). ⓇⓌⒻⒹ Pump-out, Calor, Unigas, AIG gas, cruiser hire, day hire boats, long-term mooring, winter storage, slipway, boatbuilding, boat and engine repairs, houseboats. Ⓜ

Ⓑ **Aston Boats** (Hoseasons Holidays) Bridge Wharf, Beccles (713960). ⓇⓈⓌⒹ Pump-out, Butagas, cruiser hire, winter storage, slipway, boatbuilding, boat and engine repairs, toilets. Ⓜ *Closed Sun afternoons.*

Ⓑ **Arrow Boats** (Blakes) Puddingmoor, Beccles (713524). ⓌⒹ Pump-out, Unigas, cruiser hire, long-term mooring, winter storage, slipway, boatbuilding, boat and engine repairs, houseboats. *Closed Sun afternoons, winter weekends and all Dec and Jan.*

MOORING

There is a public overnight mooring near the Locks, Geldeston. Other suitable moorings will be found at: Geldeston Dyke; Beccles Yacht Station; north of Beccles Bridge, both banks.

PUBS AND RESTAURANTS

🍺 **Locks** Riverside, Geldeston (Kirby Kane 414). A fine, unspoilt pub with benches and settles, scrubbed tables and log fires. A good choice of real ales; bar snacks, terrace and garden. Children welcome. *Closed weekdays in winter.* Approaching from the village entails a 200-yard walk along a gravel track.

🍺 **Wherry** The Street, Geldeston (Kirby Kane 371). 16thC pub of character, serving Adnams real ale and food (*L&D*). Garden, children's room.

There are many fine pubs in Beccles.

🍺 **Waveney House Hotel** Puddingmore, Beccles (712270). Adnams and Greene King real ales in the riverside bar of a hotel, parts of which date from 1584. Bar food (*L&D*), children's room, garden.

🍺 **The Loaves and Fishes** Fen Lane, Beccles (713844). Well-converted maltings where Adnams and Greene King real ales may be enjoyed in the bar. Meals (*L&D*), garden.

🍺 **White Horse** New Market, Beccles (713570). 16thC coaching inn serving Whitbread Wethered real ale and bar food (*L&D*). Note the old Lacons Brewery clock in the bar. Garden.

🍺 **Bear & Bells** Old Market, Beccles (712291). Dating from 1620, this fine old inn offers Norwich Brewery and Websters real ales. Bar food (*L only*), children's room, garden.

A very remote but attractive stretch of river, with a wide expanse of marshland either side and not a road in sight until the Waveney Inn is reached.

Aldeby

Norfolk. A tiny village with some modern housing. The church of St Mary is a Norman building, with evidence of restoration. It has a nicely decorated 14thC porch. By Aldeby Hall are the remains of a Benedictine Priory and an ancient burial ground.

Worlingham

Suffolk. Stores. The eastern continuation of Beccles. There are some handsome monuments in the churchyard of All Saints.

Burgh St Peter

Norfolk. PO, stores. A scattered village which adjoins Wheatacre, where the church of All Saints is situated. The sturdy brick and flint Perpendicular tower has been built with a bold chequerboard pattern beneath a battlemented top. The interior of the nave and chancel suggest 14thC origins and the font and font cover are both notable. The actual village church of Burgh St Peter lies 1½ miles to the east, on a slight prominence between the River Waveney and Burgh

Marshes. The charming 13thC thatched nave is unfortunately dominated by a grotesque folly of a tower – four brick boxes piled up wedding cake style. Built c1800 on a 16thC base, its pointed windows simply accentuate its awfulness. 14thC font.

Barnby

Suffolk. PO, stores. 1½ miles south of the river. The 14thC thatched church of St John Baptist has a 13thC font and a Banner Staff Locker with a traceried door – possibly a unique feature.

BOATYARDS

ⓑ **Waveney Hotel Marina** Burgh St Peter (Aldeby 217). Ⓡ Ⓦ Ⓟ Ⓓ Pump-out, gas, long-term mooring, boat and engine repairs, slipway, provisions, books, maps, caravan site, showers, toilets. Ⓜ Also see 'Pubs'.

MOORING

There are public overnight moorings at Worlingham Staithe. Other suitable moorings may be found at: north bank near Aldeby Hall; above Cove Staithe; off Castle Marsh; Waveney Hotel Marina.

PUBS AND RESTAURANTS

🍺 **Lion** Aldeby (369). Adnams and Woodfordes real ales in a welcoming country pub, with log fires when the weather is cold. Food (*L&D*) and garden.

🍺 **Waveney Inn** Burgh St Peter (Aldeby 217). To the east of the village. A charming old inn by the staithe, serving Adnams real ale and bar meals (*L&D*). Children's room, garden. Ⓜ

The Waveney continues its lonely course across the marshes. Oulton Dyke, an artificial channel, joins from the south, a link with Oulton Broad and the sea, via Mutford Lock.

NAVIGATIONAL NOTES

Tides If you are making the passage through Great Yarmouth onto the Northern Broads you should aim to enter the Bure one hour after low water slack, thus avoiding any problems with low bridges.
Somerleyton Swing Bridge and **St Olaves Bridge** both have very low headroom at high water.
Oulton Broad Navigation authority is Waveney District Council. Speed limit 10mph.

Lowestoft
Suffolk. EC Thur, MD Fri. All shops and services, BR station. A town whose fortunes were made by the discovery of the Dogger Bank and other North Sea fishing grounds in the mid 19thC. The building of the railway in 1847 brought the rich London markets within easy reach, thus putting the Thames estuary fishing ports out of business. Today, alongside the fishing fleet are cargo ships carrying timber and grain – there are fascinating guided walks around the quays and fish market, organised from the Tourist Information Office *each Mon, Wed and Thur morning*. The original fishing village was sited just north of Hamilton Dock and, although this area is now an industrial estate, it is still possible to explore the Scores – narrow cobbled lanes which once led down to the herring curing houses of the old settlement. With such a solid fishing heritage it is not surprising that the Lowestoft Lifeboat was founded as early as 1801, preceding the establishment of the Royal National Lifeboat Institution by 23 years. Of course, Lowestoft's alter ego is that of a popular east coast resort, with excellent sandy beaches, two piers, plenty of parks and gardens, a theatre and all the usual seaside entertainments, extending both north and south of the harbour. At Lowestoft Ness one can stand at the most easterly place in England.
Lowestoft Maritime Museum Sparrows Nest Park, Whapload Road, near the lighthouse (Lowestoft 61963). Housed in an extended brick cottage the exhibition charts the history of fishing and seafaring. *Open daily 10.00–17.00 May–Sep.*
St Margaret's Church St Margaret's Road, Lowestoft (off B1074). A spacious building with an imposing tower of c1300 and much flushwork decoration. Lions and angels wait at the entrance to the south porch, which is rib-vaulted inside. Graceful arcades line the continuous nave and chancel. Admire the fine east window, and the stained glass in the window to its right, done in 1819 by Robert Allen; he worked at the Lowestoft china factory, which enjoyed a transient existence from 1756–1803. See also the medieval brasses of skeletons in shrouds.

Oulton Broad

Suffolk. EC Thur. PO, stores. A continuation of Lowestoft but a resort in its own right. The Broad is one of the country's premier boating lakes, covering 130 acres and navigable virtually throughout. Sailing, cruising, powerboat racing (*Thur evenings in summer*), windsurfing and rowing provide an ever changing spectacle. The handsome maltings in the north east corner have been well-converted into dwellings. In Nicholas Everitt Park there are tennis courts, bowling greens, a children's playground and an open air swimming pool. An interesting local museum is kept in Broads House, in the park. The Sports Centre in Water Lane (Lowestoft 69116) has an indoor pool, solarium and squash courts. Oulton regatta week is held *in late Aug.*

Tourist Information Centre The Esplanade, Lowestoft (65989). *Open 10.00–17.30 May–Sep.*

East Anglia Transport Museum Chapel Road, Carlton Colville (the south westerly extension of Lowestoft, on the A146). (Norwich 625412). Motor, steam and electric vehicles on display. Narrow gauge railway, tram rides, working vintage vehicles. *Open Sat afternoons Jun, Jul & Sep. Mon–Sat afternoons Aug.* Admission charge.

Carlton Marshes Nature Reserve South of Oulton Broad. A pleasant walk along the public footpath to see marshland birds such as snipe, lapwing, bearded tits, ducks and geese.

BOATYARDS

ⓑ **Yacht Station** Oulton Broad, Lowestoft (4946). Ⓦ Friendly and helpful advice regarding tides and navigation. Ⓜ

ⓑ **Broadsway Cruisers** (Blakes) Commodore Road, Oulton Broad, Lowestoft (65063). Ⓡ Ⓦ Ⓓ Pump-out, Unigas, Butagas, AIG gas, cruiser hire, slipway, dry dock, books and maps, boat and engine repairs, toilets, showers, houseboats. Ⓜ

ⓑ **Newson Boats** (Hoseasons Holidays) Commodore Road, Oulton Broad, Lowestoft (64598). Ⓡ Ⓦ Ⓓ Pump-out, Unigas, cruiser hire, long-term mooring, slipway, books and maps, boatbuilding, boat and engine sales and repairs, toilets. Ⓜ

ⓑ **Hampton Boats** (Hoseasons Holidays) Caldecott Road, Oulton Broad, Lowestoft (4896). Ⓡ Ⓦ Ⓓ Pump-out, Unigas, cruiser hire, winter storage, slipway, books and maps, boatbuilding, boat and engine repairs, toilets. Ⓜ *Closed Sun afternoons.*

ⓑ **A D Truman** (Hoseasons Holidays) Old Maltings Boatyard, Caldecott Road, Oulton Broad, Lowestoft (65950). Ⓡ Ⓢ Ⓦ Ⓟ Ⓓ Pump-out, Calor, AIG gas, cruiser hire, sailing craft hire, long-term mooring, winter storage, slipway, boatbuilding, boat and engine sales and repairs, toilets. Ⓜ

ⓑ **Topcraft** (Hoseasons Holidays) Caldecott Road, Oulton Broad, Lowestoft (63719). Ⓡ Ⓦ Ⓓ Pump-out, Unigas, cruiser hire, winter storage, slipway (20 tons × 60ft), boatbuilding, boat and engine repairs, toilets. Ⓜ *Closed Sun afternoons.*

MOORING

There are reasonable moorings in Oulton Dyke by Carlton Marshes, but those most convenient are to be found at the Yacht Station, at the head of Oulton Broad – contact the Harbour Master.

BOAT TRIPS

Waveney River Tours Mutford Lock, Bridge Road, Oulton Broad, Lowestoft (4903). Trips aboard 'Waveney Princess' and 'Enchantress' to Burgh St Peter (*not Sats*). Special *all day Fri* trip to Beccles market.

Dayboats Hire – Oulton Broad Lowestoft 513087. Drive yourself launches.

PUBS AND RESTAURANTS

🍺✕ **Wherry Hotel** Oulton Broad, Lowestoft (3521). Large, beautifully decorated, waterside hotel catering well for holidaymakers. Websters and Norwich Brewery real ales, restaurant (*L&D*) and coffee house. Weekend discos, sail and motor boat hire. Very popular with smart young people. Ⓦ Pump-out nearby. Ⓜ

✕🍷 **The Moorings** Oulton Broad, Lowestoft (2995). Restaurant meals and coffee shop (*L&D*).

🍺 **Lady of the Lake** Near the Yacht Station, Oulton Broad (Lowestoft 4740). During the summer there is live music here. Bar meals (*L&D*), children's room, garden.

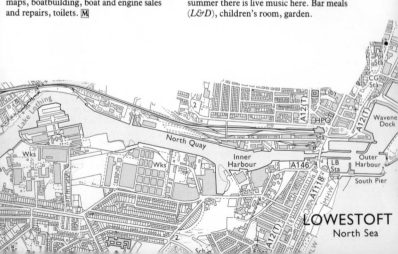

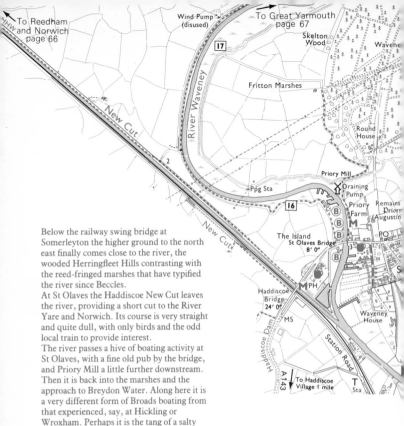

To Reedham and Norwich page 66

To Great Yarmouth page 67

Wind Pump (disused)

17

Skelton Wood

Waveney

Fritton Marshes

Round House

River Waveney

New Cut

2

Priory Mill

Ppg Sta

Draining Pump

16

Priory Farm

Remains Priory (Augustin

New Cut

The Island
St Olaves Bridge
8' 0"

B
B
B
M
PO

B

Below the railway swing bridge at Somerleyton the higher ground to the north east finally comes close to the river, the wooded Herringfleet Hills contrasting with the reed-fringed marshes that have typified the river since Beccles.

At St Olaves the Haddiscoe New Cut leaves the river, providing a short cut to the River Yare and Norwich. Its course is very straight and quite dull, with only birds and the odd local train to provide interest.

The river passes a hive of boating activity at St Olaves, with a fine old pub by the bridge, and Priory Mill a little further downstream. Then it is back into the marshes and the approach to Breydon Water. Along here it is a very different form of Broads boating from that experienced, say, at Hickling or Wroxham. Perhaps it is the tang of a salty breeze, suggesting the thrill of the sea.

Haddiscoe Bridge 24' 0"

MS

Haddiscoe Dam

Waveney House

Station Road

A 143

To Haddiscoe Village 1 mile

T Sta

M PH

NAVIGATIONAL NOTES

Tides If you are making the passage through Great Yarmouth harbour onto the Northern Broads you should aim to enter the Bure one hour after low water slack, thus avoiding any problems with strong tides and low bridges. If you are in any doubt, check with the boatyards at St Olaves or Burgh Castle.

Somerleyton

Suffolk. EC Wed. PO, store. An irregular estate village, built by Sir Morton Peto, and designed by John Thomas, who was also responsible for the Hall (see below) and the flint and stone church, a modern reproduction in the style of the local churches. To the north west is St Margaret's Herringfleet, a Norman structure, with a round tower and original Norman windows.
Herringfleet Mill ¾ mile west of the church. A unique survivor. This timber-smock drainage windpump was built to a very early design, driving a 16ft diameter scoop wheel. It once had cloth sails, turned into the wind by a marshman who was expected to appear whatever the weather to perform this task – indeed a couch and fireplace were provided so he could attend the mill non-stop if required. It is maintained in working order, and if the wind is blowing, can be seen in action three times each year.
Somerleyton Hall The home of Lord and Lady Somerleyton. A splendid and extravagant Victorian mansion in mainly Jacobean style around a Tudor shell. It was

built by John Thomas in 1846 for Sir Morton Peto, an extraordinarily successful man who began his career as a builder's apprentice and who, by the age of 31, was responsible for building Nelson's Column, St James's Theatre and railways in the Argentine, Australia and Canada. Knighted in 1855 he was bankrupted in 1886 and the house was sold to Sir Francis Crossley. Liberal dressings of stone imported from Caen and Aubigny, superbly carved and recently restored, adorn the brickwork. The splendid interiors contain paintings by Landseer, Wright of Derby, and Stanfield, with wood carving by Willcox and Grinling Gibbons. In the 12 acres of gardens, planted with azaleas and rhododendrons, is a maze dating from 1846 which is one of the finest in the country. The stable clock was the original model of a clock designed for the Houses of Parliament by Vulliamy in 1847. The glasshouses are by Paxton, designer of the Great Exhibition building of 1851. Miniature railway, teas. *House open afternoons Sun, Thur and B.Hols, Easter–Sep, also Tue & Wed, Jul & Aug. Garden open Sun–Fri.* Admission charge. No dogs.

St Olaves

Suffolk. EC Wed. PO, stores. A pretty Broadland village. To the north are the remains of an Augustinian Priory, founded in 1216. The undercroft, with its brick ceiling, survives, although many of the other buildings have been used since the Dissolution as a source of building stone. *Open daily.*

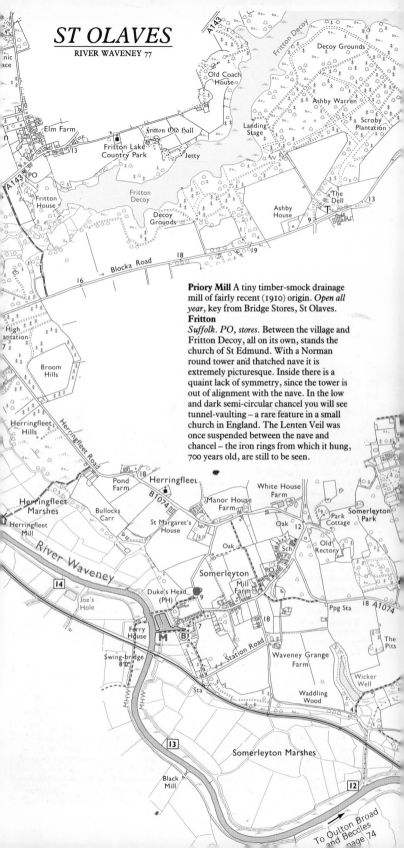

Priory Mill A tiny timber-smock drainage mill of fairly recent (1910) origin. *Open all year*, key from Bridge Stores, St Olaves.

Fritton

Suffolk. PO, stores. Between the village and Fritton Decoy, all on its own, stands the church of St Edmund. With a Norman round tower and thatched nave it is extremely picturesque. Inside there is a quaint lack of symmetry, since the tower is out of alignment with the nave. In the low and dark semi-circular chancel you will see tunnel-vaulting – a rare feature in a small church in England. The Lenten Veil was once suspended between the nave and chancel – the iron rings from which it hung, 700 years old, are still to be seen.

Fritton Decoy A three-mile-long lake set amidst trees, once called Gunhilde's Mere (she was an aunt of King Canute). 'Decoy' derives from the time when wild ducks were lured onto the lake by feeding them with grain. Trained tame ducks would then swim into a funnel-shaped net, followed by their unsuspecting wild cousins. The net was then closed, and the wild ducks killed and sent off to market.

Fritton Lake Country Park (Fritton 208). Boating, fishing, windsurfing, pony rides, putting, adventure playgrounds, walks, wildfowl collection, basket makers workshop, tea room and visitors' centre, all in 170 acres of garden and woodland walks. *Open 09.00–19.00 daily Apr–Sep.* Admission charge. No dogs.

Haddiscoe
Norfolk. A village 1½ miles south of Haddiscoe Bridge which gave its name to the new cut between Reedham and St Olaves, built in 1832 as part of an ill-fated scheme to allow coastal vessels access to Norwich without passing (or paying) Great Yarmouth. If you have time, it's worth a pleasant walk along the road across the marshes to see the church of St Mary. Its 11thC Saxon/Norman round tower is adorned with battlements and chequer work. Above the fine south door is a rare Norman sculptured figure, and in the nave a floor stone commemorates 'Bele', the wife of the Dutchman who planned the drainage of many of the marshes hereabouts.

BOATYARDS

Ⓑ **Ripplecraft** (Blakes) Somerleyton, Lowestoft (730335). Ⓡ Ⓦ Ⓓ Pump-out, Unigas, cruiser hire, long-term mooring, winter storage, slipway, boatbuilding, boat and engine repairs, toilets. Ⓜ *Closed Sun afternoons and winter weekends.*

Ⓑ **Beaver Fleet** (Blakes) Reeds Lane, St Olaves, Great Yarmouth (Fritton 254). Ⓡ Ⓢ Ⓦ Ⓓ Pump-out, Butagas, cruiser hire, winter storage, dry dock, books and maps, boatbuilding, boat and engine repairs. Ⓜ

Ⓑ **Priory Craft Marine** (Hoseasons Holidays) St Olaves, Great Yarmouth (Fritton 203). Ⓡ Ⓦ Ⓓ Pump-out, Unigas, Butagas, cruiser hire, long-term mooring, winter storage, slipway, books and maps, boat and engine repairs, toilets. Ⓜ *Closed weekends.*

Ⓑ **Castle Craft/D W Marine** (Blakes) Reeds Lane, St Olaves, Great Yarmouth (Fritton 675). Ⓡ Ⓢ Ⓦ Ⓓ Pump-out, Calor, cruiser hire, day hire boats, long-term mooring, winter storage, slipway, chandlery, provisions, books and maps, boatbuilding, boat and engine sales and repairs, houseboats. Specialists in power boat racing and boat transport. Ⓜ *Closed Thur, Sat and Sun afternoons.*

Ⓑ **Albatross Marine** (Hoseasons Holidays) Albatross Works, St Olaves (Great Yarmouth 79629). Ⓡ Ⓦ Ⓓ Pump-out, Butagas, cruiser hire, boat and engine repairs. Ⓜ *Closed Sun and winter weekends.*

Ⓑ **Johnson's Yacht Station** (Blakes) St Olaves Bridge (Great Yarmouth 79218). Ⓡ Ⓦ Ⓟ Ⓓ Pump-out, Calor, Butagas, Unigas, cruiser hire, long-term mooring, winter storage, slipway, boatbuilding, boat and engine repairs. *Closed winter weekends.*

MOORING

There are public overnight moorings at: Haddiscoe Bridge; Somerleyton Staithe; Herringfleet; St Olaves; Priory Mill.

PUBS AND RESTAURANTS

🍺 **Duke's Head** Sluggs Lane, Somerleyton (Lowestoft 730281). Family pub serving Whitbread Wethered real ale and good food (*L&D*). Garden, children's room.

🍺 **The Bell** St Olaves Bridge (Fritton 249). An old timberframe building with red-brick herringbone infills, said to be the oldest pub on the Broads. There was a ferry here in the 14thC, maintained by a fisherman who was paid in herrings and bread to the value of 20 shillings each year. What is now The Bell was probably the ferry hermitage. The low-ceilinged bar has an open fire and plenty of beams and comfortable seats. Whitbread Wethered real ale is served along with good bar food (*L&D*). Garden. Ⓜ

🍺 **Crown** The Street, Haddiscoe (Aldeby 368). Large pub serving Norwich Brewery real ale and snacks. Garden.

🍺 **The Bridge** Haddiscoe Bridge (Fritton 380). Certainly an unlikely looking pub, but do not be put off. Inside all is friendly, comfortable and welcoming. Greene King real ale, bar food (*L&D*), family room with amusements, garden. Ⓜ nearby.

Somerleyton Hall is well worth a visit

THE RIVER NENE

The River Nene rises near Daventry and empties through an artificial channel into The Wash north of Wisbech. It is navigable for 91 miles below Northampton, with 37 locks between there and Peterborough, where the Old Nene takes a more southerly course, eventually losing itself in the Middle Level Navigations. In the late 15thC Bishop Morton built his leam, or straight cut, from Peterborough to Wisbech, via Guyhirn, to enhance both drainage and navigation on the lower river.

Schemes to further improve the navigation were formulated during the 16thC and again in the mid-17thC, but it was not until 1726 that work actually started, with Robert Wright and Thomas Squire making improvements between Peterborough and Oundle, which were completed in 1730. Six years later the works were extended to Thrapston, finally reaching Northampton in 1761. As was so often the case, toll receipts fell short of expectations, and frequent disputes with mill owners added to the problems. However, the Nene Commissioners hoped their salvation would come with the building of the Northampton Arm of the Grand Junction Canal. The link was made, in 1815, but not before the GJCC had tried to make do with a railway connection, which raised toll receipts on the Nene a little, but not enough to satisfy the traders of Northampton.

Falling steeply through 17 narrow locks from Gayton, the Northampton Arm proved to be very much a mixed blessing. Toll receipts on the river rose a little, but repair bills soared. The canal boats did not properly fit the river locks and caused a great deal of damage. Around 1818 the canal boats were ordered not to navigate the river, with goods being trans-shipped onto barges at Northampton for the journey downstream. When the railway was opened from Blisworth to Peterborough in 1845, traffic on the river halved. Tolls were cut in competition with the newfangled railway, but by now the writing was on the wall; having to negotiate 34 locks, 11 staunches and 33 water-mills between Northampton and Peterborough, coupled with constant water shortages, now seemed dreadfully inefficient. There were also problems on the lower river – not least from flooding, which rendered farmland adjacent to the river useless for six months out of twelve. The resultant dampness was blamed for much of the disease, and the area's high death-rate.

Smith's Leam, built in 1728, was now the main navigation channel below Peterborough; below Wisbech there was only an unreliable, shifting channel through the sands. Various small works did little to improve the outfall until a new channel, engineered by Telford and Rennie, was completed in 1831. In the 1850s two dams and a submerged weir (the 'throttle') were built across the river at Wisbech to save the banks above the town. Such hindrances to navigation caused an uproar, and by 1859 they were removed.

By the late 19thC the whole river was in a sorry state: in 1930 the Nene Catchment Board found the river totally dilapidated. An extensive programme of works was put in hand, which included rebuilding all the locks, plus a large sluice and lock at Dog-in-a-Doublet to separate the fresh water from the salt. Tested by the floods of 1947, the new structures proved to be entirely successful. Even some commercial traffic returned. Now the river is given over entirely to pleasure traffic – most of the countryside between Northampton and Peterborough is very pleasant, and the small towns and villages close by are a particularly interesting group.

Navigation authority

Anglian Water
Oundle Division
North Street
Oundle
Peterborough PE8 4AS

Oundle 73701

Regulations and byelaws are available on request.

Registration and licensing

Both long and short term licences, registration and the vital Yale-type key which unlocks the locks, can be obtained from the Finance Manager at the above address by writing well in advance and enclosing £4. They can also be obtained on demand at Gingers Canal Stores, Long Buckby Wharf, (Long Buckby 843063), or Blisworth Tunnel Boats, Blisworth (858868). Both are on the Grand Union Canal main line. Lock keys can also be obtained from Aqua House, Town Bridge, Peterborough, during office hours. 28-day permits are issued for craft already registered with another authority (only one per annum), 14-day permits are issued for craft not registered with another authority (also only one per annum).

Water regulation

The locks on the river are used to control the discharge of water. Paddle indicator boards show how the paddles should be set after you have passed through (although some are missing due to vandalism). If the mitre gates are chained open and the guillotine is raised, the lock is 'reversed' – do not attempt to navigate.

If the water level is seen to be increasing, after heavy rain perhaps, the state of navigation can be checked by ringing Oundle 74242 for a recorded report, which will also include any closures.

The local radio stations, Hereward (225MW, 95.7VHF) and BBC Northampton (271MW, 96.6VHF) also broadcast information on conditions. The Northampton barrage has an automatic warning system.

Weed ropes

These may be found across the river from *June–Sept*. You may release them to pass through, but ensure they are securely re-fastened when you leave.

Dimensions

Length   78ft 0in
Beam   13ft 0in
Headroom 7ft 6in

Locks

Most have mitre gates at the upper end, with a guillotine at the lower. Locks should be left with the gates shut and the guillotine raised. You will require a Grand Union-sized 1¼in windlass and the Yale-type key (see 'Licences').

Speed limit

7mph. Slower if your wash is breaking.

Mooring

There are no problems finding moorings although permission must be sought from the riparian landowner, and any fee paid. Allow for changes in the water level when tying up, and do not moor within 39 yards of a lock or weir (110 yards at Dog-in-a-Doublet Lock and Bedford Road Sluice, Northampton).

Tidal river

Below Dog-in-a-Doublet Lock (Peterborough 202219) the river is tidal, and is not described in this book. If you wish to make the journey to Wisbech and the sea, ring Oundle 73701, 24 hours in advance so that the lock-keeper can be informed. Ensure that your boat is suitably powered and properly equipped. Passage through the lock is free from *07.30 to sunset every day*. Outside these hours a charge of £6 is made; again prior notice must be given.

For passage advice or mooring in Wisbech, ring the Port Manager, Wisbech 582125.

Middle Level Navigations

Entry to the Middle Level connection with the River Ouse is via Stanground Lock, maximum length 49ft. 24 hours notice is required.

Grand Union Canal

Short-term licences are available from the Section Inspector, BWB, Gayton Yard, Blisworth (858233). Maximum dimensions on the Northampton Arm are: length 72ft 0in, beam 7ft 0in, headroom 7ft 0in.

Dog-in-a-Doublet Lock

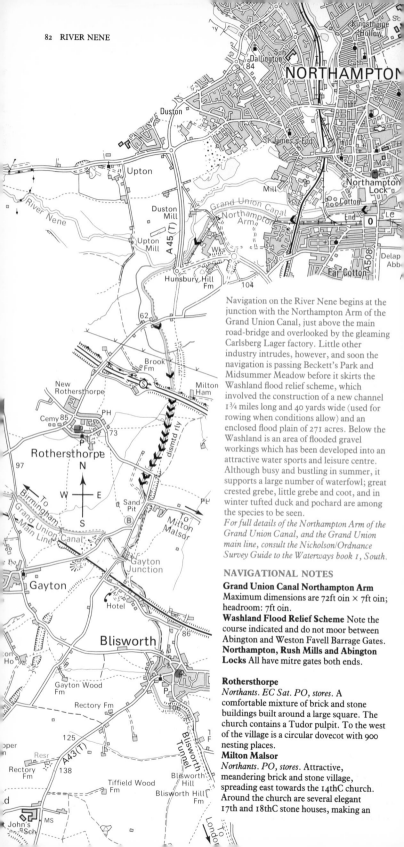

Navigation on the River Nene begins at the junction with the Northampton Arm of the Grand Union Canal, just above the main road-bridge and overlooked by the gleaming Carlsberg Lager factory. Little other industry intrudes, however, and soon the navigation is passing Beckett's Park and Midsummer Meadow before it skirts the Washland flood relief scheme, which involved the construction of a new channel 1¾ miles long and 40 yards wide (used for rowing when conditions allow) and an enclosed flood plain of 271 acres. Below the Washland is an area of flooded gravel workings which has been developed into an attractive water sports and leisure centre. Although busy and bustling in summer, it supports a large number of waterfowl; great crested grebe, little grebe and coot, and in winter tufted duck and pochard are among the species to be seen.

For full details of the Northampton Arm of the Grand Union Canal, and the Grand Union main line, consult the Nicholson/Ordnance Survey Guide to the Waterways book 1, South.

NAVIGATIONAL NOTES

Grand Union Canal Northampton Arm
Maximum dimensions are 72ft 0in × 7ft 0in; headroom: 7ft 0in.
Washland Flood Relief Scheme Note the course indicated and do not moor between Abington and Weston Favell Barrage Gates.
Northampton, Rush Mills and Abington Locks All have mitre gates both ends.

Rothersthorpe

Northants. EC Sat. PO, stores. A comfortable mixture of brick and stone buildings built around a large square. The church contains a Tudor pulpit. To the west of the village is a circular dovecot with 900 nesting places.

Milton Malsor

Northants. PO, stores. Attractive, meandering brick and stone village, spreading east towards the 14thC church. Around the church are several elegant 17th and 18thC stone houses, making an

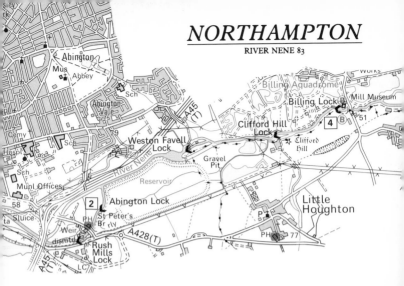

exploration on foot worth while. New houses have been well incorporated with the old.

Northampton

Northants. EC Thur, MD Wed/Sat. All shops and services, BR station. A modern Midlands town which has expanded rapidly during the last 10 years. Few old buildings, and yet of some historical interest. It was a Saxon town sacked by the Danes, and the Normans made it a centre of their communications, building a great castle here where the railway station now stands. Thomas à Becket was tried here before being exiled to France in the 12thC. Since King John bought a pair of boots here for ninepence in the early 13thC, the boot and shoe trade has flourished. It has been said that every English army since the Civil War has been shoed by Northampton. The Central Museum has the finest collection of historical footwear in Europe. The medieval market square is thought to be the largest in England.

There was a great fire in 1675, which destroyed almost all of medieval Northampton. Northampton's churches are its most interesting feature. The Church of the Holy Sepulchre, built by a returned crusader in 1100, is one of only four round churches in England (*open afternoons, closed Sun*). The 19thC St Matthew's Church, Kettering Road, contains a serene 'Madonna and Child' by Henry Moore, and a perturbed 'Crucifixion' by Graham Sutherland. St Peter's, Marefair is a beautiful Norman church with no structural separation between nave and chancel. Its intricate detailing includes much zigzag decoration in the arches, and carving on capitals; pillars alternate in shape in the distinctive nave. There are notable Saxon and Norman sculptures, and a Victorian reredos. The Norman tower was rebuilt in the 17thC. The Royal Theatre and Opera House, known locally as the 'Rep' and established in 1927, provides a continuous programme of entertainment of the highest standard.

Central Museum and Art Gallery Guildhall Road, Northampton (34881). Archaeology, antiquities, paintings, furniture and an outstanding collection of historical footware, including Queen Victoria's wedding shoes, the ballet shoes of Nijinsky and Margot Fonteyn, and even one shoe which was made for an elephant! *Closed Sun.*

Abington Museum Abington Park, Northampton (31454). Period rooms, toys, bygones, Northampton lace, ceramics and natural history, exhibited in a 15thC manor house, partially rebuilt in 1745. *Closed Sun mornings in summer and all day Sun in winter.*

Museum of Leathercraft The Old Blue Coat School, Bridge Street, Northampton (34881). Leather in use from ancient Egypt to the present day. 16thC caskets, saddlery, costume, luggage and sports equipment. *Closed Sun.*

Delapre Abbey London Road, Northampton. South of the bridge. A former Cluniac nunnery founded in 1145, the abbey underwent major alterations in the 16th and 17thC. *Open Thur afternoons.* South of the abbey park is the Eleanor Cross, one of the three surviving crosses erected by Edward I in 1290 to mark the last resting places of Queen Eleanor's body on its way from Harby in Leicestershire, where she died, to burial in Westminster Abbey.

Battle of Northampton 10th July 1460. Between Delapre Abbey and Hunsbury Hill, an Iron Age hillfort of some 4 acres. A significant battle in the Wars of the Roses in which the Lancastrian, King Henry was defeated by Edward of York. Beaumont, Shrewsbury, Egremont and Buckingham were slain and many bodies floated in the River Nene. The keenest fighting took place in the area of Nunn Mills Road, close to where the factories now stand.

Tourist Information Centre 21 St Giles Street, Northampton (22677).

Little Houghton

Northants. PO, stores. A village of attractive period houses around the church of St Mary, originally 13thC but virtually rebuilt in 1873 using warm brown stone. There are stocks to the south east. Clifford Hill, by the lock, is a large motte, remarkable only in that there is no trace of a bailey.

BOATYARDS

ⓑ **Billing Aquadrome** Little Billing, Northampton (408181). Ⓡ Ⓢ Ⓦ Ⓟ Ⓓ Calor gas, long-term mooring, winter storage, slipway, chandlery, provisions, books, maps, boatbuilding and sales, boat and engine repairs, engine sales, showers, toilets Ⓜ. Fishing, sailing and windsurfing.

ⓑ **Marine Secol Trading** Little Billing, Northampton (890559). Ⓦ Boat sales, chandlery.

ⓑ **BWB Gayton Marina** On the Northampton Arm of the Grand Union Canal (Blisworth 858685). Ⓡ Ⓢ Ⓦ Ⓓ Pump-out, gas, hire fleet, long-term mooring, winter storage, some boat and engine repairs, toilets. *Open daily in summer.*

PUBS AND RESTAURANTS

The first four pubs are actually by the Grand Union Canal

🍺 **Royal Oak** High Street, Blisworth (858372). 17thC listed building with plenty of beams and an inglenook. Manns real ale and bar meals (*L&D*) are available. Garden.

🍺 **Greyhound** Towcester Road, Milton Malsor (Blisworth 858449). A fine village pub in 17thC cottages, once occupied by workers from the brewery next door (now closed). There is an open fire in the bar, where Manns real ale and bar meals (*L only*) can be enjoyed. Garden.

🍺 **Compass** Green Street, Milton Malsor (Northampton 858365). Small 18thC village local dispensing Manns real ale. Snacks (*L&D, not Sun*) and garden.

🍺 **Chequers** North Street, Rothersthorpe (Northampton 830892). There is an open fire on chilly days in this village pub which serves Manns real ale and snacks (*L&D*).

The following is just a selection of the many pubs and eating places to be found in Northampton. Walk north from the bridge.

🍺🍴 **Plough** Bridge Street, Northampton (38401). A plush Victorian hotel offering Wilsons real ale in the comfortable lounge. Bar meals (*L only*), restaurant (*closed Fri–Sun*) and carvery (*D and Sun L*).

🍺 **Bull and Butcher** Bridge Street, Northampton (35904). Sturdy local pub dispensing Manns and Wilsons real ales, and bar snacks (*L, not Sun*). Accommodation.

🍺 **King William IV** Commercial Street, off Bridge Street, Northampton (21307). A truly exceptional range of real ales in this pub, owned by CAMRA Investments. Bar meals (*L only*).

🍺 **Saddlers Arms** Bridge Street, Northampton (32940). 18thC listed building with a wood-panelled bar, a cosy snug and a large lounge. Davenports real ale is there to be enjoyed, along with bar meals (*L only, not Sun*) and snacks. Accommodation.

🍺🍴 **W & R Shipman** The Drapery (northerly continuation of Bridge Street), Northampton (36739). Old and long-established wine bar just off the Market Square, with many unique and interesting features. Wines, spirits, and Sam Smith's real ale in half pints only. Snacks (*L only*). *Closed Sun.*

🍴🍷 **Royal Bengal** 39 Bridge Street, Northampton (38617/36100). A very good Indian restaurant doing all the things you would expect, and catering for vegetarians as well. *Open daily L&D.*

🍴 **Lawrence's Coffee House** 35 St Giles Street (turn right at the top of Bridge Street), Northampton (37939). Sandwiches, savoury snacks and freshly baked cakes and pies. *Open 8.00–17.30 (16.30 Sat), closed Sun.*

🍴🍷 **Vineyard** 7 Derngate (left at the top of Victoria Promenade), Northampton (33978). Authentic French cooking. *Open L&D, closed Sun.*

🍺 **Brittania** St Peter's Bridge, Bedford Road, Northampton (30437). An old riverside pub recently redecorated in rustic style. Manns real ale and draught cider are available, as are bar meals and snacks. Discos some evenings. Terrace. Ⓜ

🍺 **Old Cherry Tree** Cherry Tree Lane, Great Houghton (Northampton 61399). At the end of the lane to the side of the White Hart. 17thC pub, recently renovated. Charles Wells real ale, meals (*L only Mon–Fri*) and garden.

St Mary the Virgin, Whiston

Leaving Billing Aquadrome the river passes below Cogenhoe, built on a hill to the south, and meanders gently along, sometimes accompanied by pastureland, but more often by gravel pits and their attendant machinery. Thankfully the A45 trunk road keeps its distance. The town of Wellingborough lies back from the river, although warehouses and factories bring a brief reminder of the navigation's commercial past.

The Nene valley near Northampton

Cogenhoe
Northants. Shop. Very pretty around the church of St Peter, which is just a short walk from the mill and the lock. The south and north doorways survive from the 12thC; the monument of a cross-legged knight is 13thC.

Whiston
Northants. The church of St Mary the Virgin stands apart from this tiny village, accessible only on foot. It is the work of one man,

WELLINGBOROUGH

Anthony Catesby, and remains as built in the 16thC. An ironstone and ashlar banded tower, bristling with gargoyles, demons and angels is set strikingly on a hilltop. The interior is graceful, though it has no structural chancel. The timber roof is richly carved with bosses and shields, and there are monuments sculptured by Nollekens, one of which has a tearful cherub in attendance.

Earls Barton
Northants. PO, stores. Best approached from White Mills Lock (1½ miles), and even worth crossing the A45(T) to see the unforgettable sight of the mighty Saxon tower of All Saints. Highly decorated with pilaster strips, some of which fan out to form triangles, it has windows with wonderfully sturdy balusters and long-and-short work clambering up the angles. The tower, with its fine clock, is such a commanding and individual presence that it makes it difficult to look at anything else, although Norman additions include the south doorway and blank arcading in the chancel with dazzling zigzag decoration. To the north, encroaching upon the churchyard, is a Norman castle motte with a large ditch, built at the time of the Conquest, ie after the church. Fortunately, the motte was little used and thus the church survived.

Great Doddington
Northants. PO, stores. Built on rising ground above the river, with the A45(T) mercifully passing to the north. The lower part of the tower of St Nicholas' church is 12thC, with most of the rest of the building dating from the 14thC. Inside there are good wall

church of All Hallows, and now used as the church hall. The medieval church finds itself in a peaceful tree-shaded setting away from the traffic and is remarkable for the brilliant and bold stained glass of 1961 by Patrick Reyntiens to the design of John Piper. The symbols of the evangelists are brought vividly into focus by background colours of red, emerald, gold and sapphire. Note too the splendid Decorated east window, the 15thC screens, and stalls with misericords. Of more recent origin but certainly worth a visit is St Mary's, built by Sir Ninian Comper in 1908–30 in lofty Perpendicular style. Stalactite-like pendants decorate the elaborate fan-vaulted nave roof and the rood screen is very fine. At the end of the High Street is Broad Green, an attractive open space with mature trees.

Irchester Country Park
Wellingborough (76866). South of the river. Between the park and the river is the site of a Roman town, with a ditch and bank enclosing an

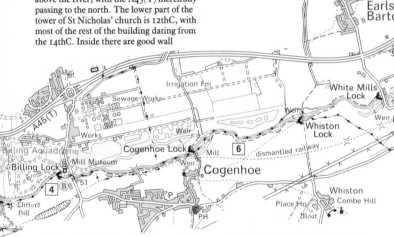

paintings of the Virgin and St John, with the head of Christ above, some 14thC stained glass and a Jacobean pulpit. The 17thC vicarage was formerly a manor house.

Wellingborough
Northants. EC Thur, MD Wed/Fri/Sat. All shops and services, BR station. A town established around shoemaking and engineering industries. It was here that Oliver Cromwell stayed at an inn, now the Hind Hotel, on his way to the Battle of Naseby in 1645. New development has made an impact on the town centre, although some good period buildings survive; notable amongst these is the Old Grammar School, dated 1617, standing north west of the

area of about 20 acres. Excavations have revealed the foundations of many buildings, and finds include a tombstone, some Castor ware, slate from the Collyweston quarries, painted wall plaster and coins from Claudius to Constantine. With the building of the railway in 1873, a cemetery containing 300 graves was uncovered to the north east. *Open daily.* Admission free.

BOATYARDS

Ⓑ **Cogenhoe Mill Caravan Site** Cogenhoe (Northampton 890579). The following facilities are available to those who moor here: Ⓡ Ⓢ Ⓦ (containers only). Gas, toilets, showers, provisions. Ⓜ

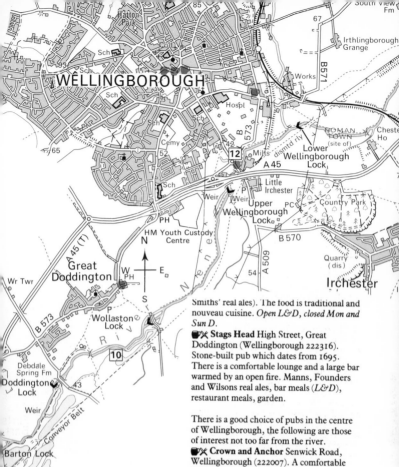

PUBS AND RESTAURANTS

🍺 **Red Lion** Little Houghton (Northampton 890247). There is a full range of traditional pub games, plus Manns, Wilsons and Founders real ales to enjoy here. Bar meals (L&D) and snacks. Patio.

🍺 **Royal Oak** Station Road, Cogenhoe (Northampton 890125). Village pub with plenty of brasses and two log fires. Manns real ale is served, and bar meals (L&D) are available. Disc jockey on *Sun evenings*. Garden.

🍺 **Boot** West Street, Earls Barton (Northampton 810640). Local pub serving Manns real ale, bar meals (L&D) and snacks. Garden.

🍺 **Stags Head** High Street, Earls Barton (Northampton 810520). 17thC listed building with a beamed ceiling. Manns real ale and bar snacks (L only). Garden.

✕🍺 **Dunkley's** South of the river at Earls Barton (Northampton 810546). A smart restaurant in a converted railway station, and using two handsome carriages as a coffee lounge and bar (Charles Wells and Sam

Smiths' real ales). The food is traditional and nouveau cuisine. *Open L&D, closed Mon and Sun D.*

🍺✕ **Stags Head** High Street, Great Doddington (Wellingborough 222316). Stone-built pub which dates from 1695. There is a comfortable lounge and a large bar warmed by an open fire. Manns, Founders and Wilsons real ales, bar meals (L&D), restaurant meals, garden.

There is a good choice of pubs in the centre of Wellingborough, the following are those of interest not too far from the river.

🍺✕ **Crown and Anchor** Senwick Road, Wellingborough (222007). A comfortable local pub warmed by open fires, serving Manns real ale and bar and restaurant meals (L&D). Garden. Ⓜ close by.

🍺 **Golden Lion** Sheep Street, Wellingborough (222333). Parts of this pub are over 400 years old; it is in fact two separate buildings. One of the bars is manorial in style, with a minstrels gallery and a large stone fireplace. The walls are decorated with suits of armour and associated weaponry. Manns real ale can be enjoyed here, and there are bar snacks (L&D) and a patio.

🍺 **Horseshoe** Sheep Street, Wellingborough (222015). Traditional pub with plenty of stained glass, wood panelling and bar billiards. Bass and Springfield real ales, bar meals (L only) and patio.

🍺✕ **Hind Hotel** Sheep Street, Wellingborough (222827). Built in 1645 on the site of an earlier inn, this establishment can apparently list amongst its patrons Oliver Cromwell, Winston Churchill and Charles de Gaulle. There is said to be a secret tunnel to Croyland Abbey. Recently refurbished, it offers bar food, restaurant meals (L&D) and accommodation.

🍺 **Jug and Bottle** 54 Midland Road, Wellingborough (71134). To the east of Sheep Street. A real ale off-licence, with a wide selection from which you may stock your boat. *Open 09.00–21.30 Mon–Sat; 12.00–14.00, 19.00–21.00 Sun.*

Continuing in a north easterly direction, the
Nene is still accompanied by the gravel
workings which have persisted since
Northampton. Indeed it is not until the
factories of Irthlingborough fade into the
distance that the Nene begins to fulfil its
early promise. Gentle green hills enclose the
flood plain, with pretty brown stone villages
dotted at regular intervals. Slender church
spires thrust out from amongst trees,
inviting the navigator to moor and take to
the footpaths. Virtually all the churches are
of interest and the village pub is never far
away.

NAVIGATIONAL NOTES
Ditchford Lock Radial gate and mitre gates.

Irthlingborough
Northants. EC Thur. PO, stores. A small
industrialised town lying to the west of the
impressive 14thC 10-arched bridge. The
church of St Peter, between the town and the
river, is a most striking sight, with its 14thC
lantern tower all but detached from the
church. The nave arcades and lancet
windows are of the 13thC, and there are
14thC windows with reticulated and flowing
tracery. Also notable are the alabaster
effigies, the stalls and the Perpendicular
font. There are guided tours to the top of the
tower, for a breathtaking view up and down
river.

Higham Ferrers
Northants. PO, stores. The substantial
remains of a 14thC market cross stands in
the triangular market place at the heart of
this fine stone-built town, still part of the
Duchy of Lancaster. Banks and ditches – all

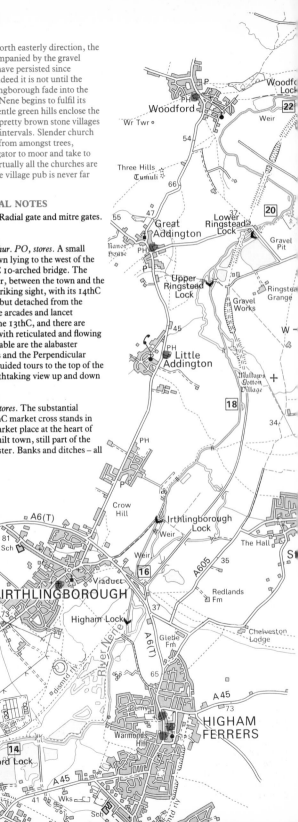

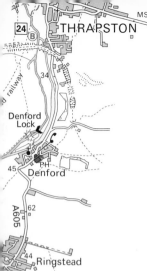

that now remains of a castle built by Peverel in the 11thC – can be seen to the north of the church. In 1266 this fortification was granted to Edmund Crouchback, Earl of Lancaster, by Henry III; the town's former importance is owed to this association with the House of Lancaster. Archbishop Chichele founded a college here in 1422, and the Bede House and School connected with it can be visited. Prominent among these ecclesiastical buildings is the church of the Blessed Virgin Mary. Its doorway, at the base of the 13thC tower, is splendidly carved and the bell openings lavishly shafted. Above is a dainty Decorated frieze, openwork flying buttresses and a tall, elegant crocketed spire. The 13th and 14thC interior has a number of carved screens, stalls with misericords from the time of the college and fascinating brasses, including one exquisite example of a priest, Laurence St Maur (died 1337) whose soul is held in a napkin by angels above his head. Work by Comper includes the rood loft and crucifix.

Founded in 1428, the Bede House, built of alternating bands of ironstone and grey stone, is to the south of the church. It housed 12 poor old men, and a female attendant, and replaced some kind of existing hospital. Archbishop Chichele's school was founded in 1422, replacing a similar establishment founded some 30 years earlier. It is to the north west of the church. There are some scant remains of the college in the pleasant gardens in College Street, to the north of the market place. H. E. Bates wrote of Higham Ferrers in his novel *The Sleepless Moon* – his heroine lived in a house adjacent to the churchyard, and was married in the church.

Stanwick
Northants. PO, stores. A small, unremarkable village around the church of St Laurence, which has an unusual octagonal tower culminating in a spire. Most of the building is 13thC, restored in 1856.

Little Addington
Northants. The short spire of the 13th/14thC church of St Mary overlooks this tiny village, which stands on high ground to the west of the river. Note the richly decorated doorway

and the 13thC tracery in the aisle windows. On the east bank of the river is the site of Mallows Cotton, a deserted medieval village.

Great Addington
Northants. One mile to the west of the river. A fine Jacobean manor house and a late 13thC church, mostly Decorated, are the attractions of this rural village. Note the 13thC font and the fine alabaster and brass monuments.

Ringstead
Northants. The mostly Decorated church of St Mary has a fine 13thC west tower and a superbly proportioned east window with elegant flowing tracery. 14thC font. The village itself is of little interest.

Woodford
Northants. Stores. The church of St Mary is nicely situated overlooking the river; its origins are Norman although it seems to have been much altered before the 14thC. Inside is an oaken monument to a knight and his lady.

Also of interest are: the Rectory built in 1820; the Round House, inscribed 'Waterloo Panorama 1815' (apparently Wellington frequented the area); and Woodford House, owned in the 19thC by Charles Arbuthnot, a friend of the Duke of Wellington. Woodford Rise is a stone-built house with Collyweston and pantiled roofs very much in the traditional Northamptonshire style; originally a 17thC cottage, it is much altered and enlarged. The village green is pleasant.

Denford
Northants. PO, stores. Those on the river will enjoy the delightfully situated church of Holy Trinity, a 13thC building right on the water's edge. It has a broach spire, and lively 14thC gargoyles decorate the south side. Note also the arcading in the chancel, and the 16th and 17thC Flemish stained glass, glowing yellow and orange in the Lady Chapel.

BOATYARDS

Ⓑ **Thrapston Mill Marina** Thrapston (2850). Ⓡ Ⓢ Ⓦ Ⓟ Ⓓ close by), Calor gas, long-term mooring, winter storage, slipway, provisions, toilets, showers, club room and bar Ⓜ *Open daily, Easter–end Dec.*

PUBS AND RESTAURANTS

🍺 **British Arms** Baker Street, Irthlingborough (Wellingborough 650911). An old local decorated with regimental prints and military uniforms. The oak-beamed bar has an open fire and serves Manns, Wilsons and Founders real ales. Bar snacks and grills (*L&D, not Sun L*). Garden.

🍺 **Green Dragon** College Street, Higham Ferrers (Rushden 312088). Hotel serving Manns real ale, bar meals (*L&D*) and food in the wine bar. There is a dovecot in the garden, thought to be some 300 years old.

🍺 **Queens Head** High Street, Higham Ferrers (Rushden 312739). Excellent Bass and Springfield real ales in this popular local. Snacks (*L&D*).

🍺✗ **Griffin** High Street, Higham Ferrers (Rushden 312612). Interesting pub dating from the 14thC, with some wood panelling and an inglenook. Manns real ale, traditional homemade bar meals (*L&D, not Sun L*) and restaurant meals (*Tue–Sat, D only*). Garden.

The Bell Little Addington (Wellingborough 651700). Adnams and Ind Coope real ales, steaks and seafood specialities (*L&D*). Garden.

Hare & Hounds Great Addington (Cranford 661). Stone-built village pub serving Manns beers. Garden.

Prince of Wales High Street, Woodford (Thrapston 4733). Friendly, down-to-earth village local dispensing Marstons real ale. Fish and chip shop next door.

White Horse Woodford (Thrapston 2646). Well-situated with a patio overlooking the valley. Ruddells, Adnams and guest real ales, bar snacks and restaurant meals (*L&D*). Occasional barbecues in summer.

Cock High Street, Denford (Thrapston 2565). Stone-built 16thC pub with exposed beams and a cosy fire in cold weather. Manns real ale, bar meals (*L&D*) and barbecues. Garden.

Oundle

Below Thrapston the river skirts a very large flooded gravel pit, enlivened with the colourful sails of many small craft. Twisting and turning through low hills, this is the river at its best, and as an added attraction the villages, always just above the old flood level, come closer.

Oundle Marina, and the intense boating activity associated with it, signal that the river is about to sweep around this very fine town. It is only a short walk to the town centre from Lower Barnwell Lock, and time should be found to explore the mellow stone buildings and handsome church. Further downstream there is access to Ashton – on a sunny summer afternoon its green is the perfect place for a snooze (after a visit to the pub).

Thrapston

Northants. EC Thur. PO, stores. The village lies to the east of the nine-arched medieval bridge, and was once the site of an important grain market. Pleasant enough, its 18thC cottages are of no particular interest. The church of St James is built mainly in the Decorated style: incorporated in it is a priest's doorway, surviving from an earlier 13thC building. To the north of the town is a very large flooded gravel pit, used for sailing.

Islip

Northants. PO, stores. Thrapston's small neighbour to the west of the river has a handsome Perpendicular church dedicated to St Nicholas. The chancel screen was donated by descendants of Mathias Nichol, Mayor of New York in 1671; the bold brasses on the chancel floor are recreations by Rev H. Macklin.

Titchmarsh

Northants. The poet, dramatist and critic, John Dryden (1631–1700), born across the river in Aldwincle, spent his childhood here. He lived at the manor (now gone) with his mother's relatives, the Pickerings. There is a bust of Dryden in the medieval interior of the church of St Mary the Virgin, whose magnificent Perpendicular tower has a lavish array of statue niches and pinnacles; friezes opulently distinguish each stage of its ascent. The churchyard boundary is defined by a ha-ha, an unusual feature. The Pickering Almshouses of 1756 can be seen to the south, by the green. A rectangular moat is the only remaining evidence of a fortified manor house which once stood to the south of the village.

Thorpe Waterville

Northants. A tiny settlement to the east of the 14thC bridge. A large barn is all that remains of the fortified manor house, built by the Bishop of Lichfield in the 14thC.

Aldwincle

Northants. Stores, no pub. The poet, dramatist and critic, John Dryden, was born in 1631 in the Old Rectory opposite All Saints church, a 13th–15thC building now seldom used. Inside there is a memorial tablet. The church of St Peter incorporates parts of a 12thC building, and has some early 14thC stained glass depicting St Christopher and St George, plus a commemorative window to Thomas Fuller (1608–61), historian and theologian, born in the rectory (now gone). The old school is now a pottery; the three-arched bridge dates from 1760.

Wadenhoe

Northants. PO, stores. A very handsome stone village where the church of St Michael is prominent on high ground beside the river. Mainly 13thC with a Norman tower, the chancel arch is supported on head corbels. 13thC font. There is a circular dovecote on the Pilton road.

Achurch

Northants. Tiny estate village to the south of Lilford Hall, a 17thC mansion, bought by Sir Thomas Powys in 1711 and much altered by him. His imposing monument can be seen in the church of St John Baptist, a mainly 19thC building incorporating some 13thC features. Lilford church, demolished in 1778, has been re-erected to the south west of the churchyard.

Lilford Wildlife Park (Clopton 648/655). *Open daily, Easter to Oct.* Admission charge.

Pilton

Northants. The late 13thC church of St Mary and All Saints and the Jacobean manor house form a picturesque group. Also of interest is the Old Watch House, with its lookout reminiscent of a chimney.

Barnwell Mill

Barnwell

Northants. PO, stores. It is thought that Barnwell Castle was built in 1266 by Berengar Le Moyne and ceded to Peterborough Abbey in 1276. If this is correct, then it is the earliest example in Britain of the Harlech-type fortification, ie square in plan with four mighty corner towers. Sir Edward Montagu bought the castle at the time of the Dissolution, and built a house in the outer courtyard, which although much altered, can still be seen. Both castle and manor are now owned by the Duke and Duchess of Gloucester. St Andrew's is reached through yews and hollies; a 13thC church with a sturdy 14thC spire. On the north doorway leaves spring from a carved face, and faces also nestle in the wonderful Decorated stone reredos, which has extravagant ogee arches flourishing foliage. Willows weep and bridges crouch over the stream leading through the village to the chancel of All Saints, all that remains of the church demolished in 1825. Monuments to the Montagus are congregated here, including an obelisk on big human feet, dripping with mud; dedicated to three-year-old Henry, who drowned in a pond in 1625. Dressed as a Jacobean manikin, his effigy holds a scroll with a pathetic echo of his end in the words 'Lord, give me of ye Waters'. And the feet say 'Not of my feete only' and 'but also my hands and head'.

Stoke Doyle

Northants. A tiny village whose church bears an unusual and rare dedication to St Rumbald. Built 1722–25, it contains two superb sculptured angels near the east window, and many monuments: notable is that to Sir Edward Ward, 1714, by J. M. Rysbrack. The Old Rectory, which pre-dates the church, stands to the east.

Polebrook

Northants. The church of All Saints has early Norman origins. The chancel piscina is particularly notable, splendidly arched, with dog-tooth decoration. 14thC font. Polebrook Hall is a Jacobean building of 1626; much altered.

Oundle

Northants. EC Wed, MD Thur, PO, stores. A very charming, handsome, stone-built market town containing some of the best 17th–18thC buildings in the country; the Talbot Inn in New Street, built in 1626, being a prime example. Its frontage was constructed with materials from Fotheringhay Castle, and its oak staircase also came from that source. Grouped around the church are many of the buildings of Oundle Public School. Founded in 1556 by Sir William Laxton, a London grocer, it replaced an earlier minor grammar school. Dominating the town is the glorious Decorated tower and spire of St Peter's, rising to the giddy height of 210 feet. Graceful bell-openings meet a delicate frieze, above which battlements and turrets make a more solid impression. Then the crocketed spire makes its final ascent, accompanied by lucarnes. The 13thC Perpendicular porch is a sumptuous affair, and beyond its handsome door, with tracery panels, is the pulpit, repainted in 1965 in its original colours. The medieval screen and lectern are notable, and there are many fine monuments. Those who have arrived by boat will be interested to see the offices of the Oundle Division of the Anglian Water Authority in the former rectory, built in 1845 in North Street.

Barnwell Country Park Oundle (73435). To the south of the town. Landscaped sand and gravel workings, with an increasingly varied flora and fauna. Picnic sites and walks; information centre. *Open daily.* Admission free.

Ashton

Northants. A model village of stone and thatch built in 1900 by the Hon Charles Rothschild, second son of the first Lord Rothschild. Local labour and materials were used, and they were well ahead of their time, each cottage having electricity, a bathroom and a garden. The village is owned by Dr Miriam Rothschild, conservationist, leading authority on fleas and creator of the 'Farmer's Nightmare', a mixture of wild flower seeds which can be spread in the hedgerows and verges, to give ribbons of colour across the countryside. Of particular interest in the sporting calendar is the World Conker Championship, held on the green *on the morning of the second Sunday in October.* Clearly Ashton is not in the least intimidated by its handsome neighbour to the west of the Nene when it can stage events on this scale.

Ashton Mill Fish Museum Ashton Wold Estate, Oundle (72264). By the river. 19thC generating machinery, farm machinery, tools, bygones and fish. Teas. *Open weekend afternoons in summer, Sun only in winter.* Admission free.

BOATYARDS

Ⓑ **Oundle Marina** Oundle (72762). ⓇⓈ ⓌⒻⒹ Calor gas, long-term mooring, winter storage, slipway, crane and gantry, chandlery, books and maps, boat and engine sales and repairs, boatbuilding, outboard sales, toilets, showers, club house and bar. *First or second Sun in July* is their annual festival day, with special events, sky diving etc. *Closed Wed and Xmas week.* Ⓜ

PUBS AND RESTAURANTS

🛈✕ **Bridge Hotel** Bridge Street, Thrapston (2128). Comfortable hotel serving Whitbread Wethered real ale. Bar food and steak house meals (*L&D*). Garden, squash court, accommodation.

🛈✕ **Courthouse Hotel** Huntingdon Road, Thrapston (3618). Drink in the bar which used to be a police station, or have a meal in the restaurant which used to be a courtroom. Food (*L&D*), patio.

🛈✕ **Woolpack** Kettering Road, Islip (Thrapston 2578). Smart pub dating from the 12thC, and taking its name from the ancient Thrapston wool market. A choice of five real ales, bar food (*L&D*) and restaurant meals (*L&D, not Sun D & Mon*). Garden.

🛈 **Fox** Oundle Road, Thorpe Waterville (Clopton 274). Smart main road pub offering Charles Wells real ale and bar meals (*L&D*). Log fire, garden. Live music every *Fri evening.*

🛈 **Kings Head** Church Street, Wadenhoe (Clopton 222). 18thC village pub which has close associations with the river. In the rough-walled bar there is an inglenook fireplace. Marstons real ale is available. Large garden and Ⓜ

🛈 **Montagu Arms** Barnwell (Oundle 73726). A choice of three real ales is available in this 15thC village pub, which has plenty of exposed beams and an open fire. Bar meals (*L&D*) and garden with crazy golf and swings.

🛈 **Shuckburgh Arms** Stoke Doyle (Oundle 72339). Ivy-covered stone-built pub dispensing real ale. Garden.

🛈✕ **Barnwell Mill** Barnwell Road, Oundle (72621). The original mill on this site was built in AD875: this building dates from 1606 and was in use as a mill until the 1930s. Now a smart conversion retaining many original features, it offers Greene King real ale, bar food (*L&D*) and restaurant meals (*D & Sun L*). Garden. Ⓜ

🛈 **Ship** West Street, Oundle (73918). 17thC building containing a pub with an appropriately nautical theme. There is a beamy bar with an open fire, where you can enjoy draught cider and a good choice of real ales. Bar meals (*L&D*) and patio.

🛈✕ **Talbot Inn** New Street, Oundle (73621). 17thC coaching inn. Bar meals (*L only*), restaurant with children's menu. John Smith's beer, garden.

✕🍷 **Tyrells** 6–8 New Street, Oundle (72347). Bistro-style restaurant serving only fresh vegetables, meat, fish and game, in imaginative dishes. Vegetarian menu. Essential to reserve at weekends. *Closed L Mon and Sun D.*

🛈 **Riverside** Oundle (72231). By North Bridge. Stone-built John Smith's pub. Bar meals (*L&D*), garden with swings.

🛈 **Chequered Skipper** Ashton (Oundle 3494). Thatched pub next to the village green dispensing Adnams, James Paine and Ushers real ales. Bar meals (*L&D, not Mon, or Thur D*) and garden. It is named after a rare species of butterfly.

Meandering in wide sweeps between the hills, the river passes a succession of beautiful and historic villages, and those on the water will miss much if they just pass them by.

At Fotheringhay the light and airy church looks very fine from the river, but it is well worth mooring below the castle mound and walking up the slight hill to see it more closely.

Parkland accompanies the Nene past Elton; at Yarwell there is a very tidy and attractive caravan and camping site around the mill.

The busy A1 dual carriageway crosses the Nene at Wansford, but somehow its presence is less of an intrusion than would seem possible. Unaffected, the river continues its extravagant course towards Peterborough, and still the picturesque villages and mills regularly appear. Even the Nene's approach to the city is through a country park, with the Nene Valley steam railway crossing, and sailing boats on the lake nearby.

NAVIGATIONAL NOTES

Wansford Lock The downstream approach can be made difficult by a side weir when there is a heavy flow on the river.

Cotterstock

Northants. A tiny cluster of buildings around Cotterstock Hall, a Jacobean house with unusual rounded gables. Altered in 1658 by John Norton who added a two-storey porch with a balcony and some fine stone fireplaces. John Dryden stayed here during the summers of 1698 and 1699, writing *Fables Ancient and Modern*. In poor health, he was nursed by Mrs Elmes Steward, daughter of his first cousin, who gave him 'venison and marrow pudding'. Visits to

Cotterstock Hall are possible by written appointment only. There is a 19thC mill right on the river, with the miller's house close by, and the church of St Andrew with its Decorated chancel, stands overlooking the Nene. Light and airy, it is lit by glorious windows rich with flowing tracery. It was founded in 1338 by John Giffard, Canon of

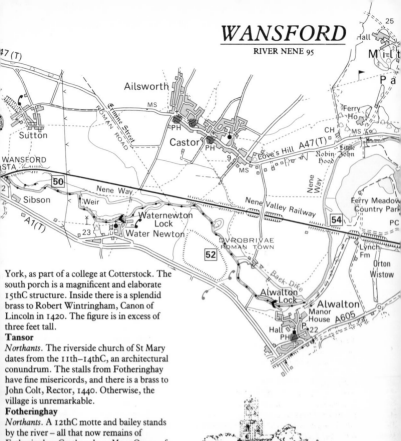

York, as part of a college at Cotterstock. The south porch is a magnificent and elaborate 15thC structure. Inside there is a splendid brass to Robert Wintringham, Canon of Lincoln in 1420. The figure is in excess of three feet tall.

Tansor

Northants. The riverside church of St Mary dates from the 11th–14thC, an architectural conundrum. The stalls from Fotheringhay have fine misericords, and there is a brass to John Colt, Rector, 1440. Otherwise, the village is unremarkable.

Fotheringhay

Northants. A 12thC motte and bailey stands by the river – all that now remains of Fotheringhay Castle, where Mary Queen of Scots was held from 1586 until she was beheaded on 8 February 1587, at the age of 45. After spending 19 years of her short life imprisoned, her hair had turned completely grey. The castle is thought to have been built c1100 by Simon de St Liz, first Earl of Huntingdon and Northampton, and rebuilt in the late 14thC by Edmund Langley, son of Edward III. By the early 18thC most of the structure had disappeared and today the mound has a melancholy air. Thistles, said to have been planted by Mary, flower each year.

In its heyday the castle must have been a formidable sight, towering over the river and the collegiate church of St Mary and All Saints. The church was originally conceived by Edmund Langley and finally founded in 1411 by his son, Edward of York, who was killed at Agincourt four years later. Its great choir was demolished in the 16thC, but the tower and nave, with graceful flying buttresses, are splendid. Windows stretching to form walls of glass create an interior brimful of light. The loveliest of lantern towers, topped with the gilt falcon, emblem of the House of York, stands high above. Inside there is a fine roof, a Perpendicular font and a pulpit with a glorious vaulted sounding board. There is also the tower's beautiful fan-vault and monuments to the second and third dukes of York, erected by Elizabeth I in 1573. The village street is lined with houses built of warm brown stone.

Warmington

Northants. PO, stores. The large church of St Mary is a fine example of a unified Early English design, built between 1180–1280 and largely unaltered. The short spire has projecting lucarnes (dormer-type windows) which give it a rather lumpy appearance. On the east wall of the chancel look out for the beautiful 13thC corbel, a sculpture representing the deadly sin of Wrath. Eaglethorpe House, to the north of the village, contains a doorway said to have been taken from Fotheringhay Castle.

Elton

Cambs. PO, stores. An attractive stone-built village of 17th and 18thC houses and cottages built around a green to the north of Elton Park. All Saints church is a predominantly Perpendicular affair externally, with a 14thC interior and a font of the same date. There are monuments to the Sapcotes and the Probys, original and present-day owners of Elton Hall. In the churchyard are two Anglo-Danish crosses, both with wheelheads and interlace work.

Elton Hall Elton (223/468). Built by Sir Richard Sapcote in 1475 and home of the Proby family (later Earls of Carysfort) since 1660. In ruins at the time of the Restoration, Sir Thomas Proby undertook a massive rebuilding programme (although he retained the 15thC Gatehouse Tower); subsequent 18th and 19thC work has created a building representing a remarkable procession of periods. Inside there is a fine library, and excellent furniture and paintings, including works by Constable and Frans Hals. Teas. *Open various afternoons during the summer, including Wed and B.Hols, May–Jul; and Suns in Aug.* Admission charge.

Nassington
Northants. PO, stores. There is easy access for boaters from a backwater which touches the village close to the pub. The church of All Saints has a Saxon nave, and a Perpendicular tower above Norman arches, topped by a recessed spire of 1640 with leaf crockets and lucarnes. Inside, above the chancel arch, is a wall painting of the Last Judgement, c1350.

Yarwell
Northants. PO, stores, holiday caravan site. A lovely stone-built village. There is an attractive 17thC house with mullioned windows, but the church is unremarkable, having been largely remodelled in the 18thC. The attractive old mill close to the lock is surrounded by a well-tended caravan park.

The Haycock Inn, Wansford

Wansford
Cambs. PO, stores. The original village, once bisected by the Great North Road, lies to the south of the wonderfully irregular bridge, whose arches are variously dated 1577, 1672–74 and 1795. To the north is the church of St Mary, its 13thC tower topped by a 14thC spire. Inside is a circular Norman font, c1120, decorated with carved figures beneath arches. The Haycock Inn is astonishingly spacious. Built of local freestone in 1632, its roof is said to support over an acre of Collyweston slate (see Pubs and Restaurants below). To the east is Stibbington Hall, which has a Jacobean

façade; dated 1625 it is a particularly fine example. The eccentric gatehouse can be admired from the road. The church of St John the Baptist dates from 1848–49, although it incorporates some original Norman features. 12thC font.

Nene Valley Railway Wansford Station to Orton Mere Station (Stamford 782854). A standard-gauge private steam railway 5 miles in length, using British, French, Danish, German, Swedish, Italian, Belgian and Norwegian locomotives. The route itself is not as interesting as the motive power. For train times ring Stamford 782921.

Water Newton
Cambs. The lock-keeper's cottage and late 18thC watermill are attractively grouped downstream of the church of St Remigius, which is itself right at the water's edge. On the west side of its Early English tower is a niche containing a small praying figure. East of the village is the site of Durobrivae, a Roman town defended by a wall, bank and ditch, and bisected by Ermine Street. There was an extensive pottery industry here.

Castor
Cambs. PO, stores. A stone and thatch riverside village built on the site of a vast 3rdC Roman villa whose reception and dining rooms stood behind the church. It is not surprising, therefore, that Roman brick appears in the north transept of St Kyneburgha's church. This is a unique dedication: she was a daughter of Penda, King of Mercia, who founded Peterborough Abbey. The central Norman tower of the church is mightily impressive, and unforgettable in its lavish ornamentation of arches. The parapet and spire were added in the 14thC. An ancient inscription over the priest's door in the chancel records the conservation of the church in 1124. Inside, the capitals of the tower pillars are rich with intertwining patterns and a variety of subjects, including scenes of vigorous action. In the chancel there is a Saxon carving of a saint, and in the north aisle, 14thC wall paintings depicting the story of St Catherine. The church was refashioned in the 13thC.

Alwalton
Cambs. PO, stores. A riverside village with some fine period dwellings and, surrounded by trees, a mainly 13thC church, with a Norman south doorway and a 12thC interior. North east of the church is the porch of Dryden's mansion Chesterton, built c1625. An unusual structure, it is currently being restored. Chesterton was demolished in 1807, but some of the windows were kept and incorporated into Lynch Farm, about ¾ of a mile to the north east.

Ferry Meadows Country Park
Peterborough (234443). 500 acres of river valley, grassland and lakes for boating, fishing, sailing, horse riding, walks, nature trails, picnics, camping and caravanning. Bird reserve, café, restaurant and visitor centre. There is also a garden centre.

BOATYARDS

ⓑ **Yarwell Mill** The following facilities are

available to those who moor here: W S
Toilets, showers. M

PUBS AND RESTAURANTS

🍺 **Falcon** Main Street, Fotheringhay
(Cotterstock 254). Excellent English cooking
(*L&D, not Mon*) and a choice of Elgood and
Greene King real ales in this fine 18thC pub.
Open fire, garden.

🍺 **Red Lion** Warmington (Elton 362)
Village pub serving John Smith's beer. Bar
meals (*L&D*), garden with children's
playthings.

🍺✕ **Black Horse** Overend, Elton (240).
The fact that this was once the local lock-up
and morgue should not discourage potential
visitors to this welcoming 17thC pub. There
is an inglenook fireplace, exposed beams,
and Sam Smith's real ale to enjoy. Meals in
the cellar (*L&D, not Sun or Mon D*), garden.

🍺✕ **Black Horse** Fotheringhay Road,
Nassington (Stamford 782324). Dating from
1674 it has a large stone fireplace, which
possibly came from Fotheringhay Castle,
and wood panelling from Rufford Abbey.
Greene King, Adnams and Tolly Cobbold
real ales, excellent bar and restaurant meals
(*L&D*). Garden.

🍺 **Queens Head** Station Road, Nassington
(Stamford 782289). Comfortable riverside
pub with an open fire dispensing Greene
King and Ruddles real ales. Bar meals
(*L&D, not Sun and Wed*). The garden
stretches down to the water's edge – barge
horses were once stabled here.
Accommodation. M

🍺✕ **Angel** Main Street, Yarwell (Stamford
782582). Greene King and Tolly Cobbold
real ales in a 300-year-old pub warmed by a
wood burner. Bar meals (*L&D*) and
evenings à la carte, children's room,

children's menu, garden.

🍺✕ **Cross Keys** 21 Elton Road, Wansford
(Stamford 782266). Village pub with a
nautical theme serving Manns real ale, bar
food (*L&D, not Sun*) and restaurant meals
(*D only, not Sun*). Garden and
accommodation.

🍺✕ **Paper Mills Inn** London Road,
Wansford (Stamford 782328). One of the
bars here is actually in a boat moored next to
the riverside garden. Bar snacks and
restaurant meals (*L&D*).

🍺✕ **Haycock Inn** London Road, Wansford
(Stamford 782223). A 17thC coaching inn by
the old 12-arched bridge, which can count
among its past patrons Mary Queen of Scots,
and Queen Victoria, who stayed in the
Gainsborough Room, before she was
crowned. There is a carpeted bar (no wellies)
with an inglenook fireplace, where you can
enjoy a choice of real ales. Riverside garden
and courtyard for warmer days. Excellent
bar food and restaurant meals (*L&D*).
Accommodation.

🍺✕ **Fitzwilliam Arms** Peterborough Road,
Castor (251). Large, picturesque, thatched
main-road pub, dispensing Ind Coope real
ale, bar and restaurant meals (*L&D*).
Garden and children's room.

🍺 **Royal Oak** 24 Peterborough Road, Castor
(217). A thatched pub with a cosy open fire,
dispensing Ind Coope real ale and bar food
(*L only, Mon–Fri*). Garden.

🍺 **Prince of Wales** Peterborough Road,
Castor (389). Manns real ale served in what
was once a shoe and boot shop. Bar snacks,
garden.

🍺 **Wheatsheaf** Oundle Road, Alwalton
(Peterborough 231056). Friendly unspoilt
pub with an open fire. Ind Coope real ale,
bar meals (*L only*), very fine garden.

Locking through at Yarwell

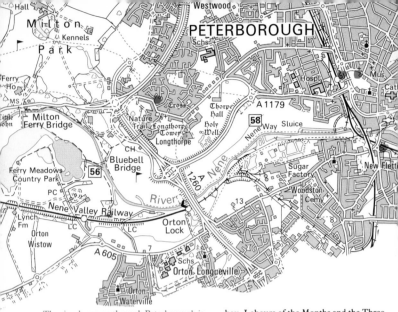

The river's course through Peterborough is, on the whole, attractive, with The Embankment and Customs House below the bridge making a very pleasant scene and a good mooring. A short way below the town bridge and just beyond the new road bridge, King's Dyke branches off to the south east – this gives access to the Middle Level Navigations, and ultimately the River Ouse, through Stanground Sluice.

The main course of the River Nene, now in an artificial cut between grassy banks, makes directly for Dog-in-a-Doublet Lock, and the tidal section below (see page 104).

NAVIGATIONAL NOTES

Stanground Sluice (Peterborough 66413) 49ft 0in × 11ft 6in, max depth over cill 2ft 3in. There is sometimes a dangerous undertow – do not enter without permission. Notify the lock-keeper 24 hours in advance of a passage through.

The recommended route through to the River Ouse is via Whittlesey, Floods Ferry, March, Upwell and Outwell to Salters Lode. The distance is 28½ miles.

Dog-in-a-Doublet Lock See page 103 for details.

Longthorpe
Cambs. PO, stores. A charming village which has become annexed to Peterborough. St Botolph's was originally a Saxon church, built at Westwood but taken down and rebuilt at Longthorpe in 1263. A chapel of ease to the church of St John the Baptist in Peterborough until 1850, it contains a superb Bishop's chair, an excellent rood screen and some fine stained glass.

Longthorpe Tower A 14thC tower, which was added as a fortification to a 13thC manor house. Square, three storeys high, with walls 7 feet thick, it was here, in 1945, that the best complete surviving set of medieval wall paintings in the country was discovered under a layer of whitewash. Dating from about 1330 they depict Biblical scenes, including the Nativity, a monk teaching a

boy, Labours of the Months and the Three Living and the Three Dead, amongst many others, all liberally adorned with birds and flowers. *Open daily Wed–Sat, Tue & Sun afternoons. Closed Mon. Small charge.*

Thorpe Hall, Peterborough

Thorpe Hall A very solid cream-coloured stone house set in 70 acres of parkland, built 1653–56 by Peter Mills (who was twice master of the Tylers' and Bricklayers' Company) for Oliver St John, Lord Chief Justice to Oliver Cromwell. Its style has been referred to as 'Artisan Mannerism'. Inside the main rooms of what is considered to be one of the most important surviving Commonwealth houses, are richly decorated ceilings and fireplaces. Craft centre. For opening times ring Peterborough 265820.

Orton Longueville
Cambs. PO, stores. A picturesque village of charming period houses. Orton Hall, once the home of the Marquess of Huntley, was built around 1835, on the site of an earlier structure. It is approached along a tree-lined avenue some 700 yards long, and is now a girls' school. The church of the Holy Trinity dates from about 1275 and is mainly Decorated. Inside is an excellent 16thC wall painting of St Christopher, and some fine

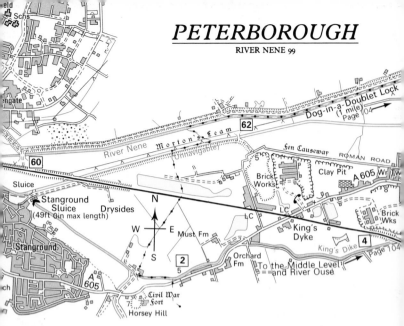

stone effigies, one, of a knight in armour,
dates from the 13thC. The tower contains a
sanctus bell, and some of the other bells are
of Plantagenet origins. Orton Waterville is
the westward continuation, and like its
partner village, is undergoing a rapid
expansion. Its own church, St Mary,
contains a sumptuous and magnificently
carved Elizabethan oak pulpit.

Peterborough

*Cambs. EC Thur, MD Wed, Fri, Sat. All
shops and services, BR station.* The only
cathedral city to be designated a new town.
Strategically placed in the East Midlands,
with good transport links. The Development
Corporation has succeeded in attracting
much new industry, and as a consequence
the population has expanded rapidly.
Businesslike and prosperous, it has at its
heart the wonderful cathedral, a very fine
17thC Guildhall, and the vast new
Queensgate shopping centre. The first river
crossing was built here in 1308 by Abbot
Godfrey of Croyland – it lasted one year. His
second attempt lasted 12. Subsequent
wooden structures were finally replaced by
an iron bridge in 1872; the present concrete
bridge dates from 1934. A new bridge to the
west was built in 1974 and a further crossing
to the east is currently underway. A major
attraction in Peterborough is the East of
England Ice Rink, opened in 1981. It was
here that Jayne Torvill and Christopher
Dean (British, European, World and
Olympic Champions) trained for their
National Skating Association Gold Star, and
put together most of their 'Barnum on Ice'
routine, with the aid of Michael Crawford.

Peterborough Cathedral (Peterborough

43342). A monastery was first founded on
this site in the 7thC and this eventually
became the Benedictine Abbey of St Peter
wherein the Anglo Saxon Chronicle, up
to 1155, was written. The present
Barnack-stone building dates from the early
12thC and is one of the most impressive
Romanesque buildings in England. Henry
VIII gave the abbey church cathedral status
in 1541 and his first wife, Catherine of
Aragon, lies buried in the north choir aisle.
A memorial marks the place where Mary
Queen of Scots was buried after her
execution at Fotheringhay; her remains were
later removed to Westminster Abbey. The
most striking feature of the exterior is the
13thC west front. The spacious nave has a
unique painted roof, dated c1220 which is
magnificently decorated with figures. There
is some early Norman work in the sanctuary,
the oldest part of the building. Look out for
the Hedda Stone, a piece of Anglo-Saxon
sculpture dated cAD800. More recently, the
cathedral was the setting for the BBC
serialisation of *The Barchester Chronicles*.

St John Baptist Moved from east of the

cathedral to be rebuilt in the Perpendicular
style on its present site in 1402–07. The old
church was often cut off by floods, and
Abbot Gyenge and Henry Beaufort, Bishop
of Lincoln, granted permission for the move.
Materials from the nave of the Chapel of St
Thomas of Canterbury were also
incorporated. Of particular interest are the
bells, which are said to have guided Matthew
Wildbore through the fenland mists to
safety. On his death he made a bequest to the
church to enable the bells to be rung each
year on the 15th March. Known as
Wildbore's Day, the custom continues.

Peterborough Museum and Art Gallery

Priestgate, Peterborough (43329).
Archaeology, history, natural history,
geology, paintings, ceramics and glass.
Victorian rooms, old shop and garage,
military gallery and 18thC watchmakers
shop. Of particular interest is the bone and
straw marquetry work made by French
prisoners of the Napoleonic Wars at Norman
Cross prison. Also visiting exhibitions of art
and general interest subjects. *Open daily
Tue–Sat and B.Hols. Closed Sun, Mon and
mornings in winter.*

PUBS AND RESTAURANTS

Moathouse Hotel Thorpe Wood, Peterborough (260000). Plush bar with a fine stone fireplace. Wilsons real ale, bar meals (*L only*), garden and putting green. Licensed restaurant, accommodation.

Fox & Hounds Thorpe Road, Longthorpe (Peterborough 264126). Friendly local pub offering Manns real ale, bar food (*L&D*) and carvery. Play area in garden.

There are, of course, plenty of (real ale) pubs to choose from in Peterborough: most are north of the bridge.

Great Northern Hotel Station Road, Peterborough (52331). Right by the railway station, as the name suggests. Elgoods and Bass real ales, meals (*L&D*) in the coffee shop. Garden.

Wortley Almshouses Westgate, Peterborough (48839). Sam Smith's real ale and bar meals (*L Mon–Fri*) in an excellent conversion of old stone-built almshouses. Near the bus depot.

Still Cumbergate, Peterborough (68531). Comfortable pub in the Queensgate Shopping Centre offering a wide range of real ales, fetched from the cellar in jugs. Bar meals (*L only*). *Closed Sun and B.Hols.*

Eastern Garden Tandoori Restaurant 39 Lincoln Road, Peterborough (48840). All the usual dishes, and a take-away service as well. (*L&D daily*).

Topo Gigio The Almshouses, Cumbergate, Peterborough (311133). Pasta, pizza, chicken and fish Italian-style. Cocktail bar. (*L&D, closed Sun L*).

Grain Barge Quayside, Embankment Road, Peterborough (311967). A converted 235-ton grain barge, now a Chinese restaurant (*L&D daily*).

Port Out, Starboard Home London Road, Peterborough (60048). South of the bridge. Those who could afford their steamship tickets to India 'Port Out and Starboard Home', and thus be on the cooler side of the vessel away from the sun, were considered 'Posh'. Whitbread real ale, draught cider, and bar food (*L only*).

Woolpack 29 North Street, Stanground (Peterborough 54417). Locals pub with an open fire and a riverside garden. Whitbread Castle Eden real ale.

Relaxing at Wadenhoe

THE MIDDLE LEVEL NAVIGATIONS
Including the Bedford Rivers

Occupying much of the lowland area between the River Nene and the River Ouse to the east of Peterborough, this complex drainage system dating from the mid-17thC, was mainly the work of the Dutch engineer Sir Cornelius Vermuyden. Prior to Vermuyden's scheme the course of the River Ouse was very different to that which exists today. In time of flood, water would be forced up the Aldreth River, a tributary, to pour into the River Cam at Stretham. This part of the Ouse is called the Old West River, since it once flowed in that direction, and not to the east as it does today. The waters of the Cam and Ouse were then combined in a new channel between Littleport and Stowbridge with the result that the original course of the river began to silt up. With the cutting of the Old Bedford River in 1631 and the New Bedford River (or Hundred Foot Drain) in 1651 it finally became extinct. Meandering through the artificial drainage channels is the old course of the River Nene; the new channel, or leam, from Peterborough to Wisbech via Guyhirn having been cut by Bishop Morton in 1470, and further improved in the late 1500s and early 1600s. Well Creek, a canalised river eight miles in length and restored to navigation in 1975, was once the main outfall of the old course of the Nene. It was used as a transport route by the Romans, and Barnack stone for the construction of Ely Cathedral was shipped along this route. With the restoration and extension of earlier drainage channels the system as it exists today came into being. Many are named after their original dimension – hence 'Sixteen Foot Drain', 'Twenty Foot Drain' and so on.

Although the prime function of the Middle Level channels is drainage, they have always been widely used for the movement of goods – indeed until early this century many of the farms and pumping stations in the area could only be supplied by water. In 1754 an Act of Parliament finally established this right of navigation, and the building of the 5¼ mile long Wisbech Canal in 1796 between Outwell and Wisbech provided a valuable final link between the Ouse and the Nene. Initially carrying a good deal of traffic, silt from the Nene continued to accumulate, particularly at Wisbech Sluice. Repair bills consumed the profits and gradually trade diminished until a new lock at Wisbech was built in 1834 and tolls on coal were reduced. As usual, it was railway competition which dealt the final blow, and abandonment came in 1926. Part of the Outwell basin still exists, but all else has disappeared.

Agricultural produce, bricks, peat and coal for the pumping stations continued to be carried well into this century, in strings of lighters towed by steam tugs. Sugar-beet traffic to Ely, a recent addition, was the last to stop, in 1959. The last water-borne oil consignment was delivered to a pumping station in 1971.

Navigation Authority

Middle Level Commissioners
Middle Level Offices
March
Cambridgeshire

March 53232/53021

No licence is required for pleasure craft. There are no tolls.

The recommended route between the Nene and Ouse is: through Stanground Sluice (49ft length) Peterborough, and then:King's Dyke; Whittlesey Dyke; Old River Nene; Well Creek and Salters Lode Lock to Denver Sluice. The distance is 28½ miles.

Navigation is prohibited on the Middle Level Main Drain between Three Holes Bridge and St Germans.

From June onwards, weed-ropes may be encountered – these can usually be pushed down with the boat-hook, allowing the boat to ride over.

Locks are open during daylight hours – please advise the lock-keepers in advance, by telephone, if you wish to pass through.

These waters are used extensively by anglers, who appear in great numbers at weekends. Afford them the usual courtesies. Particularly low bridges are marked on the map, but remember that water levels can vary (and rise) a great deal. Approach all bridges with caution.

(The Bedford Rivers are controlled by Anglian Water)

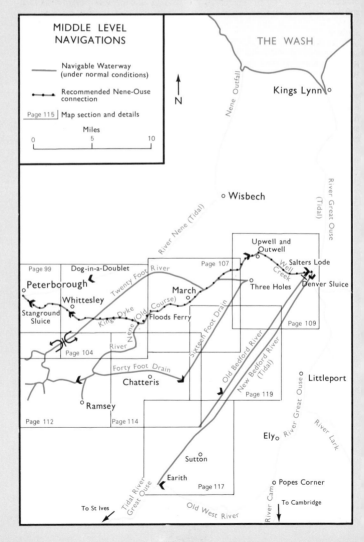

The Nene – Ouse link, passing through Whittlesey, March, Upwell, Outwell and Nordelph makes a truly fascinating journey, well worthy of exploration in its own right. Recent improvements have deepened the channel, and thousands of bulbs have been planted at Upwell and Outwell, accentuating its obvious similarity with the Netherlands. Off this route, the other waterways in this section consist mainly of straight channels across the drained peatland, now intensively farmed and often hidden from view by high grassy banks. Birdlife, a vast expanse of sky and a surprising number of pubs sustain the navigator on this peaceful, invigorating and away-from-it-all experience. A pleasant change from the crowded canals of the Midlands. But if the east wind blows – wrap up!

NAVIGATIONAL NOTES

Stanground Sluice (Peterborough 66413). 49ft 0in × 11ft 6in, max depth over cill 2ft 3in. Notify the lock-keeper 24 hours in advance of passage through. Sometimes there is a dangerous undertow – do not enter without permission. See page 99 for map.

King's Dyke Beware of shallows.

Whittlesey Briggate Take care at this notoriously sharp corner. Width between walls only 14ft 0in.

Ashline Lock (Peterborough 202975). Attended, 64ft 0in × 11ft 6in. Overspill weir at upstream end – do not enter without permission.

Bevill's Leam Navigable only as far as the pumping station.

Dog-in-a-Doublet Lock River Nene (Peterborough 202219). Attended, please telephone (Oundle 73701) 24 hours in advance if a passage through is required. Also see page 81. The river is tidal below this point – for information regarding a passage, ring the Port Manager, Wisbech 582125.

Whittlesey

Cambs. EC Thur. All shops and services, BR station. The waterway creeps through the town in a high-walled narrow channel, almost hidden. In the market place is the 17thC Butter Cross, the focal point of this little industrial town which once had so many pubs that names were dispensed with and letters were substituted – the Letter B in Church Street being the sole survivor of this regime. The rapid expansion of Peterborough has made Whittlesey virtually a suburb of its larger neighbour, with the brickworks bridging the gap between. St Mary's Church has a splendid crocketed spire atop an ashlar-faced 15thC tower. The rest of the building dates from the 13thC. The church of St Andrew is mainly Decorated, with a 16thC tower.

Whittlesey Museum Town Hall, Market Street, Whittlesey. Local history, archaeology and brick-making. Also Sir Harry Smith, hero of the battle of Aliwal, fought in India in 1846. *Open Fri and Sun afternoon, Sat morning.* Small charge.

A fine village sign

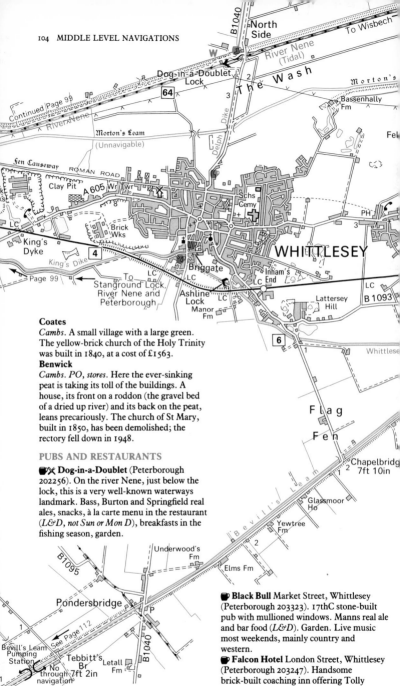

Coates
Cambs. A small village with a large green. The yellow-brick church of the Holy Trinity was built in 1840, at a cost of £1563.

Benwick
Cambs. PO, stores. Here the ever-sinking peat is taking its toll of the buildings. A house, its front on a roddon (the gravel bed of a dried up river) and its back on the peat, leans precariously. The church of St Mary, built in 1850, has been demolished; the rectory fell down in 1948.

PUBS AND RESTAURANTS

Dog-in-a-Doublet (Peterborough 202256). On the river Nene, just below the lock, this is a very well-known waterways landmark. Bass, Burton and Springfield real ales, snacks, à la carte menu in the restaurant (*L&D, not Sun or Mon D*), breakfasts in the fishing season, garden.

Morton's Fork Whittlesey (Peterborough 203393). Not far from Morton's Leam. Cold carvery and hot dishes (*L&D*), children's room, garden.

Boat Inn 2 Ramsey Road, Whittlesey (Peterborough 202488). Friendly local pub right by the water. Elgoods real ale, bar food (*D only*) and children's room. Garden, accommodation.

Black Bull Market Street, Whittlesey (Peterborough 203323). 17thC stone-built pub with mullioned windows. Manns real ale and bar food (*L&D*). Garden. Live music most weekends, mainly country and western.

Falcon Hotel London Street, Whittlesey (Peterborough 203247). Handsome brick-built coaching inn offering Tolly Cobbold real ale and bar food (*L&D*). Accommodation.

Letter B Church Street, Whittlesey (Peterborough 203358). The last remaining 'lettered' pub, dispensing Greene King, IPA and Burton real ales, plus excellent bar food (*L&D*).

Hero of Aliwal Church Street, Whittlesey (Peterborough 203736). Manns, Websters and Watneys real ales, and draught cider in a friendly pub by the river. Bar meals (*L&D*) and garden. The hero is Sir Harry Smith.

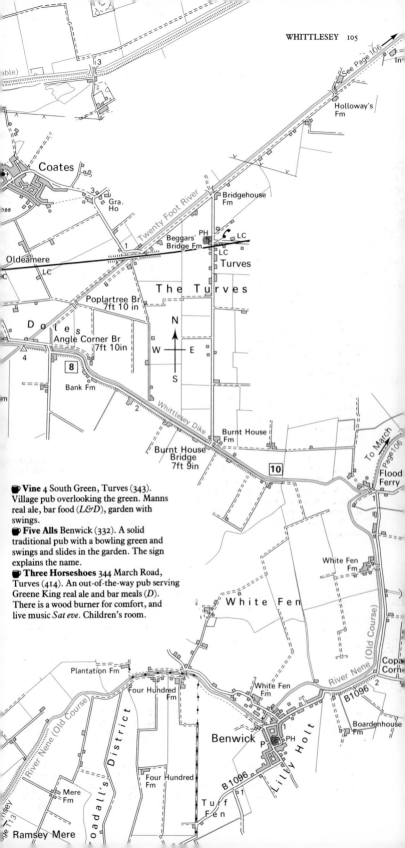

See Page 106

In

Holloway's Fm

Twenty Foot River

Coates

Gra. Ho

Bridgehouse Fm

PH

LC

Beggars' Bridge Fm

LC

Turves

Oldeamere

LC

C

The Turves

Poplartree Br 7ft 10 in

N

Doles

Angle Corner Br 7ft 10in

W — E

8

S

Bank Fm

Whittlesey Dike

Burnt House Fm

Burnt House Bridge 7ft 9in

10

To March

Flood Ferry

See Page 106

Vine 4 South Green, Turves (343).
Village pub overlooking the green. Manns
real ale, bar food (L&D), garden with
swings.

Five Alls Benwick (332). A solid
traditional pub with a bowling green and
swings and slides in the garden. The sign
explains the name.

Three Horseshoes 344 March Road,
Turves (414). An out-of-the-way pub serving
Greene King real ale and bar meals (D).
There is a wood burner for comfort, and
live music *Sat eve*. Children's room.

White Fen Fm

White Fen

River Nene (Old Course)

Copa Corn

Plantation Fm

Four Hundred Fm

White Fen Fm

B1096

River Nene (Old Course)

District

Oadall's

Benwick

P

PH

Boardenhouse Fm

Lily Holt

Mere Fm

Four Hundred Fm

B1096

Turf Fen

Ramsey Mere

March

Cambs. EC Tues, MD Wed/Sat. All shops and services, BR station. A small Tudor port which became a railway town in the mid-19thC with the building of the Ely to Peterborough line, and the later branches to Wisbech, St Ives and Spalding (now closed). In 1921 one quarter of the male population was employed by the railway company. The mechanised marshalling yard to the north, built in 1930, was once amongst the largest in the country. There are market places on both sides of the river (although one is now a parking area), with some pleasant Georgian houses in the High Street. The riverfront with its picturesque cottages is particularly charming. Note also the elaborate, Victorian-style, cast-iron George V memorial fountain. The church of St Wendreda in Church Street, at the southern extremity of the town, is justly famous for the glorious

wings, illuminated by the clerestory, to the tall tower arch and lovely flowing tracery of the west window. But do not be too impatient to go inside – the exterior is also finely decorated. The Fenland District Council has its offices in March, as do the Middle Level Commissioners; there is a small local museum (March 55300) *open Sat, and Wed morning.* As you pass under March Bridge glance upwards and you will see, inset in the structure, a long description of the subscribers to the bridge-widening scheme of last century. Why it was hidden

hosts of hovering angels in its double hammer-beam roof, with the Decorated and Perpendicular features of the church forming a beautiful vessel for them. From the 19thC chancel it is possible to gaze through three tiers of feathery outspread

away in this manner remains something of a mystery. There are good overnight moorings by the park, which has an indoor swimming pool.

BOATYARDS

Ⓑ **C T Fox** 10 Marina Drive, March (52770). Ⓦ Ⓓ Calor gas, long-term mooring, boatbuilding, boat and engine repairs, slipway, 17-ton hoist. Ⓜ

March waterside

PUBS AND RESTAURANTS

White Horse Riverside, March (53054). Norwich Brewery and Websters real ales in this pleasant, thatched, riverside pub and restaurant. Bar food and restaurant meals (*L&D, not Sun*). Garden with play area. M

Red Lion 15 High Street, March (54510). Elgoods real ale in this town-centre pub, which has discos on *Sat evenings*. Bar snacks and Market Day 'Special' (*Wed L*).

Ship Nene Parade, March (56999). Thatched, beamy riverside pub said to be the oldest in the town, offering Greene King real ale and bar meals (*L&D*).

Cock 106 High Street, March (52294). Traditional pub with exceptional hand-pumps, serving Elgoods real ale and bar food (*L&D*). Bar billiards, garden, accommodation.

The Acre March (57116). By the bridge. A lovely riverside pub with a garden. The inside is airy and comfortable, and the bar meals are excellent (*L only*). Greene King real ale and a friendly welcome. M

Nishan March (53388). Curry house around the corner from the George V memorial. *Open L&D daily.*

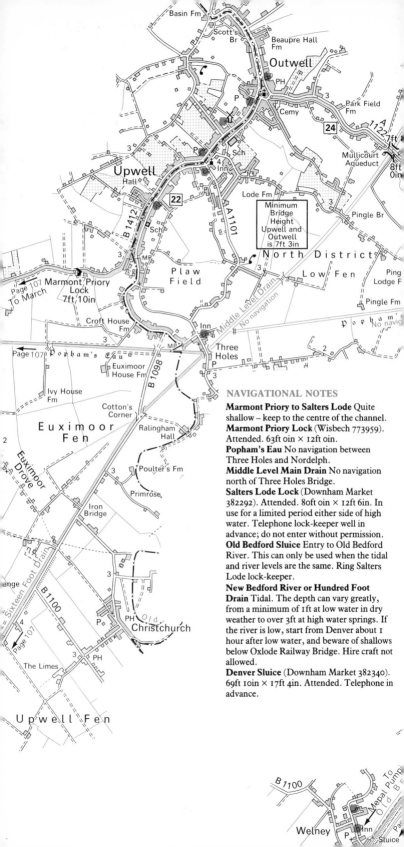

Map Labels

Basin Fm

Scott's Br

Beaupre Hall Fm

Outwell

PH

P

Cemy

3

24

Park Field Fm

A 1122

7ft

Mullicourt Aqueduct

8ft 0in

3

P

Sch

Upwell

4 Inn

Hall

22

B 1412

Sch

A1101

Lode Fm

Pingle Br

Minimum Bridge Height Upwell and Outwell is 7ft 3in

North District

Low Fen

Ping Lodge F

Pingle Fm

MP

Plaw Field

3

Middle Level Drain
No navigation

Popham's No navig

2

← Page 107
To March
Marmont Priory Lock 7ft 10in

Croft House Fm

3

Inn

Three Holes

Popham's Eau

MP

3

← Page 107

Euximoor House Fm

B 1098

Ivy House Fm

Cotton's Corner

Euximoor Fen

Ralingham Hall

Euximoor Drove

2

Poulter's Fm

Primrose,

3

Iron Bridge

Sixteen Foot Drain

ange Foot Drain

B 1100

3

PH

Old Christchurch

PH

P

4

← Page 107

3

PH

The Limes

Upwell Fen

B 1100

Wepal Pump To Old B

Welney

P

Inn

Sluice

NAVIGATIONAL NOTES

Marmont Priory to Salters Lode Quite shallow – keep to the centre of the channel.

Marmont Priory Lock (Wisbech 773959). Attended. 63ft 0in × 12ft 0in.

Popham's Eau No navigation between Three Holes and Nordelph.

Middle Level Main Drain No navigation north of Three Holes Bridge.

Salters Lode Lock (Downham Market 382292). Attended. 8ft 0in × 12ft 6in. In use for a limited period either side of high water. Telephone lock-keeper well in advance; do not enter without permission.

Old Bedford Sluice Entry to Old Bedford River. This can only be used when the tidal and river levels are the same. Ring Salters Lode lock-keeper.

New Bedford River or Hundred Foot Drain Tidal. The depth can vary greatly, from a minimum of 1ft at low water in dry weather to over 3ft at high water springs. If the river is low, start from Denver about 1 hour after low water, and beware of shallows below Oxlode Railway Bridge. Hire craft not allowed.

Denver Sluice (Downham Market 382340). 69ft 10in × 17ft 4in. Attended. Telephone in advance.

Upwell and Outwell

Cambs (west bank)/Norfolk (east bank). All shops and services (but no W*).* The Old River Nene, often regarded as part of Well Creek, passes through the centre of these two villages, where fine period houses face each other across the water and roads accompany its course on both banks. Over 1000 years ago the two villages were one settlement –

Wella – an important port and fishery. About AD970 the seaward end of the settlement became known as Out-Wella, the inland end Up-Wella. At that time rents in the area were paid in sticks of eels, bundles of 25, probably salted. It was not until 1130 that money was used.

St Peter's Upwell is a handsome building of Barnack stone and ragstone, mainly

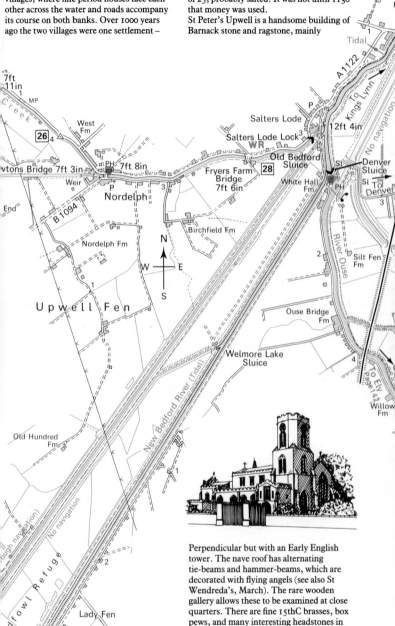

Perpendicular but with an Early English tower. The nave roof has alternating tie-beams and hammer-beams, which are decorated with flying angels (see also St Wendreda's, March). The rare wooden gallery allows these to be examined at close quarters. There are fine 15thC brasses, box pews, and many interesting headstones in the churchyard including one marked only with the letter 'C' – a communal grave for the victims of a cholera epidemic. The church is kept locked; see the notice for details of key. St Clement's Outwell is similarly built of Barnack stone and ragstone, with a battlemented 13thC tower. The tie-beam and hammer-beam roof is lavishly adorned with angels – in the north chancel chapel they carry shields; 14th and 15thC monuments, 16thC brass and an unusual Jacobean poor box. It overlooks the entrance basin of the Wisbech Canal, which joined Well Creek here but was formally abandoned in 1926; the Wisbech and Upwell Tramway opened in 1883 (and dismantled in 1968) contributed substantially to its demise. Well Creek was saved from infilling, and restored to navigation in 1975 by the Well Creek Trust. The Trust has also provided the public landing stages which are found along its course. On his voyage around the Fens in 1774 the third Earl of Orford commented to Lord Sandwich, First Lord of the Admiralty, on how ugly were the women of Upwell, Outwell and March, compared to those of Ramsey. A Dutch ancestry was, he said, to blame. He would surely not make such a comment today.

Welle Manor Hall Upwell (Wisbech 773333). Behind the church. Welle Manor was given by Royal Charter to the Benedictine monks of Ramsey in AD974. The hall dates from 1202, and is a rare example of a fortified medieval prebendary manor house. Curio museum, chapel with relic of the True Cross, work and equipment of the Victorian photographer Lafayette, mulled Norfolk punch (made here) and natural spring waters. Organised parties by appointment at any time. Guided tour (*1½ hours*) *on first Sun of each month at 15.00*. Charge.

Nordelph
Norfolk. PO, stores. An attractive village facing the river at its junction with Popham's Eau. It was from here, around 1880, that Mr Whybrow ran his packet boat to Wisbech, charging a fare of two pence from Outwell. Petrol can be obtained from the riverside garage.

Welney village and Nature Reserve See page 118.

PUBS AND RESTAURANTS

🍺 **Red Lion** Downham Road, Outwell (Wisbech 773368). Beamy riverside pub dispensing Elgoods real ale and snacks. Open fire and pub games.

🍺 **Five Bells** Small Lode, Upwell (Wisbech 772268). A fisherman's pub. Real ale, garden.

🍺 **Globe Inn** School Road, Upwell (Wisbech 772405). Riverside, by New Bridge. Elgoods beers, bar meals (*L&D*).

✕🍺 **Old Mill** Outwell (Wisbech 772614). A handsome converted tower mill with real ale in the bars, snacks, and meals in the restaurant (*D*). Accommodation.

🍺 **Chequers** Nordelph (286). A fine waterside pub serving Bass and Greene King real ales and bar food (*L&D*). All kinds of pub games, garden.

🍺 **Jenyns Arms** Denver Sluice. See page 143.

🍺 **Red Hart** Three Holes (Wisbech 773328). Near the junction of the Sixteen Foot Drain and Popham's Eau. Elgoods beers, bar snacks, garden, accommodation and children's room. *PO, stores* opposite.

The green at Ramsey

Upwell

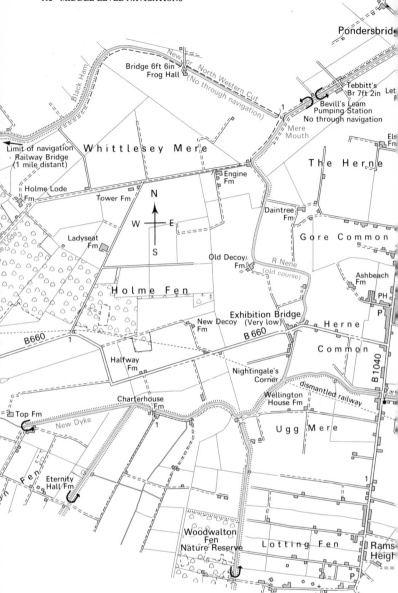

NAVIGATIONAL NOTES

Monk's Lode Can be extremely weedy.
Bevill's Leam No through navigation due to the presence of the pumping station.
Lodes End Lock Unmanned. A standard Grand Union-size windlass is needed.
High Lode Craft longer than 25ft will be unable to turn at Ramsey. There are pleasant moorings by the mill.
Exhibition Bridge The lowest on the Middle Level, its height varies from one side to the other.

Ramsey

Cambs. EC Thur. All shops and services. A market town which grew up around the remains of an abbey founded c969 by Ailwin. The abbey became one of the leading English monastic houses in the 12th and 13thC; at the time of the Dissolution the buildings were given to Cromwell, who built a house on the site of the Lady Chapel. This is now a school. The Elizabethans removed stones from the buildings, using them to build the towers of churches at Godmanchester, Holywell and Ramsey. All that now remains, apart from Cromwell's House, is the 16thC Gatehouse (NT). An ornate building containing an effigy of Ailwin, carved in Purbeck marble (*open daily in summer, closed Mon & Fri early and late season*). The nearby church of St Thomas à

Becket is a splendid building. Built originally as the abbey guest-house, or hospitium, in the late 12thC, the conversion to a church confers great interest on it. The Norman chancel is rib-vaulted and the nave arcades verge upon the 13thC in their details. The lectern has open-work tracery and a rotating top; the fine stained glass is by Morris & Co. The tower of 1672 incorporates 13thC fabric and this, together with the 13thC font, pinpoints the date of transformation from a guest-house. The area

Holme Fen Post In 1851, an iron post taken from the Great Exhibition, was set in Holme Fen, its top level with the peat, its base sunk in oak piles in the clay subsoil. It was replaced by a new post set to the level of the old in 1963. Today the top of the post stands 13ft above the ground, demonstrating that

around the abbey, the church, the green and the duck pond is very picturesque, and there is a fine mill building at the end of High Lode.

Ramsey Forty Foot
Cambs. Stores. A charming, small, fenland village on the Forty Foot Drain, with some attractive 18thC houses.
Woodwalton Fen Nature Reserve 514 acres of original fenland habitat, spared from reclamation. *Entry is strictly by permit only* from the NCC, Norminster House, Peterborough (40345).
Holme Fen Nature Reserve A preserved area of birch woodland. *Entry is strictly by permit only* from the NCC (see above).

the Fens, once 5ft *above* the silt level, are now 8ft below. It is without doubt one of the most low-lying places in Britain.

PUBS AND RESTAURANTS

- **Jolly Sailor** Great White, Ramsey (813388). Friendly local pub decorated with hundreds of horse brasses. Manns and Wilsons real ales.
- **The George** Ramsey Forty Foot (Ramsey 812775). Right by the bridge. Websters beers, garden with swings.
- **Railway** Ramsey (812597). Across the road from the end of High Lode. Manns beers, garden, bar meals (*L&D*) and accommodation.

Grange Fm

White Fen
Fm

White Fen

Keyworth
House Fm

N

W   E

S

River Nene (Old Course)

Copalder
Corner

White Fen
Fm

Four Hundred
Fm

B1093

Broadall's District

Benwick

PH

P

Lilly Holt

Four Hundred
Fm

B1096

Turf
Fen

The Limes

Benwick Mere

Beezling Fen

Swingbr

Bank Fm

Stanley
Hall Fm

To Ramsey Forty Foot

Puddock Br

Ash Drain

Dawson's
Fm

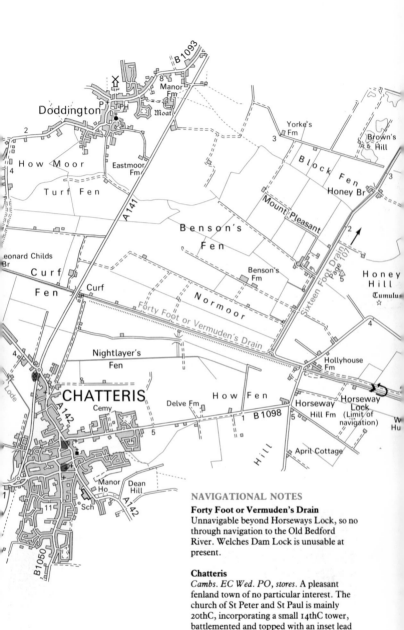

NAVIGATIONAL NOTES

Forty Foot or Vermuden's Drain
Unnavigable beyond Horseways Lock, so no through navigation to the Old Bedford River. Welches Dam Lock is unusable at present.

Chatteris
Cambs. EC Wed. PO, stores. A pleasant fenland town of no particular interest. The church of St Peter and St Paul is mainly 20thC, incorporating a small 14thC tower, battlemented and topped with an inset lead spire.

PUBS AND RESTAURANTS

- **Cock** 41 London Road, Chatteris (2026). Norwich Brewery and Websters real ales in a friendly pub where 'Petanque' is played. Bar meals (*L&D*), garden.
- **Ship** Pound Road, Chatteris (3695). Adnams, Marstons and Tetleys real ales, in a friendly old local pub. Garden. Bar snacks (*L&D, Mon–Fri*).

SUTTON

NAVIGATIONAL NOTES

Old Bedford River or Hundred Foot River
No navigation from Earith.

New Bedford River Tidal. Craft making the
passage to Denver should enter at high water
to get the benefit of the tide and an adequate
depth of water. Hire craft not allowed.

Earith
Cambs. PO, stores. A workmanlike village
with some attractive cottages situated at a
point vital in Fenland drainage. The Old
Bedford River leaves the Ouse here to run
twenty one very straight miles to Salters
Lode, having been built in 1631 by the
fourth Earl of Bedford. The New Bedford
River was built alongside 20 years later, and
empties at Denver Sluice, with the tract of
land between – the Ouse Washes – being
used to take up excess flood water when the
need arises. Where both leave the Ouse is the
Bulwark, a Civil War earthwork.

Sutton
Cambs. PO, stores. Well-situated on the
southern slope of a low ridge, with the
wonderful tower of St Andrew's visible for
miles. Inspired by Ely Cathedral, it has a
14thC two-stage octagonal lantern.
Gargoyles guard the clerestory and south
aisle with its beautiful vaulted porch, in
which prominent bosses figure, as do the
arms of the 14thC bishops of Ely, Barnet and
Arundel, who built this opulent church.
Blank arcading covers the aisle and chancel
walls, and niches flank the lavish east
window. Head corbels look out from the
lofty arcades and the tower vault is decorated
with bosses. At the Burystead, to the west of
the village, is a 14thC building, formerly a
chapel.

Mepal
Cambs. PO, stores. A small fenland
settlement around a much-restored Early
English church.

Mepal Outdoor Centre (Chatteris 2251).
Sailing, sailboarding and canoeing on the
flooded gravel pits, rockclimbing on a tower.
Picnic area. Trout-fishing available on the
other side of the road.

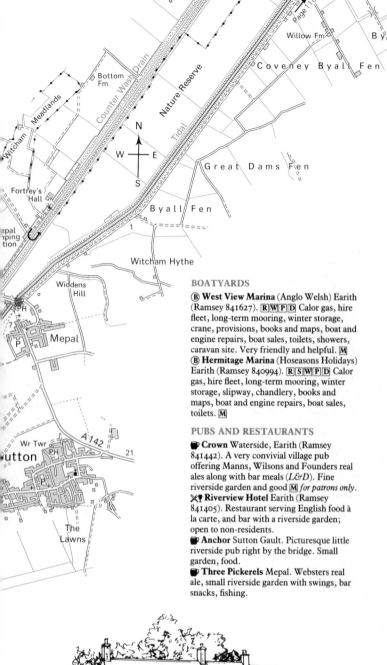

Page 116

Page 118

BOATYARDS

Ⓑ **West View Marina** (Anglo Welsh) Earith (Ramsey 841627). Ⓡ Ⓦ Ⓟ Ⓓ Calor gas, hire fleet, long-term mooring, winter storage, crane, provisions, books and maps, boat and engine repairs, boat sales, toilets, showers, caravan site. Very friendly and helpful. Ⓜ
Ⓑ **Hermitage Marina** (Hoseasons Holidays) Earith (Ramsey 840994). Ⓡ Ⓢ Ⓦ Ⓟ Ⓓ Calor gas, hire fleet, long-term mooring, winter storage, slipway, chandlery, books and maps, boat and engine repairs, boat sales, toilets. Ⓜ

PUBS AND RESTAURANTS

🍺 **Crown** Waterside, Earith (Ramsey 841442). A very convivial village pub offering Manns, Wilsons and Founders real ales along with bar meals (*L&D*). Fine riverside garden and good Ⓜ *for patrons only*.
✕🍷 **Riverview Hotel** Earith (Ramsey 841405). Restaurant serving English food à la carte, and bar with a riverside garden; open to non-residents.
🍺 **Anchor** Sutton Gault. Picturesque little riverside pub right by the bridge. Small garden, food.
🍺 **Three Pickerels** Mepal. Websters real ale, small riverside garden with swings, bar snacks, fishing.

The Anchor, Sutton Gault

NAVIGATIONAL NOTES

Vermuden's Drain Unnavigable west of
Welches Dam Lock.
Old Bedford River Limit of navigation is
Mepal Pumping Station, about 2½ miles
south of Welches Dam Lock.
New Bedford River Tidal. No hire craft.

Welney

Norfolk. Stores. A typical fenland settlement
to the west of Delph Bridge. There is some
bold stained glass to see in the church, but
little else of interest.

Welney Nature Reserve The Wildfowl
Trust, Pintail House, Hundred Foot Bank,
Welney, near Wisbech, Cambs (Ely 860711).
The entrance is 1¼ miles north east of the
Suspension Bridge on the New Bedford
River. The Ouse Washes, a strip of land 21
miles long and half a mile wide between the
Old and New Bedford Rivers, are designated
a 'Wetland of International Importance'.
The Wildfowl Trust's reserve covers 850
acres at the north eastern end. In times of
flood the whole area forms a vast reservoir
storing the excess water until such time as it
can drain away without inundating the
surrounding land. During the spring, when
the water levels fall, the Washes provide
outstanding summer pasture and an ideal
environment for many ground-nesting birds.
Birds that ceased breeding in Britain, such as

the ruff, black-tailed godwit and black tern,
have returned, due to careful management,
and in excess of 60 species are now nesting.
An important staging post on the migration
route from the north east to the south west,
winter counts have shown 30,000 wigeon,
4000 Bewick's swans and thousands of
pochard, tufted duck, teal and pintail.
Scaup, gadwall, smew and goldeneye have
also have seen. Lapwing, ringed and little
plover, gulls and raptors complete the
spectacle. During the summer there is a rich
flora, and butterflies abound. Excellent
viewing arrangements include 20 hides and
an observatory overlooking the Bewick's
swan lagoon, which is floodlit *in winter*.
Naturally if you wish to see the migratory
wildfowl, then winter is the time to come,
but a visit at any time will be amply
rewarding. Accommodation is available at
Pintail House (maximum six persons), also
self-catering lets available. No dogs. *Open
every day 10.00–17.00 (except Xmas Eve and
Xmas Day). Evening visits (swans under
floodlight 18.45–19.45) by advance booking
only.* Charge.

RSPB Reserve, Welches Dam Warden:
Cliff Carson, Limosa, Welches Dam,
Manea, March (78212). 1958 acres of the
Ouse Washes. Hides open and available for
use *at all times*. Visitor centre *open weekends
10.00–17.00*. Admission free.

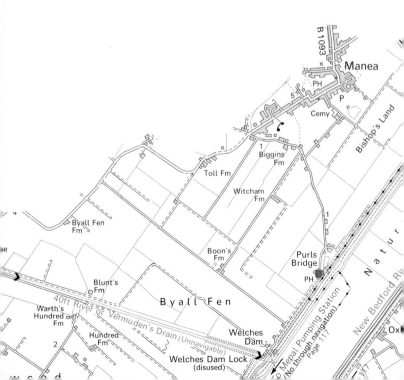

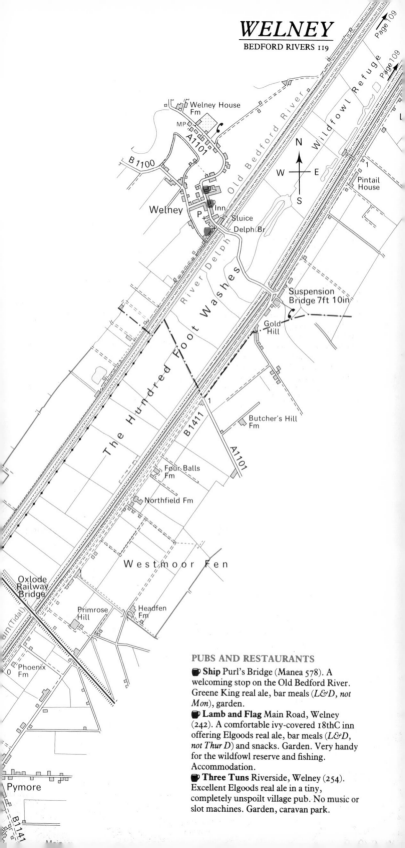

WELNEY
BEDFORD RIVERS 119

Page 109
Page 109

Welney House Fm

MP

A1101

B 1100

Welney

Inn

P

Sluice

Delph Br

Old Bedford River

Wildfowl Refuge

Pintail House

1

N
W · E
S

River Delph

The Hundred Foot Washes

Suspension Bridge 7ft 10in

Gold Hill

B1411

1

A1101

Butcher's Hill Fm

Four Balls Fm

Northfield Fm

Westmoor Fen

Oxlode Railway Bridge

an(Tidal)

Primrose Hill

Headfen Fm

Phoenix Fm

0

Pymore

B1141

PUBS AND RESTAURANTS

🍺 **Ship** Purl's Bridge (Manea 578). A welcoming stop on the Old Bedford River. Greene King real ale, bar meals (*L&D, not Mon*), garden.

🍺 **Lamb and Flag** Main Road, Welney (242). A comfortable ivy-covered 18thC inn offering Elgoods real ale, bar meals (*L&D, not Thur D*) and snacks. Garden. Very handy for the wildfowl reserve and fishing. Accommodation.

🍺 **Three Tuns** Riverside, Welney (254). Excellent Elgoods real ale in a tiny, completely unspoilt village pub. No music or slot machines. Garden, caravan park.

THE
RIVER GREAT OUSE

From its source 2 miles west of Silverstone in Northamptonshire the River Ouse crosses Buckinghamshire, and is navigable from Bedford to King's Lynn, where it meets the sea. The course taken by the lower reaches has been much altered since the Middle Ages, and never more so than in the 17thC when the major Fenland drainage schemes were underway (see the Middle Level Navigations, page 101).

During the 17thC, navigation was usually possible to Huntingdon – corn being the major export cargo. Schemes to make the river navigable to Bedford, a major corn market, were the next stage in the development of the Ouse, but it was not until 1689 that the plan was realised. The works, having progressed to Great Barford by 1640, ground to a halt and were not re-started for some 40 years.

Trade blossomed in the riverside towns, and this brought with it a new boatbuilding industry. Prior to the construction of Denver Sluice, large Humber keels could pass upstream unhindered, but when the Sluice was built in the mid-17thC the size of craft which could operate on the river was restricted, and as a result a special craft, the Fen lighter, evolved. Sturdily built of oak and elm, they were about 42 feet long with an 11 foot beam. Capable of carrying a 25-ton load, the lighters were operated in gangs of five, towed by a horse. Their construction changed little over the following three centuries, although in the 19thC a cabin for the crew was built into a 'house-lighter', with a smaller craft for ferrying horses bringing up the rear. The damage these towing horses caused to the river banks greatly upset riparian land-owners, until the Haling Act of 1789 brought them a measure of compensation, and controlled towing methods in order that as little damage as possible was caused.

With the building of the canals, and subsequently the Leicester, Bedford and Hitchin Railway, it was possible to bring coal to Bedford from the Midlands at much cheaper rates than had hitherto been possible. Toll receipts on the river fell dramatically, and in 1869 it was sold at auction for £1500. This was no bargain, and with little trade to generate income, it soon fell into disrepair. A brave attempt at revival in 1893 eventually failed, and it was not until the Great Ouse Catchment Board took over navigation rights in 1935 that major restoration began.

Navigation to Bedford was finally fully restored in the late 1970s, given impetus and financial assistance by the Great Ouse Restoration Society. Although a first class river for pleasure boating, the main priority of the Anglian Water Authority is now land drainage, and all other considerations are secondary to this.

Navigation Authority

Anglian Water
Cambridge Division
Great Ouse House
Clarendon Road
Cambridge CB2 2BL

Cambridge 61561

Registration and licensing

All craft must be registered and licensed. Apply to the Boat Registration Section at the above address.

Dimensions

Length 85ft 4in
Beam 10ft 4in
Headroom 7ft 6in (up to Bedford Lock)

Craft visiting the river should also note the following dimensions:
Denver Sluice (access from the sea) 69ft × 17ft
Stanground Sluice (access from the Nene via the Middle Level Navigations) 49ft × 11ft 6in.

Closures and stoppages

Contact the Recreation and Conservation Officer at the above address for details.

Locks

A Great Ouse Lock handle is required (1½ inch fitting) above St Ives Lock, obtainable from Anglian Water at the above address, from their area offices in Bedford, Ely and King's Lynn (Wisbech Road) and from many marinas.
Most of the locks have the usual mitre gates at one end, with a guillotine gate at the other.
Lock-keepers hours are as follows:
09.00–16.00 November, December, January, February
09.00–17.00 March, October
08.00–19.00 April, May, September
08.00–20.00 June, July, August
Closed for lunch 12.30–13.30

Manned locks are closed on Wednesdays from Nov–Mar inclusive.

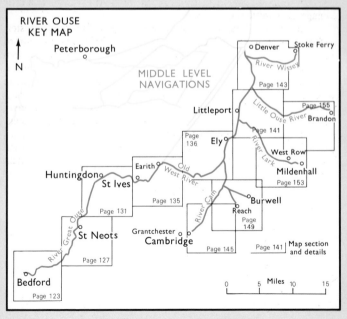

The River Ouse in Bedford flows through an area of park and gardens overlooked by the embankment – an outstanding riverscape and a recreational area much appreciated by the local people, who fish, walk, sit and row boats here. Excellent moorings can be found, clearly indicated. Skirting the large flooded gravel pits, the navigation channel

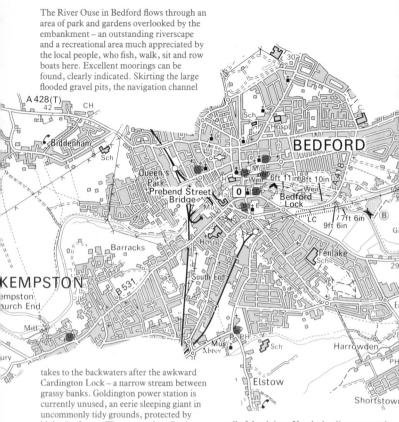

takes to the backwaters after the awkward Cardington Lock – a narrow stream between grassy banks. Goldington power station is currently unused, an eerie sleeping giant in uncommonly tidy grounds, protected by high wire fences. The approach to Castle Mill Lock is surprisingly rural, as the river narrows and loops and winds around an area afforested with deciduous trees – if you are lucky you will see kingfishers here. Over the fields to the south the vast airship hangars at Cardington stand out prominently on the horizon.

Below the new Willington Lock are the substantial remains of an old lock – there are moorings in the backwater here at the Old Mill. Now the tower of Great Barford church can be seen, and the long low bridge appears. There are good moorings below, but the passage through its narrow navigation arch is difficult (see below). By the lock you will see an unusual sculpture, made from parts of the earlier sluice, showing the date 1844.

NAVIGATIONAL NOTES

Limit of navigation This is the low railway bridge west of Town Bridge. Small craft can navigate as far as Kempston Mill.
Bedford Lock 97ft 5in × 10ft 10in. Awkward approach from above and below. Guillotine, manual. Many hire craft are not allowed through.
Disused railway bridge (eastern approach to Bedford) Use eastern arch.
Cardington Lock 93ft 6in × 10ft 4in. The upstream approach is made difficult by the

pull of the sluices. Use the landing stage and rope the boat in, even if the lock is open. Guillotine, manual.
Castle Mill Lock 96ft 10in × 13ft 2in. Fills and empties through penstocks (side paddles). Read the instructions. Manual, mitre gates.
Willington Lock 96ft 10in × 13ft 2in. Mitre gates, manual.
Great Barford Bridge The narrow navigation arches are at the north west (village) end, and the approach from upstream is made difficult by a current flowing north westerly across the face of the bridge, which can skew the boat at the last minute. Try and allow for this, and go *slowly*.
Great Barford Lock 96ft 10in × 13ft 2in. Mitre gates, manual.

Bedford
Beds. EC Thur, MD Wed, Sat. All shops and services, BR station. A modest but distinguished town. It was founded in the 10thC, and once had an important Norman castle (now just a mound), but its history since then has been largely uneventful. There is a lack of historically interesting buildings, much of Bedford being 19thC – indeed those who arrive by boat will have seen the best of the town before they disembark. Public gardens and the

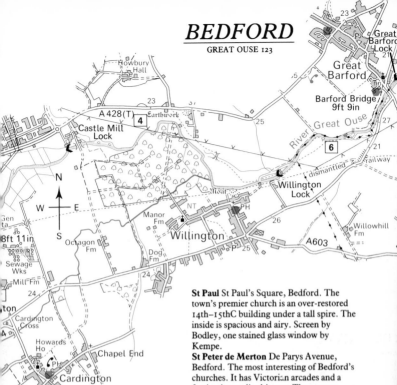

St Paul St Paul's Square, Bedford. The town's premier church is an over-restored 14th–15thC building under a tall spire. The inside is spacious and airy. Screen by Bodley, one stained glass window by Kempe.

St Peter de Merton De Parys Avenue, Bedford. The most interesting of Bedford's churches. It has Victorian arcades and a fascinating earlier history. The present chancel was the nave of a Saxon church and the tower once stood at the west end. Saxon long-and-short work (stonework alternating tall quoins with flat slabs) is visible in the tower; stones uncovered in 1890 suggested there had once been a great fire in the church, probably started by marauding Danes. The beautiful Norman south doorway was taken from the church of St Peter de Dunstable. A new chapter house was completed in 1982. The statue of John Bunyan by Sir J. E. Boehm, 1874, with three bronze panels on the pedestal illustrating *The Pilgrim's Progress* can be seen on St Peter's Green nearby.

St John's Rectory St John's Street, Bedford (south of the bridge). Adjacent to St John's church and once probably a hospital chapel, it was here that Pastor John Gifford, a reformed drunkard, converted John Bunyan. *One room is open to the public by appointment only; ring Bedford 42190.*

handsome Embankment make the riverscape outstanding among English towns, although a new high-rise building to the north of the five-arched bridge (1813) is rather intrusive to say the least. Bedford is forever associated with John Bunyan's two stays in its gaol. When in the teeth of adversity and with the help of faith, he wrote much of his great works: *Grace Abounding to the Chief of Sinners* and *The Pilgrim's Progress*. Bedford did not make amends to its 'tinker oft in quod' until it unveiled a statue to Bunyan in 1874, 200 years after the second imprisonment.

Bedford

Bunyan Museum Mill Street, Bedford
(58870). John Bunyan had his first meeting
place in Mill Street in 1672. The present
red-brick building, known as 'Bunyan
Meeting', dates from 1849, and is notable for
its bronze doors by Frederick Thrupp, 1876,
which depict scenes from *The Pilgrim's
Progress*. The museum contains relics and
possessions associated with the great man,
including his chair, walking stick and
tankard, and almost 200 translations of *The
Pilgrim's Progress*. *Open afternoons Tue–Sat,
Apr–Sep. Small charge.*
Bedford Museum Castle Lane, Bedford
(53323). Local history, natural history and
coins. *Open daily Tue–Sat and Sun
afternoons.*
Cecil Higgins Art Gallery Castle Close,
Bedford (211222). Fine collection of English
watercolours and drawings, English and
Continental porcelain and glass, costumes,
lace and furniture. *Open afternoons, closed
Mon. Small charge.*
Tourist Information Centre St Paul's
Square, Bedford (215226).
Elstow
Beds. This is the village generally associated
with Bunyan, though his birth place, now
marked by a stone, was in Harrowden Wood
to the east. The church of St Mary and St
Helen is the remnant of a Benedictine
nunnery founded c1075, and along with part
of the cloister is all that can now be seen.
Some Norman work survives amongst Sir
T. G. Jackson's extensive 1881 restoration.
Stained glass windows depict scenes from
The Pilgrim's Progress and *The Holy War*; the
font is that in which Bunyan was christened.
Some excellent brasses, especially that to
Margery Argentine, 1427. In his youth
Bunyan would ring the bell here, although
he was later to forgo this 'vain' practice.
Opposite the church is a fine row of timbered
Tudor cottages.
Moot Hall Museum Elstow (Bedford
66889). A 16thC building of timber with
red-brick infill, once used as a market house
and shops. The main hall upstairs has an
impressive tie-beam roof, and now houses a
museum of 17thC English life and traditions
associated with Bunyan. *Open daily
Tue–Sat, B. Hols and Sun afternoons. Small
charge.*
Cardington
Beds. A charming village around an
attractive green. The church of St Mary
contains many superb monuments,
including 12th–13thC coffin lids, tomb
chests with interesting brasses and excellent
busts. Also a memorial to those killed in the
R101 airship disaster in 1930. The black
basalt Wedgewood font is one of only three
in existence and was given to the church in
1783. The great airship hangars, clearly
visible from the river, lie to the south west at
Shortstown, the estate village built by Shorts
for their workers. They are now used by
Airship Industries whose Skyship 600 gained
approval to carry passengers in 1984, the
first airship so licensed since the
Hindenberg, which crashed disastrously in
America in May 1937. New materials and
the use of non-inflammable Helium gas
make this new generation of airships
extremely safe. You may be fortunate
enough to see Skyship fly over.
Willington
Beds. A riverside village with the pub at one
end and the church at the other. This Late
Perpendicular building was probably built
by Sir John Gostwick, Master of the Horse
to Cardinal Wolsey. He died in 1545, and his
tomb chest stands between the chancel and
the north chapel. There is an excellent later
memorial to Sir William Gostwick, 1615. Of
Sir John's manor house only a couple of
outbuildings remain – the dovecot, opposite
the church, is a long building with curious
stepped gables. Maintained by the NT, the
key is kept in a nearby cottage.
Great Barford
Beds. PO, stores. Parts of the irregular
17-arch bridge date from the 15thC – to the
north is the tall spiked tower of All Saints
church, an unremarkable building although
the tower screen and brasses are worth a
look. Some of the minor buildings in the
High Street are quite pleasant but the village
is at its best by the river, where the pub,
church and an endearing thatched cottage
are grouped attractively around the grassy
mooring.

BOATYARDS

Ⓑ **Harry Kitchener Marine** Priory Marina,
Barkers Lane, Bedford (51931). Ⓡ Ⓦ Ⓟ Ⓓ
Calor gas, long-term mooring, winter
storage, slipway, crane, chandlery, books
and maps, boat and engine sales and repairs,
toilets. Ⓜ

PUBS AND RESTAURANTS

The following are but a few of the many
pubs in Bedford. If you want to drink the
local beer, look out for Charles Wells; the
brewery was founded here in 1876. Not all
their pubs sell real ale, though.
🍺 **King William IV** 56 High Street,
Kempston (Bedford 854533). Charles Wells
real ales, bar meals (*L&D*) and snacks.
Garden.
🍺✕ **Embankment Hotel** Embankment,
Bedford (61332). Charrington and Paines
real ales in an attractive mock-Tudor
building. Snacks, restaurant meals (*L&D*).
🍺✕ **Kings Arms** 24 St Mary's Street,
Bedford (54494). South of Town Bridge.
Old beamy pub with small bars and open
fire. Greene King real ales, bar and
restaurant meals (*L&D*) and snacks.
🍺 **Clarence** St John's Street, Bedford
(52781). South of Town Bridge. Spacious
pub with an open fire in the lounge,
dispensing Ind Coope and Benskins real ales,
snacks (*L&D*). Garden.
🍺✕ **Swan Hotel** By the bridge (Bedford
46565). Built for the Duke of Bedford in
1794 and containing the staircase from
Houghton House. It was here, in chambers
set aside for the County Assizes, that John
Bunyan's second wife, Elizabeth, pleaded
for her husband's release from gaol.

Charringtons real ale, bar snacks and restaurant (*L&D*).

Castle Newnham Street, Bedford (53295). A short walk north east of Town Bridge. Charles Wells real ale is served in this pub which has a cosy lounge and an enormous clock in the bar. Snacks (*L&D*), garden.

Fleur de Lis 12 Mill Street, Bedford (211004). A short walk north of Town Bridge. Friendly town centre pub offering Charles Wells real ale and snacks (*L&D*). Children's room, garden.

Engine and Tender 93 Midland Road, Bedford (52665). North of Prebend Street Bridge, near the railway station. Flowers real ale in comfortable railway theme pub. Snacks (*L only*), patio.

Anchor Goldington Green (Bedford 53606). Pub with suitably nautical decor. Greene King real ale, snacks (*L&D*), garden.

Red Lion High Street, Elstow (Bedford 59687). Large wood-panelled pub very convenient for the Moot Hall Museum. A choice of real ales, bar meals (*L&D*), carvery restaurant, snacks and garden.

Kings Arms At the crossroads, Cardington (533). Whitbread Wethered and Flowers real ales served in the comfortable lounge. Bar meals (*L&D*) and snacks, garden.

Crown 17 Station Road, Willington (Cardington 308). Friendly village local. Greene King real ale, bar snacks (*L only*), garden.

Anchor At Barford Bridge (Bedford 870364). Comfortable, spacious and friendly pub serving Charles Wells real ale and excellent home cooked bar food (*L&D*). More elaborate meals in the restaurant.

Golden Cross Great Barford, on the main A428 (Bedford 870791). A pub of great character offering a good choice of real ales. Bar meals (*L&D*), garden, summer barbecues.

Below Cardington Lock

A section where the countryside, while not in any way remarkable, is none the less very pleasant. The main A1 trunk road generally keeps its distance, although it does cross the river below Roxton. The lock here was rebuilt in 1972 and is easy to work. Coping stones from the old sluice, engraved with the date 1846, have been incorporated into the new structure. Electricity pylons and flooded gravel pits mark the approach to the unused Barford Power Station, which is soon passed and soon forgotten. Surprisingly its massive bulk intrudes little. Eaton Socon is reached – look out for the Castle Hills below the lock – and then St Neots. There are excellent moorings above the bridge on the western side at Eaton Ford, by a meadow intertwined with backwaters which are crossed by little wooden footbridges. One mooring area is indicated right by St Neots bridge. Further excellent moorings alongside meadowland are provided at Island Common. St Neots Lock is in fact at Little Paxton; nestling between factories, its deep guillotine gate takes no less than *500 turns* to raise and lower. Watch out for the nasty main road crossing here. More gravel workings are passed as the main railway rushes in from the east. Above Wray House, woodland with tall trees comes down to the water's edge – a pleasant change.

NAVIGATIONAL NOTES

Roxton Lock 85ft 4in × 13ft 2in. Mitre gates, manual.
Eaton Socon Lock 103ft 3in × 10ft 7in. Guillotine gate, manual.
St Neots Lock 107ft 11in × 10ft 10in. Guillotine gate, manual, busy road crossing.

Roxton

Beds. ½ mile west of Tempsford Bridge, this quiet settlement has a church dating in part from the 14thC, and a more interesting and unusual chapel. Thatched, it has a verandah of tree trunks.

Little Barford

Beds. A village whose most famous son was Nicholas Rowe, Poet Laureate, born here in 1674. The church of St Denis stands quite close to the river, and still retains some Norman work. The Decorated south chapel is of interest. The power station, radiating pylons which fill the sky all around, is ½ a mile downstream.

Eaton Socon

Cambs. PO, stores. A town once split by the Great North Road but now thankfully by-passed. St Mary's church has a fine tall Perpendicular tower, a Norman font and brasses dating from 1450. When fire gutted the building in 1930, it was immediately restored and rebuilt. South of the church is a 19thC lock-up. On the river bank are Castle Hills, earthworks dating from the 12thC.

Eaton Socon

St Neots

Cambs. EC Tue. All shops and services, take aways, BR station. The Benedictine priory, founded c975, around which the town grew up has completely disappeared. There are some period buildings in the market place which sadly is now used as a car park, and surrounded with heavy traffic. The town's glory is the church of St Mary the Virgin. The tower of this sumptuous Perpendicular building has its ascent punctuated by friezes and decorated buttresses ending in pinnacles, with the whole thing culminating in marvellous corner pinnacles and an elaborate parapet. Inside, the roof is carved with a profusion of animals, birds and angels. The west screen of the Lady Chapel has a beautiful tangle of vine leaves and grapes, and in the chancel is the Rowley monument, with its fine ornate grille erected in 1893 by F. A. Walters. Paines Brewery is sited in the Market Place – established in 1831 as part of a malting and milling company, the brewing operation became a separate entity in 1982.

Little Paxton

Cambs. PO, stores. A village lying to the west of an expanse of flooded gravel workings. The church of St James contains some Norman work: in the churchyard is a plain memorial to John Buonarotti Papworth, architect to the King of Wurtemburg.

BOATYARDS

ⓑ **Kelpie Marine** Roxton (Bedford 870249). By Tempsford Bridge. Ⓡ Ⓦ Calor gas, long-term mooring, winter storage, slipway, 10-ton crane, boat and engine sales and repairs, toilets. Hebridean Cruisers (Huntingdon 217785) operate their hire fleet from here. Ⓜ

ⓑ **River Mill Boats** (Hoseasons Holidays) School Lane, Eaton Socon, St Neots (Huntingdon 73431). Ⓡ Ⓢ Ⓦ Ⓓ Pump-out, Calor gas, hire fleet, long-term mooring, winter storage, books and maps, boat and engine sales and repairs, boatbuilding, toilets. Pub, restaurant, tea room, beauty salon and garden centre. *Closed Mons in winter.* Ⓜ

ⓑ **St Neots Marina** St Neots (Huntingdon 72411). By the bridge. Ⓦ Ⓟ Calor gas, long-term mooring, chandlery, books and maps, boat and engine repairs, boat sales.

ⓑ **Crosshall Marine** Crosshall Road, St Neots (Huntingdon 72763). Ⓦ Ⓓ Calor gas, long-term mooring, slipway, gantry, chandlery, boatbuilding and repairs, toilets, showers. Ⓜ

PUBS AND RESTAURANTS

🍺 **Royal Oak** High Street, Roxton (Bedford 870361). Popular village pub serving Charles Wells beers, bar meals (*L only*) and snacks. Garden, pool room and children's videos.

🍺✗ **Anchor** Riverside, Tempsford (Biggleswade 40233). An excellent choice of real ales in this comfortable pub with a large garden containing an adventure playground. Flagstone floors and a warm stove, puppet shows on *summer Sun evenings*. Carvery restaurant and bar meals (*L&D*), snacks. Children welcome in the playroom.

🍺 **Wheatsheaf** 42 Church Street, Tempsford (Biggleswade 40226). Charles Wells real ale, meals and snacks (*L&D*) in a friendly village pub, thankfully by-passed by the A1. Large garden.

🍺✗ **White Horse** Great North Road, Eaton Socon (Huntingdon 74453). Rambling coaching inn of great charm. Excellent choice of real ales, snacks (*L&D*) and garden. A la carte restaurant.

🍺 **Waggon and Horses** Great North Road, Eaton Socon (Huntingdon 213373). Small, cosy pub with an open fire. James Paines real ale and snacks (*L only*).

🍺 **Wheatsheaf** Great North Road, Eaton Socon (Huntingdon 74120). Popular pub with a large garden, facing the village green. Snacks (*L&D*) and Charles Wells real ale.

🍺 **Bell** Great North Road, Eaton Socon (Huntingdon 212274). Popular pub with an open fire, serving Charles Wells real ale and snacks (*L only*). Garden.

🍺✗ **Bridge House** Market Square, St Neots (Huntingdon 72044). By the bridge. A comfortable and beamy Beefeater Steak House, offering bar food and restaurant meals (*L&D*). Children welcome in the restaurant *before 19.30.* Ⓜ

🍺 **Globe** Huntingdon Street, St Neots (Huntingdon 72590). Comfortable low-beamed pub serving Charles Wells real ale, draught cider and bar meals (*L only*). Garden.

🍺 **Kings Head** South Street, St Neots (Huntingdon 74094)). James Paines real ale in the brewery tap. Bar meals (*L only*). Live music and occasional theatre.

🍺 **Anchor** Little Paxton (Huntingdon 73199). Red-brick pub with tall chimneys at the back of a very fine riverside garden which has children's playthings. M

🍺 **Cannon** New Street, St Neots (Huntingdon 73503). Modernised Victorian local, selling Charles Wells real ale, excellent snacks (*L&D*). Children's room.

🍺 **Woolpack** 35 Church Street, St Neots (Huntingdon 212030). Charles Wells real ale, bar meals (*L&D*) and snacks. Morning coffee.

✖🍺 **Riverside Restaurant** St Neots (Huntingdon 219136). James Paines real ale, restaurant, café, toilets, pitch and putt, crazy golf, picnic area, boating lake. *Open 10.00–17.00 daily.*

HUNTINGDON
GREAT OUSE

Accompanied by the main London to Peterborough railway line the river continues northwards, passing a vast expanse of flooded gravel pits. Gradually the spire of the church at Offord D'Arcy becomes visible. The river here is wide, and quite exposed in the open countryside. On the east side, upstream of the villages, are the remains of old ridge and furrow field patterns, cut by the railway embankment. Offord Lock is approached through a maze of backwaters – below the lock is Buckden Marina, useful for supplies, and if a mooring is available a good base from which to explore the villages close by. Its entrance is on a sharp bend. Brampton Lock is reached after two more miles of wide open river – its setting is wholly rural and the mitre gates with their heavy wooden balance beams lend a touch of charm after the functional steel of the locks above. Unfortunately the upstream landing is poor – nothing to tie up to and some nasty barbed wire. The mill here is now a restaurant – note the old water wheel still turning. Good moorings can be found below the lock.

At Godmanchester there are fine moorings in the mill stream east of the lock, with good access to the village: around the next corner is Huntingdon, lying north of the river and hardly intruding, although excellent moorings are provided. Old warehouses by the bridge have been converted into dwellings. There now follows a particularly fine stretch of river, its course more narrow and intricate as it passes Houghton and the Hemingford villages. There are rowing boats for hire at Houghton Mill, and good moorings will be found above Hemingford Grey church. Just around the corner is St Ives – you can moor at the meadow above the town; at the Waits – a quiet backwater where you will have to reverse out (good for pub, launderette and fish and chips); or at the Town Quay below the bridge – better access to the town centre, and a water point.

NAVIGATIONAL NOTES

Offord Lock 100ft 0in × 11ft 2in. Guillotine, manual.

Brampton Lock 104ft 0in × 11ft 2in. Guillotine, manual. Look out for the very strong cross-current below this lock.

Godmanchester Lock 100ft 0in × 13ft 1in. Guillotine, manual.

Houghton Lock 90ft 2in × 11ft 11in Guillotine, manual.

Hemingford Lock Electrically operated guillotine. Keep to the north west of the little island below the lock.

St Ives Bridge Use the arch immediately north of the chapel.

St Ives Lock (63262). 102ft 8in × 10ft 11in. Manned. Considered to be the most tricky on the river when the sluice is running strongly. The downstream approach can be made difficult by swirling, unpredictable cross-currents – there is also a slight dog-leg in the lock, which itself is quite narrow. Go slowly, under power (and expect to bump), or rope the boat in from the landing stage. Approached from upstream, the pull from the sluice can prove irresistible – so pull in to the west bank and rope the boat in, except in the calmest conditions. *Closed Wed in winter.*

Great Paxton
Cambs. Holy Trinity's unprepossessing exterior of grey stone and cobbles gives little clue to its Saxon interior, built to a cruciform plan on a truly grand scale. It is an example probably without parallel in the country, and dates from around 1000. The south door has some interesting 13thC ironwork.

Offord Cluny/Offord D'Arcy
Cambs. PO, stores. Untidy main road villages which were once lace making centres – Cluny being so called because the abbey of that name in Burgundy owned the manor during the 11th–15thC. All Saints church (Cluny) is a Perpendicular building, built of cobbles, with some 13thC work. St Peter's (D'Arcy) dates from the same period and is also cobble built. There are some interesting brasses and monuments.

Buckden
Cambs. PO, stores. 1½ miles west of the river at Offord Cluny, this was once part of the estate of the Bishops of Lincoln, where they

built a magnificent palace in the 13thC. Today the outer and inner gatehouses and red-brick Great Tower, built by Bishops Rotherham and Russell during the 15thC, are all that remain. They stand in striking juxtaposition with the tall 15thC steeple of St Mary's, whose battlemented and pinnacled south porch is rich in medieval carving, including an animal frieze outside and a star-vault with bosses inside. Angels carved in wood and stone decorate the chancel roof. 16thC Flemish panels of the Passion may be seen on the readers' desks. The Jacobean pulpit is handsome, and monuments include an ornate 19thC Gothic triptych. In the churchyard, two uncles of Lady Jane Grey, the nine-day queen, are buried. This spacious village has some handsome brick and timber-framed buildings; note the almshouses, 1840, which bear the inscription 'Industry rewarded, Age protected'. Well-worth the walk from the river.

Brampton

Cambs. PO, stores. Brampton was much frequented by Samuel Pepys (1633–1703), keeper of the famous diary which, incidentally, was written in cipher and not deciphered until 1825. Pepys was a naval administrator at the Admiralty, a post he obtained through his uncle who was a cousin of Lord Sandwich. His uncle's house, Pepys House, is to the north east of the church. Although the diarist often expressed the wish to retire to such a pretty place, he in fact lived out his closing years in Clapham, London. The last of his family to live in Brampton was his sister, Mrs Paulina Jackson, whose monument can be seen in St Mary's church. If you visit the church, have a look at the superb misericords (ledges under hinged choir stall seats), which depict a knight and lady with a shield, a woman gleaning, a sheep shearer and a man and a woman haymaking.

The Chinese Bridge, Godmanchester

Godmanchester

Cambs. PO, stores, fish and chips. Of the Roman fort, built at the point where Ermine Street and the Via Devana crossed, there are now no visible remains, although the site of a Roman bath house was discovered in Pinfold Lane.

The picturesque heart of this market town is by the Queen Elizabeth grammar school of 1559 and the Victorian Town Hall; among many fine half-timbered buildings the most outstanding is the proud Tudor House,

dated 1600–03. The delightful Chinese Bridge, an exact reconstruction of the original 1827 structure, gives access to islands in the river and the moorings. St Mary the Virgin has a tower – built as late as 1623 in the Perpendicular style – onto a brown cobblestone church of the 13th–15thC. Of note is the remarkable mass dial in the form of a rose window on one of the buttresses of the 13thC chancel. See also the delightful animal carvings on the 15thC misericords, and the rood screen and reredos by Bodley. Details of a murderer's trial and subsequent execution are recorded on the gravestone of his victim, a 21-year old virgin, as a warning. A causeway once linked Godmanchester to Huntingdon. North of the river at Godmanchester lies Port Holme Meadow, the largest single hay meadow in England (365 acres). Still farmed as a hay meadow, it has an enormous range of plant species which have survived through traditional land management.

Island Hall Godmanchester. A fine 18thC riverside mansion with lovely period rooms and a galleried staircase. *Open afternoons Sun, Tue, Thur and B.Hols, Jun–Sep.* Admission charge.

Huntingdon

Cambs. EC Wed. All shops and services, take aways, BR station. A Saxon burgh where William the Conqueror had a castle built on an earlier Saxon mound. During the 10thC a monastery, which became Augustinian in 1113, was founded where the cemetery now is. Huntingdon's most famous son, Oliver Cromwell, was born in a house in the High Street in 1599 and the school he attended, also used by Samuel Pepys and once part of the Hospital of St John, now houses the Cromwell Museum (Huntingdon 52861). There is a good collection of memorabilia, including the Lord Protector's death mask. *Closed Mon and mornings, except Sat in winter.* During the Civil War the town became the headquarters for Cromwell and Charles I in turn. Two churches are to be seen; All Saints, a Perpendicular building by the market place is notable for its pretty organ chamber, and St Mary in the High Street, which dates from the 13thC, has an ornate Perpendicular tower and doorway. Huntingdon and Godmanchester were linked by a 17thC causeway across Port Holme, with a 13thC bridge over the river.

Hinchingbrooke House To the west of the town (Huntingdon 51121). The family home of the Cromwells which was purchased by the Montagus, later to become the home of Sir Edward Montagu (Lord Sandwich), Samuel Pepys' employer. The building is an early 13thC nunnery converted in the mid-16thC into a Tudor mansion and described by Horace Walpole as 'old, spacious, irregular, yet not vast or forlorn'. It is now a school, and is *open to the public on Sun afternoons and B.Hols, Apr–Aug.* Admission charge.

Houghton

Cambs. PO, stores. The handsome brick and timber watermill at Houghton was

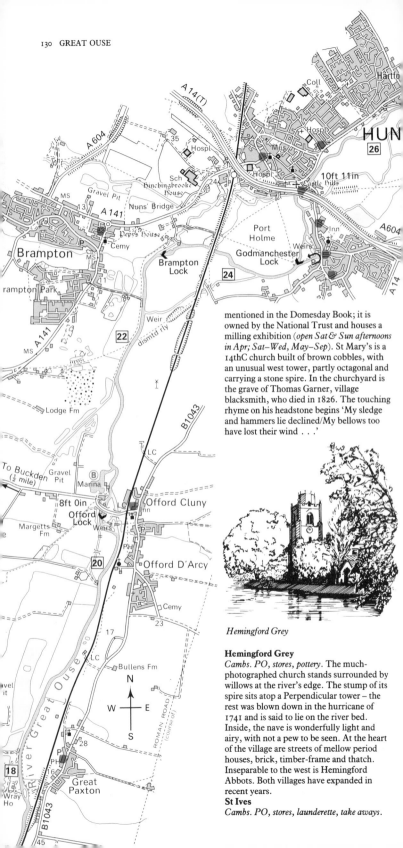

mentioned in the Domesday Book; it is owned by the National Trust and houses a milling exhibition (*open Sat & Sun afternoons in Apr; Sat–Wed, May–Sep*). St Mary's is a 14thC church built of brown cobbles, with an unusual west tower, partly octagonal and carrying a stone spire. In the churchyard is the grave of Thomas Garner, village blacksmith, who died in 1826. The touching rhyme on his headstone begins 'My sledge and hammers lie declined/My bellows too have lost their wind . . .'

Hemingford Grey

Hemingford Grey

Cambs. PO, stores, pottery. The much-photographed church stands surrounded by willows at the river's edge. The stump of its spire sits atop a Perpendicular tower – the rest was blown down in the hurricane of 1741 and is said to lie on the river bed. Inside, the nave is wonderfully light and airy, with not a pew to be seen. At the heart of the village are streets of mellow period houses, brick, timber-frame and thatch. Inseparable to the west is Hemingford Abbots. Both villages have expanded in recent years.

St Ives

Cambs. PO, stores, launderette, take aways.

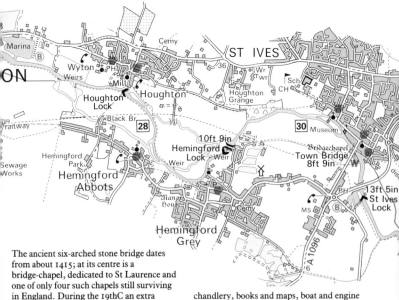

The ancient six-arched stone bridge dates
from about 1415; at its centre is a
bridge-chapel, dedicated to St Laurence and
one of only four such chapels still surviving
in England. During the 19thC an extra
storey was added when it was used as a
dwelling, but this was subsequently
removed. A sign on the door informs where a
key may be obtained if you wish to look
inside. Founded as a cell of the Benedictine
Priory of Ramsey, St Ives' prosperity in the
Middle Ages stemmed from its Easter Fair,
as important as the fairs of Winchester,
Northampton and Boston. An assortment of
period buildings make the part of the town
by the river particularly attractive, where the
tall slender spire of All Saints is dominant.
The church was built c1450 although some
parts date from the 13thC. In the market
square there is a bronze statue of Oliver
Cromwell, who farmed nearby.
Norris Museum The Broadway, St Ives
(65101). Local history, paintings,
archaeology and bygones. *Closed Mon, Sun
morning (and Sat morning in winter).*

BOATYARDS

Ⓑ **Buckden Marina** Buckden (Huntingdon
810355). Ⓢ Ⓦ Ⓟ Ⓓ Calor gas, long-term
mooring, winter storage, slipway, crane,
chandlery, provisions, sportswear,
off-licence, books and maps, boatbuilding
and sales, boat and engine repairs, toilets. Ⓜ
A fine 10-acre site planned with conservation
in mind.
Ⓑ **Purvis Marine** Hartford Road,
Huntingdon (53628). Day boat hire.
Ⓑ **Hartford Marina** Banks End, Wyton
(Huntingdon 54677). Ⓡ Ⓢ Ⓦ Ⓟ Ⓓ Calor gas,
long-term mooring, winter storage, slipway,
crane, chandlery, provisions, books and
maps, boat and engine sales and repairs,
toilets, showers. VHF base station (channel
M or 6), à la carte restaurant, club, caravan
site. Ⓜ
Ⓑ **L H Jones & Son** The Boathaven, St Ives
(Huntingdon 63463). Ⓡ Ⓢ Ⓦ Ⓟ Ⓓ Calor gas,
long-term mooring, winter storage, slipway,

chandlery, books and maps, boat and engine
repairs, boat sales, outboard sales, toilets,
showers. Ⓜ

PUBS AND RESTAURANTS

🍺 **Bell** Great Paxton (Huntingdon 72265)
Greene King real ale, good homemade bar
meals (*L&D*) and large garden.
🍺 **Swan Inn** High Street, Offord Cluny
(Huntingdon 810294). Just under ½ mile
east of the marina, over the level crossing.
Charles Wells real ale, bar meals and snacks
(*L&D*) in a friendly village pub. Children's
room.
🍺✕ **Lion Hotel** Buckden (Huntingdon
810313). Once the Old Lion and Lamb (an
old posting house) this is an extremely
comfortable inn. Bar food and restaurant
meals (*L&D*), children welcome in lounge.
🍺 **The Vine** Buckden (Huntingdon
810367). Whitbread Wethered real ale in a
very attractive pub. Snacks, garden.
🍺 **Falcon** Mill Road, Buckden (Huntingdon
811612). Welcoming village local with an
open fire, serving Charles Wells real ale and
bar meals (*L&D*). Garden, enclosed patio
and children's room.
🍺 **Black Bull** Church Street, Brampton
(Huntingdon 54193). Manns and Watneys
real ale and bar meals (*L&D*) in this popular
pub. Garden.
🍺 **Dragoon** Buckden Road, Brampton
(Huntingdon 53510). Charles Wells real ale
in a pub noted for its food (*L&D*). Garden.
✕ **China Tea Pot** 10 Causeway,
Godmanchester (Huntingdon 50413). A
splendid choice of teas accompanied by
scones or delicious cakes and pastries, with
more substantial meals at lunchtime. *Open
from mid-morning to late afternoon. Closed
Mon & Tue.*
🍺✕ **Black Bull** Post Street, Godmanchester
(Huntingdon 53310). A lovely beamy pub
with plenty of polished brass around an open

fire. Good food (*L&D*), Whitbread Wethered real ale, garden, accommodation. Children welcome in dining room.

🍺✕ **White Hart** Cambridge Road, Godmanchester (Huntingdon 53710). Timber frame and pantiled pub with a low-beamed ceiling and plenty of polished brass. Manns real ale, bar food (*L only*) and an à la carte restaurant. Garden with play park.

🍺 **Exhibition** London Road, Godmanchester (Huntingdon 59134). In the public bar the theme is steam trains; several Victorian shopfronts have been recreated around the walls of the lounge bar. Manns and Ushers real ales, bar meals (*L&D*) and garden with children's play area. 'Petanque' (the pub game of the future, apparently) is played here.

🍺 **Royal Oak** Overlooking the weir stream at Godmanchester Lock (Huntingdon 53819). Large pub with a split-level bar. Snacks. There is a useful barber's shop around the side.

🍺 **Old Bridge Hotel** 1 High Street, Huntingdon (52681). A comfortable, rambling, ivy-covered red-brick hotel, noted for its excellent food – ranging from a tempting cold spread to barbecued spare ribs (*L&D*) which can be washed down with Ruddles real ale.

🍺 **Falcon Tavern** Market Place, Huntingdon (53228). Dating from 1554, this handsome and historic inn hides up an alleyway behind an impressive wooden door. It is said to be connected to Hinchingbrooke House and the river by hidden passages and was used by Oliver Cromwell in 1643 as a recruiting centre for his Ironside army. Manns, Wilsons and Founders real ales, bar food (*L&D*), children welcome in eating area.

✕ **River View Tea Room** By Huntingdon Bridge (Huntingdon 411625). Homemade lunches and teas in a beautifully converted warehouse building. *Open daily.*

🍺✕ **George Hotel** Huntingdon (53096). An historic hotel once owned by Oliver Cromwell's grandfather, who was a brewer. In the yard of this galleried inn, *in late June*,

you may watch a Shakespeare play. Spacious lounge, good bar food (*L only*) and restaurant meals. Children welcome.

🍺 **Victoria** Ouse Walk, Huntingdon (53899). James Paines real ale in a pleasant town pub. Garden, bar meals (*L&D*) and cook your own barbecues in summer.

🍺 **Three Jolly Butchers** Houghton (St Ives 63228). 250 yards walk from a shaky looking jetty. Snacks.

🍺 **Three Horse Shoes** The Green, Houghton (St Ives 62410). Cosy inglenook bar and a comfortable lounge in which to enjoy Manns real ale and good bar food (*L&D*). Nice garden with play area and good shops close by.

🍺 **Axe & Compasses** By the church, Hemingford Abbots (St Ives 63605). A lovely thatched village pub with a cosy inglenook fireplace and lots of beams. Very good choice of real ales, and cider as well. Meals (*L&D, not Mon*), garden, and a room for families.

🍺 **Cock** High Street, Hemingford Grey (St Ives 63609). A fine local pub with an open fire in the public bar and a split-level lounge. The bar snacks are English country fare, and there is a garden with swings and a slide. Someone here supports West Ham United football club.

🍺 **Oliver Cromwell** The Quay, Wellington Street, St Ives (65601). East of the bridge. Popular old pub, dispensing Greene King and Ruddles real ales. Cobbled yard.

🍺✕ **Floods Tavern** Broadway, St Ives (67773). Greene King real ale amongst usual wine bar fare. Meals (*L&D*) and garden. Ⓜ

✕🍴 **Kushiara Tandoori** By the Bridge, St Ives (65737). Everything you would expect. *Open daily (L&D).*

🍺 **Dun Horse** Just around the corner from the Waits moorings, St Ives (64417). Manns real ale and an extensive bar menu (*L&D*) in a cosy pub. Bar billiards, children welcome. Nice little garden equipped with children's playthings.

🍺✕ **Golden Lion** Market Place, St Ives (63159). Large black and white hotel overlooking Cromwell's statue. Greene King real ale, bar and restaurant meals (*L&D*).

St Ives

The handsome mill at Houghton

The charming riverside village of Holywell is approached between extensive gravel workings – the pale orange heaps stand out conspicuously in such flat country.
Below the Pike & Eel Inn the flood protection banks close in, and in places, especially on the southern side, only the tops of slender church spires can be seen.
Brownshill Lock is passed – here, when conditions allow, there is a fine gravel beach below the sluice; a nice place for a swim according to the lock-keeper.
At Earith the useful West View Marina will be found before the Ouse widens and the Old and New Bedford Rivers leave on their respective, very straight north easterly courses. This area is a favourite wintering place for wildfowl, with up to 4000 Bewick swans arriving each year from Siberia and 200 whooper swans from Iceland. These together with the resident population of both Canada geese and mute swans make a fascinating spectacle. There are good moorings at Holywell, the Pike & Eel Inn and Earith. Below Hermitage Lock the Old West River is initially narrow and canal like, and keeps company with a road until an old pumping station is passed. High flood

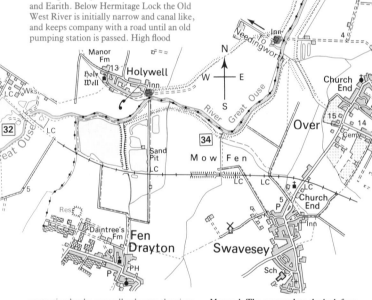

protection banks generally obscure the view, but the village of Aldreth can be glimpsed to the north. There are trees at Queenholme Farm.

NAVIGATIONAL NOTES

Brownshill Lock 101ft 0in × 13ft 2in. Guillotine, manned. Tricky circular cross-current downstream of the lock – approach slowly under power and conflicting currents should leave your boat in the right place.
Tides Between Brownshill Lock and Hermitage Lock the river is tidal, although the rise and fall is not very great (usually about 12 inches). Allow for this if tying up to a static mooring.
New Bedford River Hire craft are not allowed to enter.
Hermitage Lock 100ft 0in × 13ft 1in.

Manned. The approach to the lock from upstream is marked by a line of buoys – keep left.
Old West River Speed limit between Hermitage Lock and Pope's Corner is 4mph.
Holywell
Cambs. A compact residential village of thatch and pantiled cottages with newer properties intermingled. The old inn here was once a monastic ferryhouse, and the church tower, 1547, is said to have been built with stones from Ramsey Abbey. The chancel is 13thC, however, and is a beautiful piece of work. The well is 'dressed' each year, in a ceremony arousing much local interest and gaiety.
Fen Drayton
Cambs. A village of timbered and thatched houses. The church of St Mary is mainly

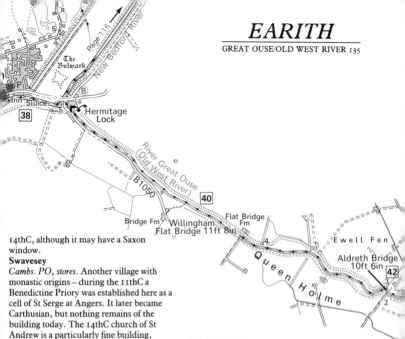

14thC, although it may have a Saxon window.

Swavesey

Cambs. PO, stores. Another village with monastic origins – during the 11thC a Benedictine Priory was established here as a cell of St Serge at Angers. It later became Carthusian, but nothing remains of the building today. The 14thC church of St Andrew is a particularly fine building, approached through an avenue of cedars. The south door heralds a spacious interior, with pretty traceried windows, admirable roofs, splendid sedilia and piscina in the chancel. There is also a grand array of carved bench ends with animals and figures. The monument to Lady Cutt, 1631, is watched over by exquisite angels.

Over

Cambs. PO, stores. An effort should be made to visit the church of St Mary, a delightfully ornate building which once belonged to Ramsey Abbey. The interior is ornately decorated, and stone seats extend round much of the walls. A small man in a big hat and a dragon devouring a man are carved on the arms of the chancel stalls, and a medieval sanctus bell hangs above the east end of the nave. The handsome 18thC vicarage stands next door.

Earith

Cambs. PO, stores. A workmanlike village with some attractive cottages situated at a point vital in Fenland drainage. The Old Bedford River leaves the Ouse here to run twenty one very straight miles to Salters Lode, having been built in 1631 by the fourth Earl of Bedford. The New Bedford River was built alongside 20 years later, and empties at Denver Sluice, with the tract of land between – the Ouse Washes – being used to take up excess flood-water when the need arises. Where both leave the Ouse is the Bulwark, a Civil War earthwork.

The Olde Ferry Boat Inn, Holywell

BOATYARDS

Ⓑ **West View Marina (Anglo Welsh)** Earith (Ramsey 841627). Ⓡ Ⓦ Ⓟ Ⓓ Calor gas, hire fleet, long-term mooring, winter storage, crane, provisions, books and maps, boat and engine repairs, boat sales, toilets, showers, caravan site. Very friendly and helpful. Ⓜ

Ⓑ **Hermitage Marina** (Hoseasons Holidays) Earith (Ramsey 840994). Ⓡ Ⓢ Ⓦ Ⓟ Ⓓ Calor gas, hire fleet, long-term mooring, winter storage, slipway, chandlery, books and maps, boat and engine repairs, boat sales, toilets. Ⓜ

PUBS AND RESTAURANTS

Ⓟ✕ **Olde Ferry Boat Inn** Holywell (Huntingdon 63227). A very old and lovely thatched pub, whose ghost is said to have been around for 900 years. A building on this site was once the monastic ferryhouse. The beamed ceilings are extremely low, there are carved wooden settles and two fires to warm you on a cold day. Clearly an excellent place to enjoy their choice of real ales and outstanding food (*L&D*). Garden, accommodation. Children welcome in the lounge.

Ⓟ✕ **Pike & Eel** Riverside at Overcote Ferry (Huntingdon 63336). Friendly and welcoming 17thC riverside inn built in mellow brown stone with lawns down to the water's edge and a sheltered terrace. Excellent bar food (*L&D*), restaurant meals and a refreshing choice of real ales. Children welcome in the restaurant, accommodation. Ⓦ Ⓟ Ⓓ Ⓜ

Ⓟ **Crown** Waterside, Earith (Ramsey 841442). A very convivial village pub offering Manns, Wilsons and Founders real ales along with bar meals (*L&D*). Fine riverside garden and good Ⓜ *for patrons only.*

✕Ⓟ **Riverview Hotel** Earith (Ramsey 841405). Restaurant serving English food à la carte, and bar with a riverside garden; open to non-residents.

The Old West River continues its lonely course between high flood banks – occasional glimpses of Haddenham and Wilburton to the north, and the odd riverside farm being the only visible signs of habitation. All the time the sky is full of birds – solitary hawks, skeins of geese and wheeling gulls are omnipresent. On the banks, the antics of moorhens, coots and various ducks provide amusement, while swans cruise along gently and lapwing pick around in the wet grass. Around Australia Farm the river meanders in an eccentric loop and you find yourself travelling southwards for a short while, looking at the distant tower of Cottenham church. An attractive pub and a small marina mark Twenty Pence Bridge. Beyond a sharp bend and an awkward bridge there is another pub and marina and the river widens considerably. The chimney of Stretham Old Engine dominates the skyline, to be followed by Ely Cathedral three miles to the north, as Popes Corner is reached. Here the River Cam joins from the south and it is a relatively uneventful cruise to the fine cathedral city of Ely.

NAVIGATIONAL NOTES

Stretham Ferry Bridge On an awkward corner and obstructed.
Rowing Keep a look out for the rowing eights at Ely during the spring.

Stretham
Cambs. PO, stores. Fenland village around a well-preserved 15thC cross. The church of St James dates from the 14thC, its stone spire visible for miles around.
Stretham Old Engine An engine house built in 1831 and containing its original steam beam engine and boilers. Built by the Butterley Company of Derbyshire, it powered a scoop wheel 37 feet in diameter, capable of raising 30,000 gallons of water per minute and consuming a ton of coal every six hours in the process. It replaced four windmills and is preserved in perfect order. There is a collection of old implements on display, including a peat cutter's spade, and an eel trap. *Open daily.* Small charge.
Ely
Cambs. EC Tue, MD Thur. All shops and services, BR station. A charming, predominantly Georgian market town watched over by a magnificent cathedral. The name derives from 'eel-eye' or 'eel

Ely Maltings

island' – folklore insists that the eels in the surrounding marsh were uncelibate priests miraculously transformed by St Dunstan. Ely was the last stronghold of revolt against William the Conqueror, led by Hereward the Wake who was eventually betrayed by the abbot of the monastery. Another famous and more successful rebel also lived in Ely: Oliver Cromwell occupied the half-timbered vicarage adjoining St Mary's church, and was responsible for collecting the tithes. There are many notable buildings in the Cathedral precincts: Ely Porta, the main gatehouse of the Benedictine Priory, begun 1397; Prior Crauden's Chapel, outstanding in the Decorated style; Prior's House, 14th–15thC with a Norman undercroft; Walsingham House, built in 1335 for Alan of Walsingham, who was responsible for rebuilding the cathedral tower. Also of interest is the Bishop's Palace, parts of which date from the 15thC, but much altered by Bishop Laney in the 17thC.
Ely Cathedral The Gallery. A religious settlement was first founded at Ely in AD673 by St Etheldreda. Her relics were placed in the cathedral choir in 1252. After the Conquest, William I laid the foundation of the present cathedral, which took 286 years to reach completion. A magnificent Gothic edifice, it has two glorious features for which it is universally acclaimed. When the Norman tower collapsed in 1322, the impressive Octagon was constructed. An engineering masterpiece, its crowning wooden lantern is a fine example of medieval carpentry. The lovely, light, Lady Chapel has some marvellous intricate carving in white stone. Note the ceiling and the detail of each of the many bosses. Associated with the cathedral is the beautiful chapel of Kings' School, which recently celebrated its millennium

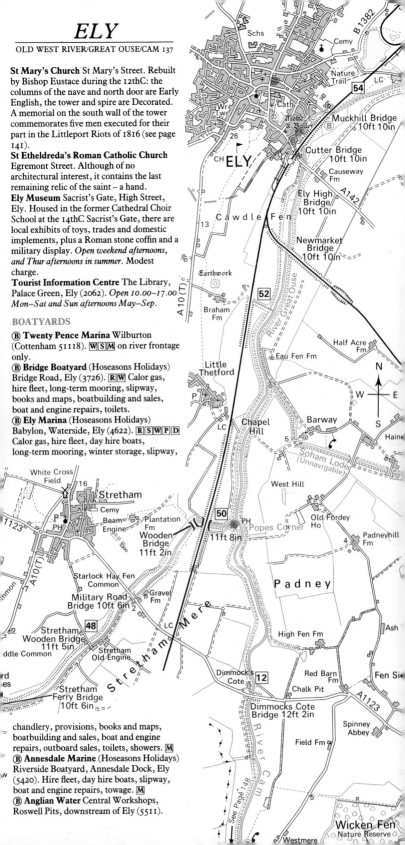

ELY

St Mary's Church St Mary's Street. Rebuilt by Bishop Eustace during the 12thC: the columns of the nave and north door are Early English, the tower and spire are Decorated. A memorial on the south wall of the tower commemorates five men executed for their part in the Littleport Riots of 1816 (see page 141).

St Etheldreda's Roman Catholic Church Egremont Street. Although of no architectural interest, it contains the last remaining relic of the saint – a hand.

Ely Museum Sacrist's Gate, High Street, Ely. Housed in the former Cathedral Choir School at the 14thC Sacrist's Gate, there are local exhibits of toys, trades and domestic implements, plus a Roman stone coffin and a military display. *Open weekend afternoons, and Thur afternoons in summer.* Modest charge.

Tourist Information Centre The Library, Palace Green, Ely (2062). *Open 10.00–17.00 Mon–Sat and Sun afternoons May–Sep.*

BOATYARDS

Ⓑ **Twenty Pence Marina** Wilburton (Cottenham 51118). Ⓦ Ⓢ Ⓜ on river frontage only.

Ⓑ **Bridge Boatyard** (Hoseasons Holidays) Bridge Road, Ely (3726). Ⓡ Ⓦ Calor gas, hire fleet, long-term mooring, slipway, books and maps, boatbuilding and sales, boat and engine repairs, toilets.

Ⓑ **Ely Marina** (Hoseasons Holidays) Babylon, Waterside, Ely (4622). Ⓡ Ⓢ Ⓦ Ⓟ Ⓓ Calor gas, hire fleet, day hire boats, long-term mooring, winter storage, slipway, chandlery, provisions, books and maps, boatbuilding and sales, boat and engine repairs, outboard sales, toilets, showers. Ⓜ

Ⓑ **Annesdale Marine** (Hoseasons Holidays) Riverside Boatyard, Annesdale Dock, Ely (5420). Hire fleet, day hire boats, slipway, boat and engine repairs, towage. Ⓜ

Ⓑ **Anglian Water** Central Workshops, Roswell Pits, downstream of Ely (5511).

Slipway and cranage, boats up to 87ft.
These facilities may soon be made available
to the general boating public.

PUBS AND RESTAURANTS

🍺✗ **Twenty Pence Inn** Twentypence Road,
Wilburton. Riverside, at the bridge
(Cottenham 50158). English and French
food, à la carte and bar meals (*L&D*).
Children welcome in the coffee lounge. Tolly
Cobbold real ale is served in what is claimed
to be the lowest bar (relative to sea level!) in
the country. Children's playground in the
fine riverside garden. M

🍺✗ **Hunters Fen** Twentypence Road,
Cottenham (50455). Good selection of real
ales and bar food (*L&D*) in an enterprising
free house. Children's playground and à la
carte meals in the restaurant.

🍺 **Royal Oak** Riverside, Stretham (314).
Less than a mile south west of the Old
Engine. Bass real ale, bar meals (*L&D*) and
snacks in this well known landmark. Teas
are also served, and there is a shop. The
riverside gardens contain a playground and
extend to a marina where there is: W M

There are plenty of pubs and restaurants in
Ely.

🍺 **Cutter Inn** Riverside, Annesdale, Ely
(2713). So named in the 1830s when the
Ouse navigation was straightened by
building Sandy's Cut, it once sold beer
brewed in the town by Hall, Cutlack and
Harlock, no less, but now dispenses

Norwich Brewery and Websters real ales,
bar meals (*L&D*) and snacks.

🍺 **Lamb Hotel** Lynn Road, Ely (3574).
Restaurant and bar meals (*L&D*, *L only at
weekends*) with a wide choice of real ales to
accompany them.

🍺 **Royal Standard** Fore Hill, Ely (2613).
Popular city pub serving Greene King real
ale, bar meals (*L&D*) and snacks.

🍺 **Angel Inn** Station Road, Ely (2462). A
real ale only pub. Bar snacks,
accommodation.

✗🍷 **Riverside at Ely Quay House** Quayside,
Ely (2415). A la carte restaurant, buttery
bar, tea bar. Children welcome. (*L&D*,
Closed Sat L, Sun D & Mon).

✗🍷 **Surma Tandoori** 78 Broad Street, Ely
(2281). For those who like their curry.
(*L&D daily*).

🍺 **Minster Tavern** Minster Place, Ely
(3994). Bass and Springfield real ales, bar
meals (*L only*) and snacks. Garden,
accommodation.

🍺✗ **Fish & Duck** Popes Corner (Stretham
580). Beautifully situated and under
enthusiastic new management, this fine
pub/restaurant offers Tolly Cobbold real ale,
bar meals (*L&D*), and haute cuisine (*D
only*). Large garden. R W M

✗🍷 **Old Fire Engine House** 25 St Mary's
Street, Ely (2582). Local recipes prepared
from fresh local produce, good fruit pies and
farmhouse cheese in a fine old house with a
sheltered garden. Adnams real ale. Essential
to reserve. *Open L&D, not Sun D*.

Stretham Old Engine

The River Ouse at Denver

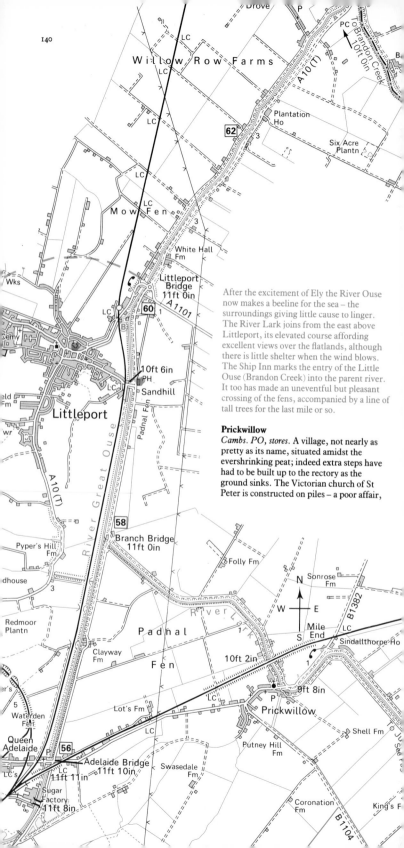

Drove

Willow Row Farms

A10(T)

To Brandon Creek
10ft 0in

PC

B

Plantation
Ho

62

Six Acre
Plantn

LC

Mow Fen

LC

White Hall
Fm

Wks

Littleport
Bridge
11ft 0in

60   A1101

LC

B

10ft 6in
PH

Sandhill

After the excitement of Ely the River Ouse
now makes a beeline for the sea – the
surroundings giving little cause to linger.
The River Lark joins from the east above
Littleport, its elevated course affording
excellent views over the flatlands, although
there is little shelter when the wind blows.
The Ship Inn marks the entry of the Little
Ouse (Brandon Creek) into the parent river.
It too has made an uneventful but pleasant
crossing of the fens, accompanied by a line of
tall trees for the last mile or so.

Prickwillow

Cambs. PO, stores. A village, not nearly as
pretty as its name, situated amidst the
evershrinking peat; indeed extra steps have
had to be built up to the rectory as the
ground sinks. The Victorian church of St
Peter is constructed on piles – a poor affair,

Littleport

A10(T)

River Great Ouse

Padnal Fen

58

Branch Bridge
11ft 0in

Pyper's Hill
Fm

Folly Fm

Sonrose
Fm

N

W   E

S

Redmoor
Plantn

River Lark

Padnal

Mile
End

B1382

Sindallthorpe Ho

LC

Clayway
Fm

Fen

10ft 2in

1

9ft 8in

LC

P

Lot's Fm

Prickwillow

Waterden
Fen

Shell Fm

Queen
Adelaide

56

P

Adelaide Bridge
11ft 10in

Putney Hill
Fm

LC

11ft 11in

Swasedale
Fm

To J U
See r

Sugar
Factory
11ft 8in

Coronation
Fm

King's F

B1104

it contains the font from Ely Cathedral. Donated by Dean Spencer in 1693, the exquisite white marble is not a little incongruous here.

Pumping Engine Museum Prickwillow. An enthusiastically maintained 1923 Mirrlees, Bickerton & Day pumping engine surrounded by artifacts and some fine old photos. *Open daily Apr–Oct, and running several weekends during the year.*

Littleport

Cambs. PO, stores, BR station. A riverside town known as the scene of the Littleport Riots in 1816, when farm workers returning from the Napoleonic wars were faced with high prices, unemployment and consequent starvation. A riot started here following a meeting in the Globe Inn. The rioters marched on to Ely armed with farm implements and preceded by a wagon bearing a punt gun. They were brutally put down by the military, many were imprisoned or transported and five were publicly hanged – they are commemorated in St Mary's church, Ely. The town's own church, St George's, is a large Perpendicular building with some Victorian additions. Its tall west tower looks out over the rich farmland all around.

Little Ouse

Norfolk. An isolated settlement with a school and a church, all hidden amongst a welcome stand of trees.

BOATYARDS

Ⓑ **The Boathaven** Littleport (Ely 860560). ⓇⓈⓌⒹ Pump-out, Calor gas, hire fleet, day hire boats, long-term mooring, winter storage, slipway, chandlery, provisions, books and maps, boat sales, boat and engine repairs, toilets, showers Ⓜ. The future of this yard is uncertain as we go to press.

PUBS AND RESTAURANTS

⬛✕ **Black Horse** Sandhill, Littleport (Ely 860328). Norwich Brewery and Websters real ales, meals in the dining room (*L&D, not Mon, Tue, or Sun L*) and bar snacks. Riverside garden.

⬛ **George & Dragon** Station Road, Littleport (Ely 860145). A brick-built pub serving Norwich Brewery beers.

⬛✕ **Ship Inn** Brandon Creek (228). Smart riverside pub and restaurant, serving Norwich Brewery real ale and meals (*L&D*). Patio. Ⓜ

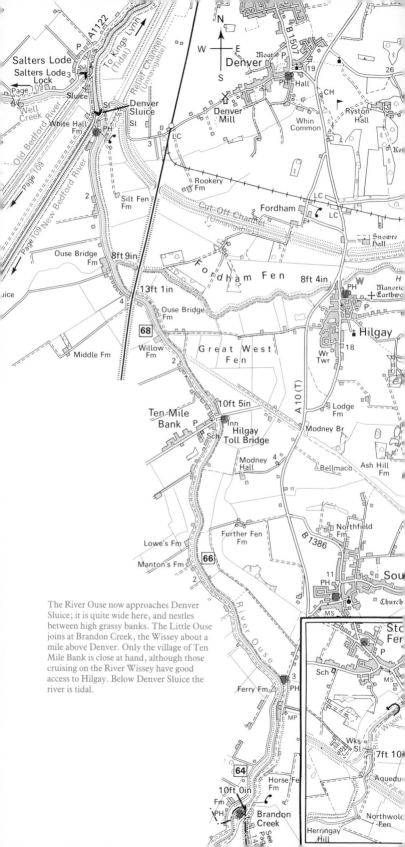

The River Ouse now approaches Denver Sluice; it is quite wide here, and nestles between high grassy banks. The Little Ouse joins at Brandon Creek, the Wissey about a mile above Denver. Only the village of Ten Mile Bank is close at hand, although those cruising on the River Wissey have good access to Hilgay. Below Denver Sluice the river is tidal.

NAVIGATIONAL NOTES

Denver Sluice (Downham Market 382340).
Approx 69ft 0in × 17ft 0in. Telephone the
lock-keeper 24 hours in advance. The river is
tidal below this point. The ideal time to pass
through en route to King's Lynn is high
water on a spring tide. A crossing to the
Middle Level (Salters Lode) can be made
between 2 hours before and 3 hours after
high water.

Salters Lode Lock (Downham Market
382292) 80ft 0in × 12ft 6in. Telephone the
lock-keeper 24 hours in advance. The river is
tidal below this point. Locking through is
possible for limited periods either side of
high water – the tidal approach is difficult.

New Bedford River Tidal. Minimum
headroom Denver to Earith is 7ft 10in at
high water springs. When the river discharge
is small, start from Denver about 1 hour
after low water.

Old Bedford River This can be entered
through the sluice when the tide makes level.
Contact the lock-keeper at Salters Lode 24
hours in advance.

River Wissey The limit of navigation is a
short way below the bridge at Stoke Ferry.

Southery
Norfolk. PO, stores. Southery, and Hilgay to
the north, are the only two Norfolk Fenland
villages mentioned in the Domesday Book.
The church of St Mary was built in 1858 to
replace an older building whose empty walls
still stand to the east. Note the fine village
sign.

Ten Mile Bank
Norfolk. PO, stores. A tiny settlement, useful
for supplies.

Hilgay
Norfolk. PO, stores. Situated at an ancient
crossing of the River Wissey. The church of
All Saints is approached along an avenue of
limes – parts date from the 14thC although it
was greatly remodelled by Street 1869–70.
The grey-brick tower was built in 1784.

Denver
Norfolk. PO, stores. A settlement of
attractive houses and cottages occupied since
Roman times, which has given its name to
the Denver Sluice, a major feature in
Fenland drainage. Constructed in 1652 as
part of a major scheme by Vermuyden,
Charles I's Dutch engineer, the sluice soon
became very unpopular as it was a hindrance
to navigation. There was great rejoicing
when it burst in 1713, due to flood water
meeting spring tides, but renewed flooding

soon necessitated its replacement in
1748–50. It has subsequently been much
rebuilt and improved, and marks the
northern limit of casual boating on the river
– fierce tides dominate below the sluice. The
church of St Mary has a late 13thC tower; to
the south east is Denver Hall, a handsome
Tudor building with a picturesque little
gatehouse, dated 1570 (private).

Denver Mill A six-storey tower mill built in
1865, with a steam mill and granary
attached. Lots of original equipment,
including a Blackstone oil engine. Also a
display of milling artifacts. Being restored as
we go to press, *for opening times ring the
Tourist Office, King's Lynn 763044.*

Stoke Ferry
Norfolk. PO, stores. The head of navigation
on the River Wissey, and an ancient crossing
point occupied since Roman times.

PUBS AND RESTAURANTS

🍺 **Ferry Boat** Riverside, Southery (Brandon
Creek 247). A very basic Trumans pub by
the Denver Cruising Club mooring.

🍺 **Old White Bell** Southery (425). Formerly
the Silver Fleece. Norwich Brewery real ale,
bar meals (*L&D*) in a tidy pub. Large field at
the back.

🍺 **Windmill** Riverside at Ten Mile Bank
(Southery 445). Modern pub offering
Websters real ale, bar meals (*L&D, not Wed*)
and snacks. Children's room, playpark, and
a waitress service to the garden. R W M

🍺✕ **Jenyns Arms** Denver Sluice
(Downham Market 383366). A pub once
popular with the 'berthsmen' who piloted
vessels on the tidal river and lodged in the
taproom here. Still equally popular, but with
a different clientele. Note the old Denver
Sluice toll board displayed on the outside
wall, and the peacocks roaming everywhere,
both in the garden and on the Sluice.
Restaurant and bar meals (*L&D*) and a
choice of real ales. A well known waterways
landmark.

🍺 **Bell** Denver. A fine old flint and cobble
village pub, serving Norwich Brewery real
ale.

✕🍷 **Cross Keys** Hilgay, by the bridge
(Downham Market 387777). Riverside
restaurant (*D only*). M

🍺 **Rose & Crown** Hilgay (Downham
Market 387668). Large and basic brick-built
village pub, south of the bridge.

🍺 **Blue Bell** Stoke Ferry (500358). In the
more attractive, north west part of the
village. Norwich Brewery real ale, bar meals
(*L&D*), garden.

Above Jesus Lock the River Cam winds through The Backs on its way to Grantchester. Those who have arrived in Cambridge by cruiser will have only a short walk from the moorings into the city centre, where narrow alleyways lead to college gardens, and fascinating shops encourage browsing. Water-borne exploration above Jesus Lock is done in the traditional way, by hiring a punt or rowing boat.

Leaving Cambridge the river is soon amongst trees as it passes Fen Ditton and approaches the very pretty Baits Bite Lock, a cheerful sight with plenty of flowers. Horningsea is veiled by trees, with the railway not far away on the opposite bank; gradually the prospect opens out, with the typical large arable fields stretching away to the horizon. Below Bottisham Lock the River Cam enters Fenland proper.

NAVIGATIONAL NOTES

River Cam Conservancy Responsible for navigation between Byron's Pool, Grantchester and Bottisham Lock. Their address is The Guildhall, Cambridge (358977). Craft need only be registered with the Conservators if they stay above Bottisham, otherwise they must be registered with Anglian Water.

Limit of navigation Powered craft should *not* pass through Jesus Lock. Although the practical limit is Magdalene Bridge, power craft are actively discouraged from mixing with the punts and rowing boats which are found in large numbers above the lock. Byron's Pool, Grantchester is the limit for unpowered craft.

Jesus Lock Manned. A toll is payable.

Baits Bite Lock 100ft 0in × 14ft 3in. Manned. A toll is payable, from 50p to £4.30 (1985 charges) depending on the size of craft.

Bottisham Lock 97ft 10in × 14ft 9in. Unmanned. Electrically operated guillotine and mitre gates (Anglian Water).

Rowing Take care between Jesus Lock and Baits Bite, Rowing eights travel surprisingly fast and cannot easily take avoiding action.

Grantchester

Cambs. PO, stores. A leisurely punt ride from Cambridge along the Cam, Grantchester was beloved of and mentioned by both Byron and Tennyson. But it is in Rupert Brooke's nostalgic and comic poem that this tranquil little village has gained immortality. Brooke lived at Grantchester before he died in Greece during the first world war, becoming one of the most famous war poets. There are thatched cottages and a fine church with Roman bricks and a Saxon window. See the clock still standing at ten to three, and note Brooke's name on the war memorial.

Cambridge

Cambs. All shops and services, BR station. Situated between the Fens to the north and swamp to the south, the site of Cambridge was established as a ford over the River Cam. It soon became a busy and important commercial centre. The Romans used Cambridge as an inland port and built a

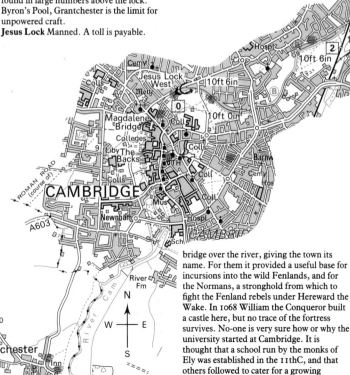

bridge over the river, giving the town its name. For them it provided a useful base for incursions into the wild Fenlands, and for the Normans, a stronghold from which to fight the Fenland rebels under Hereward the Wake. In 1068 William the Conqueror built a castle here, but no trace of the fortress survives. No-one is very sure how or why the university started at Cambridge. It is thought that a school run by the monks of Ely was established in the 11thC, and that others followed to cater for a growing

Clare College Trinity Lane. The third oldest college founded by Elizabeth de Clare in 1339. Fire destroyed the hall in 1521 and the earliest part is the east range of the old court, dated 1638. For the best view of this beautiful building, look over from the lawns of King's College.

King's College Chapel King's Parade. A glorious Gothic wonder of delicate fan vaulting and stone carving, it was begun in 1446 by Henry VI. The windows, which flood the building with an array of beautiful, coloured light, date from 1517 to the 1530s. Behind the altar sits Rubens' magnificent 'Adoration of the Magi', painted c1634 and presented to the college in 1962.

Corpus Christi College Trumpington Street. Founded by the townspeople in 1352. It was formerly called Bene't College after the partly Saxon church of St Bene't (St Benedict), which was used as the college chapel. Two of the college's most famous students were Christopher Marlowe and John Fletcher, the Elizabethan dramatists. Fletcher came to the college in 1593, the year Marlowe was killed in a tavern. Both are commemorated on a plaque on the wall of the Old Court.

Emmanuel College St Andrew's Street. Founded in 1584 by Sir Walter Mildmay, Chancellor of the Exchequer to Elizabeth I, on the site of the Dominican or Black Friars house. The chapel was designed in 1666 by Sir Christopher Wren.

Jesus College Jesus Lane. Accommodated Thomas Cranmer who was made a Fellow in 1515. The poet Coleridge was also here and writes of the college in his *Biographia Literaria*.

Magdalene College Magdalene Street. With its two charming courtyards, it is particularly known for the Pepysian Library which contains 3000 books left to the college by the diarist. His diary, written in cipher, was found amongst the collection and deciphered for publication in 1825. The books are housed in his own bookcases and his personal desk is still there too.

Pembroke College Trumpington Street. Edmund Spenser, Thomas Gray and the younger Pitt were all sons of Pembroke College. The New Chapel was the first building that Christopher Wren ever designed, commissioned by his uncle, the Bishop of Ely. The west end, quietly classical, remains unaltered, the rest has acquired considerable Victorian additions.

Peterhouse College Trumpington Street. The first of the colleges, founded in 1281 by the Bishop of Ely as a secular institution. Little remains of the original hall due to 19thC restoration but it has retained a Tudor fireplace. The William Morris windows are an attractive later addition.

One famous fellow of this college, if short-lived, was the poet Thomas Gray. With a phobia for fire, the ladder which he left permanently attached to his window proved too tempting for his mischievous fellow students. One dark night in 1742 they raised the alarm outside his window.

demand. By the 13thC several religious orders had been established, with schools attached, and in 1284 the first college proper was founded – Peterhouse. The academic community in Cambridge developed quickly and more colleges sprang up to house the growing number of students.

Cambridge has a wealth of historic buildings and much of its charm lies in the winding back streets and passages, such as Botolph Lane and St Edward's Passage. Medieval houses and cottages line Northampton and Magdalene Streets. The willow-hung 'Backs', sloping down to the peaceful riverside, make a perfect picnicking spot for a lazy summer's day. You can envy the nonchalance with which the well-practised students manipulate the poles – or rise to the challenge and take a punt out yourself. Visitors are welcome to wander around the colleges and grounds, but during term time there may be restrictions.

Christ's College St Andrews Street. Accommodated Milton from 1625 to 1632; it is believed that he wrote *Lycidas* while sitting under the mulberry tree in the gardens. The hall has been much altered, but the gatehouse survives, embellished with fine heraldic carving.

Thomas rushed down the ladder clad only in his nightshirt, and landed straight in a tub of icy water. Predictably not amused, he left for Pembroke College.

Queens' College Queens' Lane, was founded by two Queens: Margaret of Anjou, wife of Henry VI and Elizabeth Woodville, wife of Edward IV. Begun by Margaret in 1448, it was taken over by Elizabeth in 1465. It remains essentially, the same great Tudor mansion constructed then.

Arching quaintly over the river is the famous wooden Mathematical Bridge, so called because it was based upon geometric principles and constructed in 1749 without the use of any nails or bolts. A curious Victorian took it to pieces to see how it worked, did not succeed, and could not put it back together again. So now it has bolts and nails just like any ordinary bridge.

Trinity College Trinity Street. The largest and richest college, Trinity was founded by Henry VIII who added new buildings and combined the existing colleges of King's Hall and Michaelhouse. There are many grand buildings: the Great Gate of the chapel with a statue of Newton; a marvellous hall and the Great Court, the most impressive in Cambridge and said to be the largest university court in the world. Trinity men include a half-dozen Prime Ministers, the poets George Herbert, Dryden, Byron (who kept a tame bear and was sent down for bathing naked in the fountain), Tennyson and Housman, and, in the field of science, Isaac Newton and Rutherford who, for better or for worse, split the atom.

St John's College St John's Street. Second largest of the Cambridge colleges founded by Lady Margaret Tudor in 1511, but not built until after her death. Notable buildings include the splendid turreted gatehouse, the Tudor hall with its hammer-beam roof and the handsome Combination Room. Crossing the Cam is the famous Bridge of Sighs modelled on the one in Venice, and built in 1831. St John's men include Wordsworth, Palmerston, Wilberforce and Herchel the astronomer.

If you've any energy left, there's plenty more in the way of churches and museums.

Church of the Holy Sepulchre Bridge Street. Built in 1130, with its impressive Norman nave, this is the largest of the four remaining round churches in England. Much restored in 1841.

St Bene't's Church Bene't Street. The tower is one of the few Saxon survivors in England, and is thought to date from the reign of King Canute or even earlier. Note the long-and-short stonework (alternating tall quoins and flat slabs) in the tower and the tower arch inside which is decorated with many strange, mythical beasts.

The Fitzwilliam Museum Trumpington Street. One of the world's great museums, housing paintings by Turner, Brueghel, Canaletto and Constable. There is also a large Egyptian section and collections of illuminated manuscripts, sculpture,

furniture and clocks. *Open most days.* Also worth a visit is the Cambridge and County Folk Museum, Castle Street, exhibiting interesting everyday articles from medieval times until the 20thC, *closed Sun mornings & Mon.* The Scott Polar Research Institute, Lensfield Road, a memorial museum to Scott and his companions containing documents and memorabilia from their expeditions, *open weekday afternoons.*

Tourist Information Centre Wheeler Street, Cambridge (322640).

Fen Ditton
Cambs. PO, stores. A riverside settlement of very pretty brick-built thatched cottages.

Milton
Cambs. PO, stores. Separated from Cambridge by the busy A45(T), the village has managed to retain its own identity. Some Norman features are still visible in All Saints church, in spite of restoration in 1864. The communion rail was taken from King's College Chapel; there is a fine brass dated 1553 and a 19thC barrel organ.

Horningsea
Cambs. A wooded riverside village with some quite attractive brick-built cottages, although the church is not particularly good.

Waterbeach
Cambs. PO, stores, BR station. A nunnery of the Franciscan Order of St Clare was founded here in 1294, and its foundation walls are incorporated into a farmhouse and barn to the south of the church, a much-restored building. After the spire was blown down in 1821, the chancel was rebuilt and enlarged. However, inside some original 13thC work remains. The nicest part of the village is around the large triangular green.

Car Dyke Built by the Romans as a catchwater drain, it also served as a canal for carrying agricultural produce to Lincolnshire and even as far as York. It silted up and fell into disuse during Saxon times.

BOATYARDS

There are plenty of punts, rowing boats and canoes for hire by Magdalene Bridge, and along The Backs.

Ⓑ **Scudamores** Granta Place, Cambridge (359750). Ⓡ Punt and rowing boat hire, winter storage, slipway, boat repairs, toilets.

Ⓑ **Two Tees** 70 Water Street, Cambridge (65597). ⓇⓌ Calor gas, cruiser hire, long-term mooring, winter storage, chandlery, small boatbuilding, boat and engine repairs. *Closed Sun afternoons.*

PUBS AND RESTAURANTS

🍺✗ **Green Man** High Street, Grantchester (Cambridge 841178). Snug low-beamed pub with plenty of cosy corners, and an open fire in cold weather. Imaginative bar food (*L&D*) and à la carte menu in the restaurant (*Sat & Sun only*). Tolly Cobbold real ale, children allowed in when eating. Riverside garden.

🍺✗ **Red Lion** High Street, Grantchester (Cambridge 840121). Carvery and à la carte meals in the restaurant (*L&D, closed Sun D*

Baits Bite Lock on the River Cam

and Mon) and bar meals (*L&D*) are served in this big thatched pub. There are some animals in the garden to amuse the children, and a sheltered terrace. Greene King ales.

There are many good pubs and eating places in Cambridge; the following are just a few of them.

Free Press 7 Prospect Row, Cambridge (68337). Probably the only pub in the country registered as a rowing club, so no prizes for guessing what decorates the walls here. Cosy and snug, it can become crowded, since along with Greene King real ale there is exceptional bar food (*L only, reserve at weekends*). Vegetarians are catered for, young children are not.

Fort St George in England Midsummer Common, Cambridge (354327). East bank, below Jesus Lock. A Tudor pub with log fires and wooden settles, serving Greene King real ale and sturdy English bar food (*L&D*). Riverside terrace, children allowed in eating area.

Eagle Hotel Bene't Street, Cambridge (353782). A welcoming 16thC inn, with a cosy open fire and a ceiling still covered with the signatures of World War II British and American airmen. Greene King real ale and bar food (*L&D*). Open-air drinking in the cobbled courtyard, children's room.

Xanadu 7A Jesus Lane, Cambridge (311678). Lavishly decorated Middle Eastern restaurant in what was once a turkish baths. Short menu with some exotic dishes. Vegetarians well catered for. Advisable to reserve. *Open D only Mon–Sat.*

The Taj Mahal 37–39 Regent Street, Cambridge (353835). For those who must have their curry, either here or take away. *Open L&D daily.*

Shades 1 King's Parade, Cambridge (354907). Good cold food and simple hot meals in this cellar wine bar opposite King's. Restaurant upstairs. *Open L&D, closed Sun.*

Panos 154 Hills Road (continuation south east of St Andrew's Road), Cambridge (212958). Excellent Greek and French food, with the usual bouzouki music making everything jolly. Vegetarians catered for. Essential to reserve. *Open L&D, closed Sat L and Sun.*

Spade and Becket Riverside, Thompsons Lane, Cambridge (311701). Tolly Cobbold real ale and bar meals (*L&D*) in this pleasant pub. Riverside garden.

Pike and Eel Inn Water Street, Chesterton, Cambridge (350521). Riverside pub serving bar meals (*L only*). Garden.

Plough Inn Riverside at Green End, Fen Ditton (Teversham 3264). A choice of real ales, restaurant and bar meals (*L&D, not Mon D*) in an attractive riverside pub with 2½ acres of garden. Note the fine sign. Fishing M

Plough & Fleece High Street, Horningsea (Cambridge 860795). Friendly old pub serving Greene King real ale and really excellent traditional home-cooked food (*L&D, not Sun or Mon D*). Cosy open fire, garden.

Ancient Shepherds Fen Ditton (Teversham 3280). Tolly Cobbold real ale and a good range of bar and à la carte restaurant meals (*L&D*). Garden.

Bridge Hotel Clayhithe (Cambridge 860252). Riverside hotel with welcoming open fire in cold weather, and a fine garden for warmer days. Everards real ale and bar meals (*L&D*).

Star 40 Station Road, Waterbeach (Cambridge 861287). Excellent village local dispensing Greene King real ales. Open fire, good bar food (*L&D, not Sun*), garden.

Open and intensively farmed fenland stretches away from the river in all directions. At Upware, Reach Lode branches off to the south east and eventually comes to an abrupt halt by a pumping station behind the handsome village of Reach. Access to the Lodes is through a lock, with opposed mitre gates and a guillotine. Small craft may explore part of Wicken Lode. Burwell Lode ends in a very satisfactory fashion – a 'T' junction at the bottom of a pub garden. Amazingly, quite large craft are moored in the narrow channel to the north.

NAVIGATIONAL NOTES

Swaffham Bulbeck Lode Unnavigable.
Reach Lode Lock (Ely 720343). Manned. 50ft 0in (slightly longer if the river is in flood) × 13ft 11in, headroom 9ft 0in – the keeper's hours are posted on a board. Turning room is limited, especially at Reach.
Wicken Lode Small craft may navigate part of the way.

roof. The aisle roofs also harbour angels and the nave roof is carved with bosses and friezes. A palimpsest brass shows a 16thC abbot on one side and parts of a canon and deacon on the other. A monument in the churchyard recalls a terrible tragedy which took place in the village on 8th September, 1727 when a travelling puppet show was giving a performance in a local barn. The show was so popular that the barn doors were nailed shut to keep others out. There was a fire and 82 members of the audience were burnt alive. Years later a dying Fordham man admitted having started the fire in pursuance of a grudge. To the west of the church is the site of a castle. Built in 1143, it was never completed, and only the moat remains. William Heffer, founder of Heffer's Bookshop in Cambridge, was born in Burwell.

Burwell Lode is of more recent origin than Reach Lode, and was probably cut in the 17thC to replace the Old Lode, a Roman construction, nearby. With the opening of Ball's Burwell Chemical Works in the 1850s, later to become Colchester & Ball's Patent Manure Works in the 1890s, Burwell Lode became busier than Reach Lode, with up to 10,000 tons of cargo being carried annually, including coal, stone, bricks, fertiliser and sugar-beet, this last trade continuing until 1963.

Wicken Fen The oldest nature reserve in Britain, owned by the National Trust and extending over some 700 acres. Largely undrained, it has not shrunk with the surrounding peatlands and thus remains at a higher level. It retains much of the medieval character of the fens, and is rich in plant, insect and bird life. Of great interest is the four-sided, smock marsh drainage windmill with a brick base and a boat-shaped cap, which came originally from the Adventurers Fen at Burwell. Wicken Lode was only ever navigable by small shallow-draught craft, which transported sedge and peat from the wharf at the head, about half a mile from Wicken village. Wicken Fen (Ely 720464) is *open every day except Thur*. £1 admission fee for non-members.

Wicken
Cambs. The tiny secluded church of St Laurence stands among trees; it was the last resting place of Henry Cromwell, the Lord Protector's son and Governor General of Ireland. He lived for a while at Spinney Abbey, a nearby house built on the site of an abbey founded by Augustinian canons in the early 13thC. The present building on the site dates from 1775.

Swaffham Prior
Cambs. PO, stores. 1 mile south of Reach. In Swaffham Prior two churches stand together above the street – St Mary's is notable for its octagonal Norman tower which pre-dates that at Ely. Struck by lightning in the 18thC, the tower has been left open right up to the roof – a dramatic prospect when viewed from inside. The close juxtaposition of St Cyriac's makes this a remarkable sight. It also has an octagonal tower.

Reach
Cambs. PO, stores. A very handsome village giving little clue to its former importance as an inland port and trading centre. Reach Lode was built by the Romans for drainage, transport and as the continuation of the Devil's Ditch, a defensive earthwork seven and a half miles long. A 300-yard stretch of the Ditch was levelled at Reach during the 13thC to make space for a fair, an event still opened annually *on the May Day Bank Holiday weekend* by the mayor of Cambridge, who tosses coins to the children. Apparently under a charter granted by King John, Reach is a self-governing Kingdom. With the building of the sluice at Denver, coasters could no longer trade easily to this little port, and its importance diminished. The last vessels, carrying a load of clunch (a building material) left from here in the 1930s. The church of Holy Trinity was built in 1860, a time of great Victorian self-confidence. It is extremely ugly.

Burwell
Cambs. EC Wed. PO, stores, Chinese take away. A large village at the head of Burwell Lode, with many handsome 17th and 18thC houses. A splendid church whose Perpendicular tower top, upon a Norman base, was inspired by Ely Cathedral. Inside St Mary the Virgin all is light and loftiness, arches soaring to the clerestory and a rose window sparkling above the tracery over the chancel arch. Ornate canopied niches enrich the chancel walls and angels embellish the

Anglesey Abbey (NT) 2 miles west of Swaffham Bulbeck, at Lode (Cambridge 811200). Buses run to Anglesey Abbey from Burwell, Reach and Cambridge. A foundation of the Augustinian Order, part of that original building, the Canon's Parlour dating from 1236, still remains. After the Dissolution, when much of the building was demolished, it was rebuilt as an Elizabethan manor house by the Fokes family. Purchased by Lord Fairhaven and his brother in 1926, they created a 100-acre garden of particular beauty and interest. There are occasional demonstrations of the machinery in the Lode Mill. Lunches and teas. *Open afternoons Wed–Sun and B. Hols, Apr–mid Oct. Garden only open Mon & Tue mid May–Sept.* Admission charge.

BOATYARDS

Ⓑ **Norman Cole Marine** The Marina, Upware, Ely (Cambridge 860528). Ⓓ Calor gas, long-term mooring, winter storage, slipway, boat and engine sales and repairs, boatbuilding, toilets, showers. Has facilities for lifting craft up to 70ft long and weighing 40 tons. Ⓜ

Ⓑ **Upware Marina** (Ely 721930). ⓌⓅⒹ Long-term mooring, winter storage, slipway, chandlery, provisions, boat and engine repairs, toilets, showers. Ⓜ

PUBS AND RESTAURANTS

There is no pub in Reach.

🍺 **Red Lion** Swaffham Prior (Swaffham 21022). Old village local. Bar snacks (*L&D*), garden.

🍺 **Fox** The Causeway, Burwell (Newmarket 741267). Norwich Brewery and Websters real ales in an old village pub. Bar snacks (*L&D*), open fire for cold days, garden for sunny days.

🍺 **Crown** Burwell (Newmarket 741298). A lively pub with geese, chickens, ducks and a goat in the garden. Greene King real ale, bar meals (*L&D*), snacks and barbecues in the barn. Live music *Sat eves*, cream teas *Sat and Sun afternoons in summer*.

🍺 **King William IV** Burwell (Newmarket 741456). Norwich Brewery real ale, snacks, seafood and homemade dishes (*L&D, not Sun or Wed*). Garden.

🍺 **Anchor** Burwell, at the head of the Lode (Newmarket 741101). Greene King real ale in a beamy local pub. Bar snacks (*L&D*), riverside garden with swings, covered terrace. Ⓜ (turning restricted).

🍺✕ **Five Miles From Anywhere, No Hurry** Upware (Ely 721654). Large comfortable riverside pub offering a choice of real ales, bar and restaurant meals (*L&D*). Garden. Ⓜ

Reach

The Bridge of Sighs, Cambridge

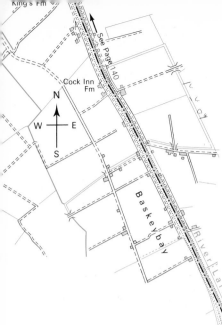

See Page 140

Cock Inn
Fm

N
W   E
S

Baskey bay

River Lark

West Row
Suffolk. The head of navigation for large
craft on the River Lark. It was near here in
1932, at Thistley Green, that a two-roomed
Roman building, including a hypocaust and
a pottery was discovered. Ten years later a
hoard of 34 pieces of 4thC AD Roman silver
was uncovered by the plough. The largest
item was a dish depicting Bacchus's triumph
over Hercules. It is thought the pieces may
have been manufactured in Rome; they are
now on display in the British Museum. To
the north is the giant Mildenhall USAF air
base.

Worlington
Suffolk. A tiny village to the south of the
river. The church of All Saints has an Early
English chancel and a Decorated west tower.
The west window is adorned with flowing
tracery.

Bà

Isleham Lock
6ft 6in
Fifty Fm

Waterside   Weir

East Fen

B1104

Priory
(rems of)

P

Pit

Isleham

Lee Brook

The Pits

The River Lark has been left high on an
embankment by the dramatically shrunken
peat. Isleham Lock is very isolated, being a
mile north of the village; the head of
navigation for large craft is reached only a
short distance beyond this point. Smaller
boats may follow the river's winding course
as far as Mildenhall.

NAVIGATIONAL NOTES

Isleham Lock (Isleham 275). Manned.
87ft 0in × 14ft 11in. Headroom 6ft 6in.
Limit of navigation Large craft – Judes
Ferry (West Row) Smaller craft –
Mildenhall.

Isleham
Cambs. PO, stores, fish & chips. A survival
little short of miraculous is the Norman
chapel of Isleham Priory (key at 10 Sun
Street), founded by Benedictine monks of St
Jacutus de Insula, near Dol in Brittany, and
abandoned by them in 1254. Absolutely
plain, it stands in stark contrast to the
church of St Andrew, which although
marred by an undistinguished 19thC tower,
is a fine and spacious Decorated building,
beautifully refashioned during the reign of
Henry VII. The blank arcading inside the
gabled south porch is notable, and the tall
clerestory makes a wonderful flourish,
complementing the roof, adorned with
angels. Shields of the Peyton family, who
built both, appear in the spandrels of the
nave arches. Many of the Peytons can be
seen in effigy, including Thomas, who died
in 1484, and his two wives, whose brasses are
elaborately detailed, one wife wearing a
richly patterned dress, and both a haughty
expression. Perhaps Thomas is praying for
silence. Also examine the marvellously
inventive carving of the Jacobean altar rail.
There is a handsome medieval Lychgate in
the churchyard.

Mildenhall
Suffolk. EC Thur, MD Fri. PO, stores.
Mildenhall defines the south west corner of
an area of sandy heath and bracken known as
Breckland. Scattered throughout the sand is
flint, the traditional building material of the
area. It was used in prehistoric times to make
tools – arrow heads, knives and scrapers, and
more recently as a component of the flintlock
musket. It was these barren stony outcrops,
known as brecks or brakes, which give the
area its name. However, the hand of man has
wrought vast changes, with large military
installations, battle training grounds and
vast tracts of forest plantation conspiring
either to destroy, or deny access to, any land
of primaeval quality.
In Mildenhall, Suffolk's largest parish, the
ancient timbered buildings at the heart of the
town are surrounded by an ugly sprawl of
untidy modern development where an
American accent seems as commonplace as
the local Suffolk burr.
The bleak heathland seems to have been

fertile ground for the spreading of the Nonconformist religions; indeed Mildenhall has three chapels, Wesleyan, Calvinist and Baptist, the latter being supported with great fervour by the American Baptists, who have organised baptisms involving total immersion in the River Lark. But all is not lost in this old market town, for the large impressive church of St Mary is a distinctive landmark. Pinnacles climb out of shafted buttresses and make their way up the tower. Flushwork chequers the north aisle and panelled battlements crown the north porch, which has niches in its buttresses, and a vault inside studded with carved bosses. The hammer-beams of the traceried nave roof are decorated with angels – wings outstretched. Though the roof escaped the worst Puritan ravages through its great height, it was peppered with shot; the angels in the north aisle roof were defaced and are without wings. Biblical scenes, saints and fabulous beasts hold their own in the spandrels. The 13thC chancel arch is particularly fine, and the east window tracery has quatrefoils which seem to dance around the rim.

PUBS AND RESTAURANTS

The Griffin Isleham (Newmarket 78447). A friendly pub offering a good choice of real ales, bar snacks and restaurant meals (*D only*). Garden, accommodation.

Judes Ferry House Inn West Row, Mildenhall (712277). A very well-known and popular landmark on the River Lark, where you can enjoy a good selection of real ales (including their own brew, Jude's Tipple), bar snacks, restaurant meals (*L&D, not Mon*) and barbecues. Children's room, large riverside garden, boat hire. M

Riverside Hotel Mildenhall (712166). A handsome place at the absolute limit of navigation on the River Lark. Restaurant and bar meals (*L&D*), summer barbecues, riverside garden. Accommodation. Children welcome.

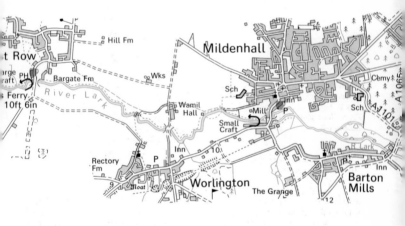

Isleham Priory

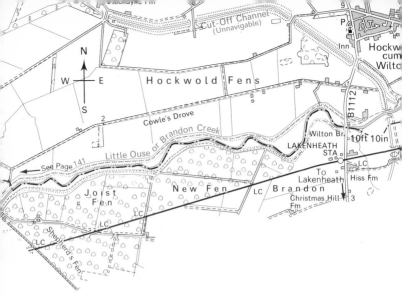

The river meanders eastwards past
Lakenheath as the railway closes in from the
south. Crossing the Cut-Off Channel on an
aqueduct it approaches Brandon, where
navigation ends short of the fine flint-faced
bridge.

NAVIGATIONAL NOTES

Limit of navigation The staunch (sluice) a
short way below Brandon Bridge. The river
is quite shallow here.
Floods Water is diverted into the Cut-Off
Channel in time of flood, thus closing the
navigation near the aqueduct.

The Little Ouse at Little Ouse

Brandon
*Suffolk. EC Wed, MD Thur/Sat. PO, stores,
BR station.* A little town with some
interesting flint buildings; it is also a centre
for flint knapping, a local trade
commemorated in the name of the pub at the
corner of Thetford Road and the High
Street. The flints, quarried from pits near
Grimes Graves, were once brought to the
yard behind the pub, to be quartered, flaked
and knapped. They were used for building
purposes, especially church restoration; for
the British Army's guns during the
Napoleonic Wars, and strangely, today, are

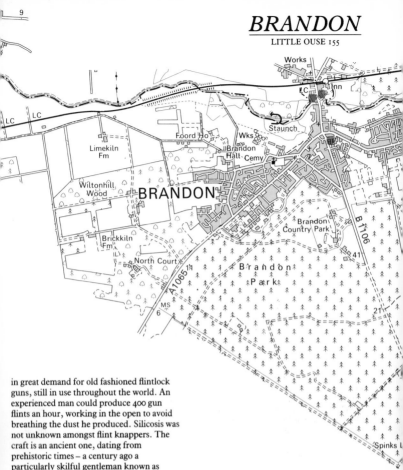

in great demand for old fashioned flintlock guns, still in use throughout the world. An experienced man could produce 400 gun flints an hour, working in the open to avoid breathing the dust he produced. Silicosis was not unknown amongst flint knappers. The craft is an ancient one, dating from prehistoric times – a century ago a particularly skilful gentleman known as Flint Jack created relics which he sold as being of Neolithic origin. Doubtless many collectors still have examples of his handiwork displayed alongside the more genuine article. Now demand is so great production has been moved from behind the Flintknappers Arms to a larger yard on the Bury St Edmunds road. Fittingly, the new bridge at Brandon, built in 1953, has been faced with local flint.

One of Brandon's most famous sons was Simon Eyre – he built Leadenhall Market, and became Lord Mayor of London.

The church of St Peter lies half-a-mile to the west of the town centre. It has an early Decorated chancel with two turrets, a Perpendicular south chapel and a 14thC font. At one time a light was displayed on the tower to guide navigators. Lighters once plyed the river beyond Brandon to Thetford, negotiating staunches on their way. These single oak gates, raised by chains, were built to hold back the flow of water. Each carrying about 25 tons, the lighters navigated in teams of five hauled by sturdy Suffolk horses. All commercial carrying ceased on the Little Ouse in 1914. Small iron steam vessels were actually built at Thetford during the 1880s, and a 25ft paddle steamer, 'Pride of the Ouse', ran a passenger service to Cambridge and other waterside towns in the area.

Grimes Graves 4 miles north east of Brandon. Not in fact graves, but Neolithic shafts sunk some 20ft into the chalk beds to extract flint from the underlying layers. Excavations in 1870 revealed antler picks and a chalk figurine, probably a fertility goddess, some 4000 years old. There may have been in excess of 700 pits – of the 16 excavated, two are open to the public, who are advised to wear old clothes and carry a torch. Flint is still extracted from pits in this area.

PUBS AND RESTAURANTS

Ram Hotel Near the railway station, Brandon (Thetford 810275). A rambling brick-built pub with an aviary. Norwich Brewery real ale, bar snacks, garden.

Flintknappers Arms Brandon. Not built of flint, but black timber-frame with red-brick infill and nice stained glass. Bar meals (*L&D*). There was once a flint-knappers yard round the back.

Brandon House Hotel Brandon (Thetford 810171). Adnams and Greene King real ales, hot and cold buttery (*L*) and restaurant (*L&D*) in a fine hotel. Garden.

Bridge House Tea Rooms Right by the bridge, Brandon. Teas in a conservatory decorated with antiques. Garden, boat hire.

USEFUL ADDRESSES

Anglian Water (Broads region)
Yare House, 62–64 Thorpe Road, Norwich, Norfolk NR1 1SA
Norwich 615161
Anglian Water (River Nene)
North Street, Oundle, Peterborough, Cambs PE8 4AS
Oundle 73701
Anglian Water (River Ouse)
Great Ouse House, Clarendon Road, Cambridge CB2 2BL
Cambridge 61561
Blakes Holidays
Wroxham, Norwich, Norfolk NR12 8DH
Wroxham 2911
Broads Authority
Thomas Harvey House, 18 Colegate, Norwich, Norfolk NR3 1BQ
Norwich 610734
River Cam Conservancy
The Guildhall, Cambridge CB2 3QJ
Cambridge 358977
Great Yarmouth Port and Haven Commissioners
21 South Quay, Great Yarmouth, Norfolk NR30 2RE
Great Yarmouth 855151
Hoseasons Holidays
Sunway House, Lowestoft, Suffolk NR32 3LT
Lowestoft 64991
Inland Waterways Association
114 Regent's Park Road, London NW1 8UQ
01-586 2556
Middle Level Commissioners
Middle Level Offices, March, Cambs PE15 8AF
March 53232
National Trust (East Anglia regional office)
Blickling, Norwich, Norfolk NR11 6NF
Aylsham 733471
Nature Conservancy Council (East Anglia region)
60 Bracondale, Norwich, Norfolk NR1 2BE
Norwich 620558
Norfolk and Suffolk Yachting Association
Hon Sec, Spring Cottage, Mill Lane, Horning, Norfolk NR12 8LL
Horning 630831
Norfolk Naturalist's Trust
72 Cathedral Close, Norwich, Norfolk NR1 4DF
Norwich 625540
The Norfolk Wherry Trust
Hon Sec, 63 Whitehall Road, Norwich, Norfolk NR2 3EN
Norwich 624642
The Norfolk Windmills Trust
Dept of Planning and Property, County Hall, Martineau Lane,
Norwich, Norfolk NR1 2DH
Norwich 611122
Royal Society for the Protection of Birds (East Anglia office)
Aldwych House, Bethel Street, Norwich, Norfolk NR2 1NR
Norwich 615920
Swan Rescue Service
Norwich 629444 (24 hrs)

INDEX